D1235204

IN THE SLEEP ROOM

IN THE SLEEP ROOM

The Story of the CIA Brainwashing Experiments in Canada

Anne Collins

KEY PORTER BOOKS

Canadian Cataloguing in Publication Data

Collins, Anne, 1952–
          In the sleep room

Includes index.
ISBN 1-55013-937-0

1. Cameron, Ewen, 1901–1967. 2. Allan Memorial Psychiatric Institute.
3. Brainwashing – Quebec (Province) – Montreal. 4. United States.
Central Intelligence Agency. I. Title.

RC339.52.C34C64   1997   616.89'0092   C97-932042-9

The publisher gratefully acknowledges the support of the Canada Council for the Arts and the Ontario Arts Council for its publishing program.

THE CANADA COUNCIL | LE CONSEIL DES ARTS
FOR THE ARTS | DU CANADA
SINCE 1957 | DEPUIS 1957

Key Porter Books Limited
70 The Esplanade
Toronto, Ontario
Canada M5E 1R2

Printed and bound in Canada

97 98 99 00 6 5 4 3 2 1

To Eric, Evan and Winston

I have always wanted to believe in the goodness of people. If not in the goodness of what people do then, at least, in the goodness of what they set out to do.

—*The Telling of Lies*, Timothy Findley

Everything is becoming science fiction. From the margins of an almost invisible literature has sprung the intact reality of the twentieth century.

—J.G. Ballard

Contents

1. The Sad Demonstration   1

2. Rejection   5

3. Disclosure   24

4. Good Science, Bad Science   44

5. The Elusive Cure   64

6. An Imperative to Treat   83

7. At Last, a Mover and a Shaker   100

8. The Automatic Cure   121

9. Mary Morrow, MD   142

10. In the Sleep Room   160

11. The Wrong Road Travelled   182

12. Fall from the Pedestal   204

13. Death at the Summit   237

Afterword to the Second Edition   244

Source Notes   247

Acknowledgements   266

Index   268

CHAPTER ONE
The Sad Demonstration

She was the only one who stopped, a small middle-aged woman wearing a beige beret that matched her winter coat, a fluffy scarf tangled in the fringes of her reddish curls. She looked wholesome and ordinary enough and, for a moment, the tiny group of demonstrators circling outside the U.S. Embassy in Ottawa on a cold October day were happy that a stranger had found their cause compelling enough to join them. They were the mad movement, a dozen ex-inmates and their supporters at the hard core of anti-psychiatry protest in Canada, and they had had enough of people's pushing past them, ignoring their testimony, their witness, their press releases. They were here to speak out against a major injustice, the strongest of the strong abusing the weakest of the weak, the CIA funding of brainwashing experiments on the inmates of a Canadian mental institution, the American invasion of the territory of the mind. But the embassy windows stared down at them, indifferent. The cold wind made their noses drip, wrenched at their placards, and turned their chant into a chorus of uncertain voices. "Victims united will never be defeated!" (and the meek shall inherit the earth).

But some things can be counted on in Ottawa, and the RCMP did turn up to try to order the tiny demonstration off the sidewalk. It had little effect except to reveal that the sole independent supporter, the small Ottawa matron, had a foul-mouthed interest in castration. Particularly castration of masculine figures of authority. A fly on Orestes' flank, she stuck to the demonstrators as they marched across the street to the rally on Parliament Hill. And even though there was no crowd, and would be no crowd, she made for the microphone and gave a garbled speech and had to be persuaded away from it by members of the mad movement whose job it was for the rest of the long afternoon to contain the crazy person they had attracted.

Still, the handful of demonstrators waited rather hopefully for the legitimate speakers to arrive. One of them was going to be David Orlikow, MP, the husband of one of the victims they had come to Ottawa to support. Val Orlikow was the leading plaintiff in a suit that nine former patients of Dr. D. Ewen Cameron and Montreal's Allan Memorial Institute had filed against the CIA for experiments the doctor had performed on them in the late fifties and early sixties. But Orlikow, when he turned up, a tiny balding fellow in his sixties dressed carefully in a navy suit, stood there tired and detached, and spoke to them for less than a minute. Thanks, he said, for your support—it's going to be a long fight. As if they didn't know that already, as if the suit hadn't already dragged on for six years since it had been filed in 1980.

They applauded politely for Orlikow, but the suspicion crossed more than one mind that he was embarrassed by them. What weight did they pull after all? They were ex-mental patients just like his wife. Victims, just like his wife. In their minds, tortured by psychiatrists just like his wife, but with no overtones of spy novels, no leftist glamour, and no famous Washington civil-liberties lawyer taking on their case. When they read about what Dr. Cameron had done to some of his patients—massive electro-shock, sensory deprivation, chemical sleep for days on end with tape machines playing endless loops of words under their pillows telling them just how awful they were, how they had to change—they could feel it in their own bodies. But that kind of empathy didn't make them necessarily the kind of allies Orlikow would want. He wanted sane society, normal society, powerful society, the side of society they thought that psychiatrists were on, to recognize the horror. Not them. They already knew, and could not even draw a crowd.

Other speakers did a better job, but only one former cabinet minister stopped to find out what was going on. As a child he had lived on the same street in Montreal as Dr. Cameron and he had played with Cameron's sons. It was all awful, as far as he was concerned, but everything in the mad business was awful. His mother had killed herself in a mental institution when he was a teenager. He did not actually listen to the speakers; he was too busy describing how he too was a victim.

Hopes were now pinned on a press conference the demonstrators had booked at 4:00 PM in a broadcast room in the Centre Block itself. All the members of the Press Gallery had been sent a release, and they wouldn't have to come out into the cold, only walk down a flight or two of stairs. But only one reporter turned up, a scarily crisp young woman who took a further hand-out and left the room. And a knife-pleated, clean-shaven young man whose fat neck turned slowly red against his starched collar as he surveyed the demonstrators settled messily awaiting attention among the microphones, some of them sitting on the floor and picnicking out of bags. This was too much—he had to do his daily live broadcast to the Maritimes, this was where he always did it, this was the time he always did it, and who were these (a pause filled by whatever derogatory term he was too angry to spit out) people cluttering up his room. Ex-mental patients who wanted to talk about brainwashing? Who cared? Who did they think they were?

He made a perfect target for the woman with castration on her mind, but in the end the Press Gallery president came down to mediate the dispute. The mad movement was allowed to stay another half hour to accommodate the reporters who never showed up. It was an uncomfortable wait, in the House of Commons basement under the corridors of power. One of the group was loudly insisting that the poor turn-out was censorship—the government must have told people not to come. Others thought that it wasn't censorship but indifference.

Dorothy, an older woman with a kerchief tied under her chin, who looked small and humble and downtrodden until you met the humour in her eyes, suspected it was a little worse than indifference because she had felt it so often before. The fear of contamination. She knew that she was stigmatized by her incarceration. Few people who haven't been in mental hospitals themselves find ex-inmates a credible source of comment on anything—even their own experiences in mental hospitals.

What none of them knew, as they downheartedly sorted themselves out, gathered their bags, and prepared to go, was that even the people they were trying to defend, the plaintiffs in the CIA suit, had been warned off them by their Washington lawyer, Joe Rauh, and his young partner, Jim Turner. Those two were smart enough to know that you don't win at power games—you don't beat the CIA—by allying yourself with the fringes. Nobody except other fringe-dwellers pays attention to the fringes.

CHAPTER TWO
Rejection

Though married to an MP, Val Orlikow herself spent a long horrible period of her life in the place where nobody listens unless you pay them to, like doctors, or unless they're trapped in a house with you, like husbands. Not that David was so trapped. He could always find pressing public business to attend to at his Winnipeg North constituency office, or even farther away, in Ottawa, when the House was sitting. He'd been an MP for twenty-six years, and for most of those years she'd been his shadow, his cross to bear, David Orlikow's mad wife.

She is seventy-one years old. In her great moon face, fringed by its grandmotherly halo of short white hair, in her dark-circled eyes, you can see the wreck of a fine and creative intelligence. When David first met her, she liked to read George Orwell and D.H. Lawrence; she could plough her way through and then discuss *Das Kapital*. Now it takes her more than a year to read light stuff. David Niven's *The Moon's a Balloon* is heavy going. Now, David says, she is only 20 per cent of her old self. But who can even remember that old self? Its slow disintegration began in 1949, when Val, at thirty-two, gave birth to her first and only child, Leslie.

The woman who had married David Orlikow at the rather late age of twenty-nine was active, aggressive, and outgoing. She liked to be that way and she had to be that way—she was in public relations, a fairly hefty job for the big department-store chain T. Eaton Company, in downtown Winnipeg. Val did the Santa Claus Parade broadcasts and wrote the scripts for a children's radio program the store sponsored. She handled all the store's fashion advertising and ran the Eaton's junior counsellor program for high-school seniors. There were dark spots in her life—everyone has dark spots. Her father, a charming Irishman with a taste for women, had left his wife and two daughters when Val was seventeen and her sister only eleven. Three females in mourning for the ne'er-do-well. Still, she had liked her life.

Two years after she and David were married, Val got pregnant and quit her job. It was all according to plan—she was going to stay home and raise their family. But the plan was severely tested by the first necessary step: Leslie's birth. Val's labour lasted three days. She haemorrhaged and had to have a blood transfusion. In the aftermath, tired and distraught, she was further tormented by a bad case of haemorrhoids—banal, maybe, but they made her feel even more mutilated and split asunder.

Then her daughter didn't digest food well. Val had to pay infinite and obsessed attention to the mysterious workings of one small alimentary canal. The world closed down to the size of that tract, but even that Val could not control: "There was constant care and having to change the food she was on…I was frightened."

And frigid, that expressive 1950s word for women who had gone off sex. Struggling through a post-partum depression of massive proportions, Val finally sought help because she was feeling frozen towards David, the man who got her pregnant. Her own lack of interest in sex didn't bother her so much: "I was primarily concerned about my husband's reaction to my reaction to sex." She went first to her internist. He gave her some hormone therapy, which slightly increased her sexual appetite, but didn't make things any easier for her. To reassure her—he really thought there was nothing much wrong with her; she had no history of emotional problems—he offered to set up an appointment for a thorough check-up at the Mayo Clinic in Minnesota, where most Winnipeggers went when they wanted state-of-the-art medicine. Val emerged from two weeks at the Mayo Clinic with a full-fledged psychiatric diagnosis—"character neurosis"—and the recommendation that she should receive psychotherapy in Winnipeg.

The trouble with the Mayo Clinic analysis was that character neurosis was a catch-all diagnosis that could mean any number of things to any number of psychiatrists. Val was not schizophrenic, not obsessive-compulsive, not manic, not thoroughly depressed—just somehow "flawed" in her character development. The "evidence" was her maladjustment to motherhood. But how did you fix a character? No one was really sure.

And there wasn't a single practising psychotherapist in Winnipeg, no one who could approximate a "talking cure". There weren't even very many psychiatrists. "I never knew anybody who went to a psychiatrist," says Val. She ended up going to weekly appointments with Dr. John Matas, a psychiatrist who definitely wasn't a psychotherapist. He didn't give her a diagnosis, or much of anything, except a prescription for Seconal so that she could sleep at night. "The secret of sleep in a capsule," as its ads ran, to "gently break the chain of wakeful nights." A barbiturate, and heavily addictive, Seconal proved a bit of a problem. It wasn't then on the restricted drug list, and David, who was a pharmacist before he became a politician, owned a drugstore with his brother, also a pharmacist. When the bottle was empty Val would take it to the drugstore, and David or his brother would fill it up. She began to forget how many pills she had taken, and if sleep didn't come soon enough she would take a few more pills, which sometimes looked pretty close to attempted suicide.

She saw Dr. Matas for four years. Throughout those years she pushed at him for treatment, for relief. Anything. It was at her suggestion that Matas tried a course of thirteen electro-shock treatments on her in 1953. Val had heard of a couple of people who had had electrotherapy (ECT) and felt better. She had no such luck.

David read of a drug called Largactil, the first of what were then called the major tranquillizers and are now called anti-psychotic or neuroleptic drugs. They weren't on the market yet, but he knew a drug salesman who got a supply for Val. Unsupervised, she took the new drug and worried: "Every time I went out into the sun I had a burning sensation on my skin and the part of my hair, I didn't know what it was." It was a common effect of taking Largactil.

To keep the walls from totally closing in, and to earn some money (the drugstore wasn't too profitable), Val took a job as a payroll and correspondence secretary for a company called Quality Pants. She was managing to take care of Leslie and work and run the house, but she couldn't shake her fatigue, her anxiety and depression, her indifference to sex. Then, in 1955, she got pregnant again, which happened whether she liked sex or not. The decision to have an abortion seemed clear-cut.

"I felt I was managing with Leslie and David, and I didn't know what another person entering our lives would do. I did not want to disrupt.... On top of which, Dr. Matas had said he didn't think it would be a good idea." When consulted by Dr. Matas, Dr. George Sisler, head of the department of psychiatry at the University of Manitoba, didn't think it would be a good idea either, and neither did Val's gynaecologist, Dr. Ruben Lyons. A thirty-nine-year-old woman struggling to cope with a six-year-old and with the potential for extreme post-partum depression and feelings of frigidity connected to her first experience of birth was not a good bet for a mother. What the triumvirate of doctors didn't tell Val and David was that they had decided among themselves that she should never have another child. They left that to the resident doing rounds in the hospital where Val was admitted to have her abortion.

"A young intern came to our room and took the medical history. And he said that I would be having this abortion and that he had a paper for me to sign for a tubal ligation. And I said, 'What's that?' And he said, 'They're going to see that you don't have any more children.' And I said, 'Well, I never discussed that with the doctors, nobody told me about that.' And he said, 'Well, I'm sorry, but that's the paper I have.' And David and I were flabbergasted and we sat there. And he said, 'I'll leave you alone for a while to think it over.' And we sat there all evening and we didn't know what to do...because we really wanted to have a family. And then we decided, well, if this was recommended, that we'd better do it. And so we signed that paper. Oh, God. And we lost our child and we never had another child and that was that."

Val stopped seeing Dr. Matas. He hadn't helped her. She was condemned to feeling like this all her life. There was nobody in the world who could help her. Finally she turned to Dr. Sisler at the university, in the fall of 1956. She wanted to go somewhere, a hospital, where she could get better. Not the provincial hospital, that was for chronic cases; she'd been miserable for seven years but she wasn't chronic, and they wouldn't have psychotherapy there anyway. Psychotherapy was what they told her she needed. Sisler suggested two places in the east where she could get help, one in Guelph, Ontario, and the other the Allan Memorial Institute in Montreal. It was affiliated with McGill University and the famous Royal Victoria Hospital, and it was famous in its own right as a cutting-edge psychiatric treatment centre, the best in Canada. Val had worked in Montreal for a couple of years during the war and she had friends there. The choice seemed simple.

In November 1956, Val Orlikow took the train to Montreal all by herself. One sight lingered in her mind: her seven-year-old daughter dancing alongside the train and waving. Leslie didn't want a mother who was sick. Dr. Sisler told Val that with the right care she'd only be away for three or four months, and that seemed like a little sacrifice if afterward she would be better.

She stayed for a couple of days with her friend Peggy Prisant. On November 26, Peggy helped her pile all her luggage in a taxi and then got in and held her hand all the way up Mount Royal to the doors of the Allan Memorial Institute. It was housed in an Italian Renaissance mansion, incongruously built out of grey Montreal limestone in the middle of the last century by the Allan family of steamship magnates. Sir Hugh Allan used to climb the central limestone tower to look down over the vista of Montreal and the harbour, watching for his ships through a telescope, a true master of all he surveyed. High above the front portico he had felt inspired to have carved the motto "*Spero!*" (I hope!).

Val's hope took a good beating at the admissions desk. Presenting herself there at the appointed time, she found the admitting clerk, Mrs. Fisher, looking past her shoulder for her husband. A wife could not be admitted and treated without her husband's consent, and David was back in Winnipeg. Through a long afternoon and evening Val negotiated. Finally at 9:00 PM, after a telegram had been received at the Allan from David Orlikow ("This is to authorize you to admit my wife Mrs. David Orlikow into your institute for treatment. —David Orlikow"), Val was allowed in.

From the outside, it was a spooky-looking place that lived up to its original name—Ravenscrag. But Val's room was not in the cramped-to-overflowing old mansion but in the new wing, T-shaped and three storeys high, out at the back of the building. It had opened just two years earlier and had been built according to the specifications of the Allan's director and founder, Dr. D. Ewen Cameron. A tall and imposing Scot with large ambitions for his profession, a past president of both the Canadian and American psychiatric associations, a key figure in the promoting and funding of psychiatric research in Canada, Cameron didn't want his institute looking like a loony-bin, or even much like a hospital. Of his new wing he wrote, "If people are to recover they must be located in settings in which reality is so arranged as to beckon and entice the individual towards full and mature living, and not confined in some stripped-down stone and steel box where the only escape is flight into his fantasy life."

Val's room looked as though it belonged in a motel; it was mirrored to prevent it from seeming too small and had its own washroom. If it hadn't been so hard to check in she could imagine herself on a trip, the car outside the door waiting to take her down the highway to the next town. A nurse took her on a quick tour of the facilities—a lounge on her floor, a beauty parlour, the snack bar, and the dining-room. The institute didn't appear formidable. She might even be comfortable here, if she could only, for the first time in seven years, get comfortable with herself.

But comfort was the last thing on the minds of the doctors, nurses, and psychologists who ran Val Orlikow through the standard paces of tests and examinations for the two weeks after she entered the Allan. Val and her long-standing misery were a mystery to them, to be cracked open, gotten to the heart of, and the cracking would hurt. Her brain waves were inspected in the EEG lab, a sophisticated facility rare in mental hospitals. Her sedation threshold was established; a doctor working at the Allan had discovered a correlation between categories of mental disease and how much barbiturate it took to put you to sleep. Val's was a little hard to judge because she'd been taking barbiturates for years.

She was taken a few steps down the mountain to the neighbouring Royal Victoria Hospital, an even more formidable pile of grey stones, for a complete physical. In the cramped basement of the Allan, psychologists asked her to draw and fingerpaint and look at Rorschach blots, and to interpret them all. And she was interviewed, by the resident doctor assigned to her, by the chief resident, and at long last by Dr. Cameron himself.

She had seen Cameron only on rounds, an imposing figure trailing a wake of students, forceful, good-humoured, and opinionated in an accent still noticeably Scots; busy and important—internationally important—he was always being hailed to take a telephone call from far away. The crack along the wards as he passed by was, there but for the grace of God goes God. Val took it almost literally. When Cameron asked to see her a second time, and then asked if he could switch on the giant tape machine, a huge floor model he always kept in his office, to record their hour together, Val was flattered. She even boasted a little to the nurses that Cameron, himself, had taken her on as a patient.

She was interviewed under the influence of sodium amytal, something commonly called a truth drug, but which the psychiatrists called an abreactant agent: it was supposed to get under her skin, free her from inhibitions, get her talking about her past, bring to light the inklings of repressed trauma. The doctors called what came out of Val "material", and out of it they were slowly building the beginnings of a firm diagnosis and suggestions for treatment. For Val, it was like falling into a mud-hole: nothing she said was taken at face value, and if she struggled against their interpretations she was considered hostile.

Her reaction to Leslie's birth, her troubles since, even her feelings about Dr. Matas—her belief that he couldn't help her—were viewed by the doctors writing notes in her chart as protest behaviour. Their insight was as follows: "The patient stated that she failed to develop any understanding of her difficulties and felt quite disillusioned by the course of treatments. This seemed to us probably to represent her underlying hostility which was present not only in respect to all her therapists but also with respect to authoritative figures even during her childhood and her girlhood years and may well, we thought, constitute a serious problem in the satisfactory carrying-out of therapy." In other words, if the treatment didn't help her, they were more likely to suspect not that it was the wrong treatment but that she didn't want to be helped. Resistance to therapy, repression of childhood traumas, was something Freud had recognized early on.

The therapeutic team became certain fairly quickly that Val was suffering from "essentially distorted father and mother figures". A note in her chart is almost poetic on the subject: "The mother means work; perfection and discipline and burdening. This always ended up in abandonment, injury and death threat through childbirth. The father means charm, pleasure, a mess and unsatisfied needfulness. The patient shuffled between these two extremes and tried to remain something of a mess, but not quite father, something of a perfectionist, but not quite mother.... Childbirth itself was experienced as both a mutilation and an annihilation." These unresolved feelings, they believed, were distorting her relationships with her child and with her husband— how else to explain her long-standing depression, her frigidity? The problem was how to get Val to accept, to work on, her primary relationships. The Mayo Clinic had said psychotherapy; Dr. Sisler in Manitoba had said psychotherapy, a long-term talking cure. Val was bright and articulate enough to talk her way through almost anything.

But psychotherapy as it was traditionally practised was slow, and Dr. Cameron didn't like anything that was slow. He didn't have the patience for it, his mind skittered ahead. He had come up with a technique he thought could speed up the whole process; sometimes he called it automatic psychotherapy, but in a paper published just that year in the *American Journal of Psychiatry* he'd called it psychic driving. What it meant was that he'd tape interviews with chosen patients and then, with the help of his long-time technician and electronics whiz, Leonard Rubenstein, he'd edit extracts from that hour—Val talking, and him responding or asking further questions— into a tape that Rubenstein would present to the patient to work on. Patients were to listen two hours in the morning, two hours in the afternoon, and two hours at night, every day until their next hour with Dr. Cameron. If that hour was revealing, they'd get a new tape. Working meant not only listening but writing everything that came into their heads and, at the end of each day, giving all their papers, their productions, to the nurse to carry down to Dr. Cameron's office. It took him far less time to read their thoughts, said Cameron, than to listen to them say them.

So Val wrote, sometimes only two pages a day, and sometimes up to thirty. Every so often the enigmatic Rubenstein—not a doctor, in fact a confusing combination of vegetarian, Orthodox and deeply religious Jew, practical joker, and technician—would arrive at her door with a new tape: "Dr. Cameron wants you to listen." And if she didn't work hard enough, or if she didn't work on the right things—her relationship to her mother or her husband—or if she tore up either her papers or her tapes in frustration, Cameron would withhold the two things that by then she couldn't do without: her sleeping pills or his presence. Forcing her down the road towards health with a behaviourist carrot and stick.

When, one morning in January, the doctor appeared in her room with a syringe full of she didn't know what, it wasn't surprising that Val allowed him to inject it. He patted her on the shoulder, turned on her tape-recorder, and walked out of the room, saying, "Write whatever comes into your mind." And shut the door.

The notation on her chart says that Val's reaction to this injection was "very intense indeed". In the syringe was gamma 50 LSD-25 and 10 mgs of Desoxyn: in other words, a moderate-sized hit of acid combined with a little speed.

The kind thing for Cameron to do would have been to warn Val of some of the things she might experience; he hadn't tried the drug himself, though he had used it on patients, and other doctors at the Allan had tried it. But kindness wasn't the point. Cameron was using LSD as one more abreactant agent, one more potential hammer to break down Val's walls, to get to the place in her psyche that needed fixing. Her distress, her panic and fear, might turn out to be useful signals of the danger zones, the "hot spots", as he liked to call them: the more emotionally aroused she was, the better the chances, he thought, of changing her. But for Val the LSD was too terrible: "I had absolutely no control over me. And I felt that all my bones were melting. And it seemed to me that I would go in a funny kind of way, zigging and zagging around like a squirrel in a cage. I couldn't get out. I tried to climb the walls. And I felt that if I was to lie down, I'd never get up."

Cameron came the next day and had to put his arm around her and walk her around the halls before she'd consent to another injection. She remembers his saying, "Well, lassie, you know that we would never give you any medication that we can't stop, so if you can't stand it you come out in the corridor and you call a nurse. Now be a good girl and write from your tapes." She tried that once, calling a nurse, but all she was given was sodium amytal, and it didn't stop anything.

Cameron believed that Val was making progress. His notes say that she took her third LSD injection with "considerable reluctance but is proving reasonably cooperative. She is beginning to deal with some of the fundamental problems with which she is faced....We hope to get her to the point where she can at least live outside."

By the first week of February, Cameron was still worried by the difference between the way Val viewed her husband and the way Cameron thought he really was: "The husband had now been seen, he was rather different from the picture which the patient had portrayed, instead of being the warm, affectionate, definite and steadfast person, he was rather quizzical, aloof, highly tentative, and quite ambivalent, save insofar that he was definite that he could not go on living with his wife unless she should mend her ways."

By the middle of February, Cameron was beginning to feel that he had got Val to confront what they all thought was the dark heart of the matter: "The patient's references to her unconscious homosexual feelings concerning the mother were much more frequent…about her mother being hot, moist and sticky and the feeling that her mother was smothering her."

But persuading her to take the injections was harder and harder. Says Val, "Dr. Cameron would say, 'Come on, lassie, we'll walk down the hall.' We would walk down the hall. He would put his arm around my shoulder and say, 'Now, lassie, you want to get better. Come on, lassie, you're going to take this injection for me. You know you are.' And I would say, 'Okay, I'll do it, but I don't want to do it. It's killing me. It's killing me.' "

That sequence of events happened fourteen times—the needle, her fear, his persuasion, the injection. After the last shot Val fell into what she calls the black hole. Three days of it, unmoving, her tears streaming, total panic, until a psychologist she'd finger-painted for, whom she liked, came to her room and said, "Come, let's do some painting. I'll take you down the back stairs and no one will see your tears."

Then Cameron came with another needle, on daily rounds. When Val heard his footsteps and those of his entourage she hid in her washroom. "I could hardly stand up. I didn't care whether I lived or I died." He coaxed her out of her washroom, but she wouldn't take the shot. She refused him in front of the others, and he turned on his heel and said, "Fine, we'll go on." And he didn't come back to her.

She was soon discharged from the Allan. If she wouldn't work, Dr. Cameron wasn't going to let her stay in the institute. In part, the discharge note sent to Dr. Sisler read: "We are still not sure why the protest behavior which seems to summarize much of her difficulties appeared during the time of her pregnancy with her only child. It is clear moreover that her reaction to the termination of her second pregnancy and the ligation of her tubes will also have to be brought out for discussion.

"Our final diagnosis is that of severe character neurosis."

Looking at it from the outside—at Val's disillusionment, anger, and feelings of rejection—it seems incomprehensible that she didn't pack her bags and head home to the steady old misery that she knew. But Dr. Cameron now loomed so large in her life as to overshadow all the familial relationships she was supposed to be working on. She was supposed to be thinking of her mother, her daughter, her husband, but more and more she thought of Ewen Cameron: "I breathed because he was alive." It wasn't pure love: "There were many times when I felt he was sympathetic, kindly, interested; there were times when I thought he was being brutal and harsh, disinterested and cold."

Despite the LSD injections and the fact that she heard his voice more often on tape than in the flesh, Val was caught in the psychological process called transference, in which the therapist becomes all things to the patient, the vehicle through which she works out her feelings towards the world. Cameron did try to broach the subject of Val's feelings for him, her *unique* feelings, as far as she was concerned; she felt he was being clumsy, egotistical, obtuse, embarrassing. How could she tell him, the object of her passion, that the frigid wife found him immensely sexually attractive, that she both feared him and was in love with him? She refused to talk.

So she stayed on in Montreal, living in a one-room apartment a block from the Allan and turning up throughout the summer of 1957 at a program called the Day Hospital. It was tapes and more tapes. At 9:00 AM every working day she reported to a tiny room that had once been a supply cupboard to listen and write until noon. A break for lunch and then back to the cupboard to listen and write for three more hours. At 4:00 her notes were gathered up and taken off to Dr. Cameron's office, to which she also had to report to pick up her night's sleeping pills. Cameron was not going to take the chance on Val alone in an apartment at night with a whole bottle of pills.

Five months went by like this. Then in September Cameron told her that David, her David, couldn't afford to keep her enrolled in the Day Hospital any more, and that she'd have to get a job to start paying some of her own bills. She found a job—in fact, she found three of them over the next two years—to keep her in Montreal. David bought her a tape recorder so that in her apartment for four hours each night after work she could listen to her tapes. Every morning she mailed her writings off to Dr. Cameron.

But even with her working, David had to sell the Winnipeg house to meet the bills, and he and Leslie moved in with Val's mother. Slowly it began to upset Val that Leslie was being raised by her grandmother, an old woman, while her own mother spent the nights alone with a tape-recorder, a pen, and voices, in a city far away. Three or four months away from home had turned into three years. In December 1959 Val quit her last job, as secretary to the McGill University chaplain, and went home. Dr. Cameron advised her that going back to Winnipeg was the last thing on earth that she should do—but if she was set on it, he said, she should get her own job and take her own apartment. She tried that obediently for six months, all the time wanting to be with Leslie and caring less and less that getting her family back together might, as Cameron worried, reinforce her neurotic patterns.

The Orlikow family at last had a wonderful six-week-long reunion holiday in Jamaica. Then the three of them settled down to try ordinary life, stepping around the broken eggs ten years of mental illness had strewn in their path. It wasn't easy. Val hadn't had any luck with jobs. She got fired from a position as a secretary in the biochemistry department of the University of Manitoba for not concentrating and quit a part-time job with the information department of the provincial Department of Agriculture after six weeks because she couldn't handle the work. David had given up pharmacy and was now a City of Winnipeg councilman, but his brother, Arch Orlikow, still ran a drugstore. Arch would give her a bottle of amytal capsules whenever she needed one.

When the triumph of the reunion began to shift, for Val, into lethargy and despair, her pride kicked up. She would not inflict a depression on Leslie and David. Instead she made a serious suicide attempt.

Surviving past it was a further problem. Val was sometimes able to get herself moving around the house in a rough facsimile of the old Val Orlikow, but more often couldn't. By June of 1962, when David Orlikow won a seat in the federal Parliament of Canada, Val was only able to view his electoral triumph as a chance to move to Ottawa. In Ottawa she would be close to Dr. Cameron again. By August 1963 she was in such bad shape that Cameron readmitted her to the Allan.

But he would not see her—she'd catch a glimpse of him passing on rounds, but he didn't stop to talk to her. Only the residents talked to her; and they insisted that she start the psychic driving again because Dr. Cameron wanted her to. This time the tapes were worse, an impersonal voice, not her own or Cameron's. It repeated questions in loops: "What are your earliest memories? Who did you like best, your mother or your father? What was your favourite toy?" She had to listen to the loops through headphones—she couldn't turn the machine off, or rest. And she was supposed to write the answers to these questions over and over again. Find new answers to the same old questions.

They gave her drugs to help her write. Not LSD this time (they weren't using LSD any more), but sodium amytal and methamphetamine, at first by pill—talking-out capsules they called them—and then, since she was habituated to barbiturates and the effect wasn't strong enough, by injection.

Write the answers to questions she had already answered a hundred times over; with the earphones delivering the voice straight to her brain, with the injections sending her straight up to the ceiling. Val got lost, disembodied, and then would come crashing down in a rage. But even tearing up the tape or refusing to write didn't bring Dr. Cameron to her.

No one told her that he was staying away by experimental design, that he was in the final stages of trying to automate psychotherapy— that he couldn't have personal sessions with his patients if he was to prove that the taped therapy could help them. She also didn't know that he had dubbed her Miriam, that she was being written up as part of a paper called "Automation of Psychotherapy".

In fact she was being used to prove, empirically, that a strong patient-therapist relationship could survive even on minimal contact. Describing her as "a 46-year-old woman who suffers from such intense ambivalence that it has quite destroyed her domestic life", Cameron found both her love of him ("Doctor, you are all things to me") and her rage clinically interesting. The paper quotes one outburst: "To hell, to hell, to hell with it! To hell with the whole damn thing! I am all wrong inside. If one more nurse asks me what's wrong, I'm going to hit her. I get so hot and then so cold—it's hateful. I'm so tired of it all, it makes me feel sick—I hate being sick like this. I am so nasty. I don't think I even like you anymore either."

The only break from the psychic driving, seven days a week of tapes, was performing as a subject in another series of experiments, for Leonard Rubenstein. Val and another woman on the ward were asked to buy short shorts and sleeveless tops. From July until early October, Val had to dress her bulky self up in these clothes and walk across to the mansion's old stables, where Rubenstein was set up in what Cameron called the Behavior Laboratory. Two chairs stood back to back, and one after the other Val and her friend were filmed sitting and standing up, the same postures repeated day after day. Then each would go into a sound-proof glass booth into which Rubenstein piped a variety of sounds. Some made Val jump; others she found pleasant; her reactions, physiological and otherwise, were carefully noted. All of it she found boring. The only reason she kept on was because everyone told her Dr. Cameron wanted her to.

She tried to please the distant doctor, but the psychic driving wasn't going well. She hated the tapes, the impersonal voice. Weeks went by with the residents and nurses telling her she wasn't working hard enough, she wasn't serious about getting better. The third tape was very harsh. "Do you realize," the voice asked, "that you are a very hostile person? Do you know that you are hostile with the nurses? Do you know that you are hostile with the patients? Why do you think you are so hostile? Did you hate your mother? Did you hate your father?"

They must want me to be hostile, Val thought. Well, she'd show them hostile. A patient down the hall had torn her room apart and thrown all her clothes out in the hall. Maybe she should try that. The chart notes that Val had become "childish and manipulative".

The halls were full of voices, mutterings from wall speakers in private rooms, broadcast depth probes into other patients' lives. Some patients loved their tapes, meditated on the voice, were lost without the voice, could summon the voice up to soothe themselves, even when the tape wasn't running. But they had gone on to the positive tapes; the tapes that told them that they wanted to get better, that they could get better, that the world was manageable. All Val's tape told her was that she was hostile, over and over again, until she was reduced to writing only one word in response.

Loss. Loss, loss, loss, loss. Middle-aged now, not young, and still too sick to make her daughter happy. No good for her husband, no good for herself, banished from Dr. Cameron. Loss.

That word brought Cameron to her door. If she didn't do better than that, he said, she couldn't stay. But that was all she could do. Write the word "loss". They could try ECT, he said, but he didn't think it would work.

She didn't think it would work either—she was most emphatic that it wouldn't work. ECT brought visions of the room they called the sleep room into Val's head. She always kept to the other side of the hall when she had to go by it—people were drugged into sleep for days and days in there and given ECT until they didn't know who they were or where they were or how to feed themselves, until they lost control of their bladders and bowels. She saw patients who had just come out of the sleep room standing in puddles of urine in the halls. Banging into walls as they tried to walk. The tapes played there too, through speakers under the sleepers' pillows. Val thought people really lost their minds in there. A friend of hers had disappeared after sleep treatment; someone saw her months later, nearly unrecognizable and unable to speak, at the Verdun Protestant Hospital, the place they sent the hopeless cases.

They could try different drugs, Dr. Cameron said, but she was already on most of the drugs a psychiatrist could find to use: barbiturates to let her sleep; the neuroleptic drug Permitil three times a day; the minor tranquillizer Miltown, also three times a day; and Gravol to deal with the nausea the drugs evoked. He was giving her drugs to treat both psychosis (Permitil) and depression (Miltown). The bases were covered; what more could he do?

Val didn't know. She lay on her bed after he left her gradually stiffening into twenty-four hours of catatonia. She emerged with failure wedded to the word loss in her mind, and still not knowing what to do. She tried the art-therapy program and did some nice paintings until she ran out of things to paint; then she would just go there to be in the room with the sweet art therapist, Marie Revai, and the songbirds she kept in cages, an oasis in the Allan. Until Marie told her that she was sorry but that Dr. Cameron said Val couldn't keep coming to the art room if she wasn't going to paint.

In the end, a social worker came to tell her she was being discharged once again from the hospital.

Two months later, in August 1964, Dr. Cameron himself retired from the Allan and the chair of psychiatry at McGill, after twenty years as "the Chief". He moved to live full time at his family home in Lake Placid, N.Y., and to a job as head of a research lab into ageing funded by the American Veterans Administration. But Val was still the doctor's shadow. Every Sunday, if she could, appointment or no appointment, she would get someone, usually David, to drive her to Lake Placid. Two and a half hours from Ottawa, a large part of it through the turns and twists and switchbacks of the Adirondacks. David would sit in the waiting-room of the office Cameron kept in his house, while Cameron gave Val a talking-out injection and then sat—in the flesh, and not a tape-machine—behind her as she lay on his couch. Cameron took pity on David and told Val she could drive herself. One day, heading home still under the influence of the talking-out drugs, she misjudged a curve of the road and banged her car into a railing. From then on, David drove her.

Why Cameron kept on is anybody's guess. Both he and Val found their relationship exceedingly frustrating. Cameron was a man who viewed thirty weekly sessions as long-term psychotherapy; he did not have the patience to enjoy a long psychotherapeutic haul. He had been treating Val Orlikow for ten years, and she was without a doubt worse off. He had asked a favour or two of David, in his capacity as MP— a few figures dug up from the Department of Health and Welfare, that kind of thing. Perhaps he felt he owed David something. Val's persistence was another factor.

But one Sunday in 1966, Cameron had finally had enough. Instead of giving Val her injection and settling into his listening post, he called David into the office, and said—to David—"I'm not going to see Val any longer. I find she has no motivation to recover or get any better than she is, and there is absolutely no point in me wasting my time."

David led his numbed wife out to the car and drove the 185 miles back to Ottawa. When they got home, he was tired and soon went to bed. Val stayed up, circling, raging, mooning. By 5:30 the next morning she was sure that it was all a misunderstanding, that the doctor hadn't meant what he said.

She took the car and drove back to Lake Placid. She knocked on the door at 8:00 AM, and the doctor's wife told her that Cameron was out climbing in the mountains. Val went back to her car and sat all day in the road near the house. When she saw him return she drove her car into the driveway behind him and went down the side of the house to his office door and let herself into his waiting-room.

"Finally he came into the room, and he said, 'And what did you want?' And I said, 'I just don't understand what you said to me yesterday.'

" 'Well, I thought I made it perfectly clear.'

" 'I don't understand. You've never said anything, how can I have failed? Please, I need you.'

" 'Look, if you feel at some time that you can work on your problems better than you are doing now, well, you can write me a letter. In the meantime, there is an older woman in the city whose husband has died today—they are friends of ours—and she has asked to see me. I was told you were waiting to see me, and so I've come. But who needs me more?'

   " 'Well, I guess the old woman does.' "

   Val never saw Dr. Cameron again.

CHAPTER THREE

Disclosure

Ewen Cameron died in September 1967, of a heart attack, while climbing a mountain near Lake Placid. The god had proved mortal, and Val found that she still breathed on, in the pain to which he had permanently banished her. Rage was a constant companion, uncontrollable, sparked by as little a thing as not being able to find her shoes. She felt like Pandora's box, out of which all the horrors of the world flew to heap themselves on the shoulders of the people she loved—David and Leslie.

Relief was a chimera; Val had become what she had dreaded, a chronic mental case. For a while she swallowed vitamins in megadoses, trying a therapy for schizophrenia pioneered by prairie psychiatrist Ab Hoffer. But it turned out that the vitamins only corrected a coeliac condition she hadn't known about, and the new equilibrium didn't last. For weeks and months Val lay on her bed in absolute lethargy and depression, or wandered where her barbiturate addiction and her rage led her—suicide threats, suicide gestures. In 1971, five years after her last sight of Cameron, she finally found a doctor in Winnipeg, Gordon Lamberd, who took her on in all her angry misery. Lamberd talked to her, week after week, and only talked;

24

he got her medication levels down. After Cameron, who had taken her on such a roller-coaster ride, Val found Lamberd "a caring, natural, human man". Though both she and her new doctor realized it was too late for her to achieve well-being, he helped her manage her rages and keep the suicide thoughts at bay.

That in itself was a major accomplishment, given that Val carried the weight of twenty years of private pain—her own and the hurt she had caused others. Other people can tolerate a breakdown, can even live through a few months of it with you, but twenty years of despair is isolating, very isolating. Who can follow you there, into the darkest side of private life (as dark as the horrible things she sometimes shouted at David in the middle of the night)?; who could really understand her total absence from David's public life? She was no political wife. What a joke, even the thought. Did they gossip about her, was she something that made his colleagues pity him? Two of her paintings—the only comfort she had found at the Allan was learning to paint—hung in his Ottawa office. David could point to them and tell a visitor that his absent wife was creative and let silence cover over all that she wasn't. The 80 per cent of herself that was permanently lost, according to David's calculation.

Then, one sunny summer day in August 1977, David was sitting in the cool wooden splendour of the Parliamentary Library in Ottawa, catching up on the *New York Times*, quietly absorbed in external affairs, miles from thoughts of his wife. He was reading yet another story of CIA wrongdoing, a staple of the papers in those post-Watergate days. This one topped them all for gruesome pleasures—its plot was right out of a 1950s science-fiction movie. The evil ones, it seemed, had actually been searching for the ways and means to control human minds, spurred by the cold war fear that the Soviet and Chinese communists had found the key to brainwashing—Pavlov meets Dr. Fu Manchu. As the *Times* put it, the CIA "had looked into the vacant eyes of Joseph Cardinal Mindszenty at his treason trial in Budapest in 1949 and been horrified", certain that "he was either under the influence of some mysterious mind-bending drug or that he was standing before the dock in a post-hypnotic trance".

The CIA thought it saw the same look in the eyes of returning American POWs captured by the Chinese in the Korean War. All-American air-force pilots had confessed to waging germ warfare in Korea—confessed to something they hadn't done. Ordinary soldiers had collaborated with the enemy; some had converted outright to Communism, a propaganda victory of the highest order. The folks back home found it fearsome and inexplicable, and so did the CIA—no American boy would have done what these ones had unless the Communists had found some noxious new tool to conquer the minds of the free world.

At first, the CIA impetus was defensive; they felt driven to catch up to the Communists, to understand what had happened. But as the *Times* pointed out, "the CIA quickly turned to seeking an offensive use for behavior control. It sought to crack the mental defenses of enemy agents—to be able to program them and its own operatives to carry out any mission, even against their will and against such fundamental laws of nature as self-preservation." That wasn't hyperbole on the part of the *Times* reporters—they were paraphrasing recently declassified CIA documents. It was everyone's worst dream of what a secret agency could do, funding research that violated democratic ideals from a secret bastion at the heart of the world's largest democracy. In all its lurid glory, the story was meat to an old leftist like David Orlikow.

On the front page the paper was full of details of the funding. The CIA had wanted access to researchers at the forefront of psy-chiatry, neurology, psychology—every field concerned with human behaviour—but were aware right from the beginning that not every sci-entist would leap at the chance to do brainwashing research for the CIA. Even at the height of the cold war, the agency also figured that Amer-ican citizens might not understand the need for such research, might pillory both the scientists and the CIA if the news got out. So the agency funded a lot of the work through cover organizations: the Society for the Investigation of Human Ecology (SIHE) in New York, founded by eminent Cornell University neurologist Harold Wolff; and in Washing-ton, D.C., the Geschickter Foundation for Medical Research and the Josiah Macy Jr. Foundation. All three were private institutions with no apparent connection to the CIA, though the SIHE had been set up on the agency's direct instructions.

David Orlikow followed the story as it turned to page 16 and looked with some interest at a chart of known CIA-funded programs at the top of the page. The first name listed in bold type under the heading "Society for the Investigation of Human Ecology" was familiar to him, so familiar that the sight of it stopped him cold.

Dr. D. Ewen Cameron
(Allan Memorial Institute
of Psychiatry, McGill
University, Montreal)
Brainwashing techniques
and other experiments
on patients and staff.

David's eyes drifted to the left and down into the dense, reliable *Times* text; another name jumped out at him—Leonard Rubenstein. His wife had told him about the weird Mr. Rubenstein, about his bringing her the tapes, filming her in skimpy costumes, playing sounds at her in a tiny isolation booth. Here he was in the paper saying, "It was directly related to brainwashing....They [the Society for the Investigation of Human Ecology] had investigated brainwashing among soldiers who had been in Korea. We in Montreal started to use some [of these] techniques brainwashing patients instead of using drugs." Rubenstein claimed he knew nothing about the CIA, but he remembered the society's executive director, Colonel James Monroe, an air-force officer, an expert on the "brainwashed" American POWs. An odd duck to be running an independent scientific research foundation.

The effect of that *New York Times* story on David Orlikow was nothing compared to its effect on his wife. Since Leslie's birth in 1949 there had been no reason for anything that had happened to Val outside of her own sickness, no reason for all the suffering except her own inability to cope, her failure to get well. In the revelations in the *New York Times*, in all the revelations that followed, Val found her "missing link", the reason "why I had not felt better". Cameron hadn't really been trying to help her, but to find out things about her, about how her brain worked, "to provide information [to the CIA] that could only hurt other people." At last, Val thought, she had the answer to why Cameron had cut her out of his life.

But the sense she made of it was alarmingly double-edged: Val was sure that the reason she wasn't well was that the man she had idolized had abused her trust. When she was of no more use to him— or the CIA—he had cast her off. That meant he had never cared for her. And that made her want three things more than anything: justice, vindication, revenge. Dr. Lamberd, who knew the story of her treatment at the Allan and thought Cameron's methods had been closer to "psychological torture" than therapy, still worried that Val was overreacting to the news. What would it gain her to raise the whole thing in public—more anger, more pain? Could she stand a long fight? Shouldn't she leave well enough alone, CIA or no CIA?

Val's answer was simple: "I can't. I've listened to experts all my life and you are an expert but I'm sorry, I can't take your advice. I am driven to find out what happened. I have an absolutely full sense of being driven. I can't stop. I've got to find out what happened."

Luckily for Val Orlikow, there was another person with an absolutely full sense of being driven—John Marks, a project director with the Washington-based Center for National Security Studies, a tiny watchdog group funded by the American Civil Liberties Union for the purpose of keeping an open eye on the actions of the American secret agencies. CIA-watching was a cottage industry in the United States in the 1970s, especially after *New York Times* reporter Seymour Hersh got his hands on the story that the CIA had turned its agents loose on home ground to spy on hundreds of thousands of Americans it believed supported "dissident" causes. After those revelations, Gerald Ford, in 1975, had asked vice-president Nelson Rockefeller to investigate the agency's activities within the United States and to publish the findings, leading to even more investigations of CIA dirty tricks.

Marks, a long and lanky fellow with curly hair and the face of an honest schoolboy, had already written a book on the CIA with former agent Vincent Marchetti. He had covert contacts, and he had been invaded, as a result of his long look at the intelligence community, by its paranoid, conspiratorial frame of mind. When the Rockefeller *Report* came out in June 1975, the dogs of the press went haring off after the most obvious thing in it: that "behavior-influencing drugs" had been tested on "unsuspecting" American subjects, and that one of them—an anonymous employee of the army—had been slipped a dose of LSD without his knowledge at a meeting with CIA personnel; he had freaked out and jumped from the tenth-floor window of a New York hotel several days later. The press learned and soon published that his name was Frank Olson; that his wife and family had been told that he had committed suicide because of long-standing psychological difficulties and not because of an unwitting dose of LSD. Gerald Ford apologized to the widowed Alice Olson, and Congress passed a law conferring a settlement on the Olson heirs of $750,000.

What drew Marks' attention, however, were two sentences in the report that were almost an aside: "The drug program was part of a much larger CIA program to study possible means for controlling human behavior. Other studies explored the effects of radiation, electric-shock, psychology, psychiatry, sociology and harassment substances." And, later, "All the records concerning the program were ordered destroyed in 1973, including a total of 152 separate files." The report said that drug-testing had started in the late 1940s; the files were destroyed in 1973, which meant that the program could have been running for twenty-five years.

Marks understood that the CIA, before anything else, was an enormous bureaucracy. To him it didn't seem possible that all the files pertaining to the behaviour-control program had been destroyed. By June 30, 1975, Marks had filed a request to the CIA, under the Freedom of Information Act, for all materials "furnished by your Agency to the Rockefeller Commission relating to the 'program to study possible means for controlling human behavior' ". The agency's Freedom of Information co-ordinator wrote right back to say that the CIA hadn't supplied any "documents or any other written material on this topic" to the commission. It was the first typically unenlightening exchange in a struggle that lasted two years and stopped just short of Marks' taking the CIA to court to get the files.

What Marks finally received astounded him. Frank Laubinger, an ex-CIA employee hired on a freelance basis to do the mind-control paper search, had confirmed that the main files—seven boxes of them—had been destroyed on orders from two men: CIA Director Richard Helms, who retired in 1973, and Dr. Sidney Gottlieb, the man most closely connected with the mind-control program and a long-time Helms protégé, who had also thought it wise to retire in 1973. But in the agency's Retired Records Center, Laubinger found seven boxes that had been overlooked: financial records, invoices, and expense statements, with accompanying brief descriptions of the projects— whatever it took to reassure the people who handled the books that the money was going where it was supposed to go.

In total, Marks had wrangled sixteen thousand pages of documents out of the CIA—documents in which most of the names were blacked out but in which there were identifying details; documents that sketched the progress of roughly $10 million through 80 institutions, 144 colleges or universities in the United States and Canada, 15 research facilities or private companies, 12 hospitals or clinics, and 3 penal institutions. Marks already knew that people who worked for an agency like the CIA were into control—control of their agents, control of other people's governments. But control of people's minds? The book Marks eventually wrote outlining the CIA's absolute exercise in control he could not resist calling *The Search for the "Manchurian Candidate"*.

John Marks is the only private person ever to force such large disclosures on the CIA under the Freedom of Information Act; the CIA usually side-steps potentially unpleasant requests with a simple loophole—it cannot reveal any information that might damage national security. Marks readily admits that he won the day pretty much because Admiral Stansfield Turner, the former naval officer Jimmy Carter appointed to head the CIA in 1977, wanted him to. Turner hoped that as full a revelation as possible of the operation the agency had called MKUL-TRA would be the last act of the CIA's long *mea culpa*, the nadir from which—after one more set of hearings, this time in front of joint Senate Select Intelligence and Human Resources committees—the CIA had nowhere to go but up.

Turner, recruited by Carter to restore the credibility and effectiveness of the agency, had rather bleak recent examples to consider. Richard Helms had been recruited into the Office of Strategic Services (OSS)—America's first civilian spy service—in the glory days of the Second World War and had a full career at the heart of the CIA's espionage and covert action branches. But he had displeased his president, Richard Nixon, by not acting soon enough to bring about Salvador Allende's downfall in Chile, and Nixon had posted him as ambassador to Iran. Helms then denied that the CIA had tried to overthrow the Allende government in front of the Senate Foreign Relations Committee, in order to protect Nixon, and was charged and convicted of perjury. His successor for a few months, James Schlesinger, had focused on raking all the suspected CIA dirt up from under the carpets: he asked all employees to come forward with reports of misconduct and ended up with a 683-page list of dubious dealings that came to be called the CIA's "family jewels". William Colby, another career intelligence officer first recruited in OSS days, had mostly had to concentrate on containing the damage the slow but sure leakage of those jewels caused. George Bush, Turner's immediate predecessor, thought that being head of the CIA was a great job, not seeming to notice that the agency's morale was at an all-time low, that fear of criticism and forced disclosure had brought nearly all of the CIA's risky business to a halt.

It fell to Turner to try to resolve the basic dilemma at the heart of all this: you can't run a secret agency without secrets, but secrecy itself leads to abuses because it denies public accountability. In fact, Turner was *forced* to try to resolve that dilemma because, in light of the long history of CIA abuses, Congress imposed governmental review (usually called "oversight") on the agency in the form of Senate and House Intelligence committees and the National Security Council.

After Carter was defeated and Ronald Reagan replaced Turner with the old cold warrior William Casey, Turner wrote a rather wistful book called *Secrecy and Democracy: The CIA in Transition*, recalling his attempts to establish the CIA as a professional and apolitical intelligence-gathering agency, devoted more to analysis, assessment, and advice than to covert action. Wistful, of course, because Casey and the new administration blocked any true transition, being quite fond of the CIA as it had been in the fifties and sixties. A few "harebrained enterprises" of that era, Turner wrote, had resulted in the total erosion of the CIA's status and power; that such enterprises had even got off the ground was the result of an almost total lack of checks on secret activities during those years. Of MKULTRA, he wrote (in a section of manuscript the CIA censors forced him to delete), "The unit conducting the experiment simply had such autonomy that not many outsiders could look in and ask what was going on.... In this case, the system just could not provide that kind of detached critical review and a few well-intentioned, but terribly misguided, individuals badly abused the CIA's privilege of keeping secret so much of what it does."

Turner quite simply disliked the covert style of the CIA. He strongly deplored the consequences of spookiness: "We are a democracy, one with high ethical ideals. We should never turn over the custody of those ideals to any group of individuals who divorce themselves from concern for the public attitude. The crimes against mankind perpetrated by zealots who did not need to answer to the citizens are too many....Without accountability the temptations of acting in secret [are] too great." Before being replaced by Casey, Turner was well on his way to establishing a basic ethic on secrecy: even while acting covertly, the people in charge should "feel they could defend their decisions before the public if the actions became public". In other words, act as though the public did know, as if you had already justified yourself.

But even though the CIA censors under Casey launched an attack on Turner's own manuscript, forcing him to make more than a hundred deletions, Turner didn't seem to realize that such "excesses" as

MKULTRA were not aberrations. The confessional style of the seventies and Turner's own interregnum were the aberrations in the history of an agency that soon, under Casey, was back fighting the secret Third World War. Instead of putting the CIA's behaviour-control program down to the misguided actions of Sidney Gottlieb (whom he described as a "CIA middle-level manager"), Turner should have studied MKULTRA as evidence of the agency's misguided will to power. Horrifying, silly, and spooky, flamboyant and eventually futile—the MKULTRA program of experimentation expressed attitudes and ideas that came back to haunt the CIA and America in the 1980s.

Summoned to testify before the Senate Sub-committee on Intelligence chaired by Senator Frank Church in 1975, that middle-level manager Sid Gottlieb hid behind a pseudonym (Victor Scheider) and his humanitarianism: in order to appear, he had had to fly home from the Missionary Hospital in India where he was working as a volunteer. The main files relating to MKULTRA had been destroyed on Gottlieb's orders just two years earlier, however, so the Church committee was hamstrung in its attempts to make him accountable; his answers were appropriately vague. In 1977, the joint Senate Select Intelligence and Human Resources committee hearings had the documents John Marks had managed to get declassified, with almost every name in them blacked out except for Sid Gottlieb's. No matter what the Bronx-born chemist said, his role at least was somewhat clearer than it had been in 1975. Still, before testifying, Gottlieb asked for, and got, immunity from criminal prosecution, and—because of heart problems—he was allowed to give his evidence in a small Senate antechamber away from the crush of media and interested observers.

A touch of bitterness crept into Gottlieb's prepared statement as he wondered why the CIA censors had let his name stand—an obvious cutting of losses on the agency's part. But even so, the small grey-haired man with the club-foot, the spiritual and actual leader of the CIA's quest to conquer the mind, effectively countered the committee members' desire to know what, all in all, the CIA had learned from twenty-five years of experimentation. He simply said he didn't know.

The thing that was eminently clear from his appearance at the 1977 hearings was his attitude. Gottlieb considered himself a noble warrior in the cold war: "I would like this Committee to know that I considered all this work—at the time it was done and in the context of circumstances that were extant in that period—to be extremely unpleasant, extremely difficult, extremely sensitive, but above all, to be extremely urgent and important."

Though never obviously embarrassed by the specific revelations— whether it was of San Francisco and New York safe houses outfitted like brothels in which CIA agents ran unwitting drug-testing projects under names such as Midnight and Climax, or his own role in plots to assassinate Congo premier Patrice Lumumba and others—the implication was that Gottlieb had had his qualms. He was a man, after all, whom his co-workers described as a humanist, who had a solid marriage, four children, a farm, and a herd of goats he had milked in the dawn before heading into Washington to spend days pondering how to make Fidel Castro's beard fall out. A man with a club-foot who had taken up folk-dancing as a hobby, who was clumsy when simply walking but nimble and graceful when demonstrating new folk steps he had picked up in foreign places while on clandestine missions for the CIA. A man with a pretty horrifying mission, who had the intellect and resources, the personal complexity allied with conviction, to keep others signed up to the cause.

"I realize," Gottlieb continued, "that it is extremely difficult to reconstruct those times and that atmosphere today in this room." In fact, in the droning sequence of committee interrogation, the escapades of the boys from MKULTRA caused more laughter than shock: the cold war became a 1950s comic-book. Playing up the stupid ideas, the misfires, and the Three Stooges routines may even have been a deliberate strategy on the part of Gottlieb and company to evoke just that response; John Marks reported afterwards that the small cadre of witnesses had agreed among themselves beforehand to limit their testimony to questions asked, not to volunteer anything, knowing that the committee had not had the time to digest the documents and could have missed much.

For his statement, however, Gottlieb was playing it serious, justifying himself. "Another thought that I would like to leave you with," he said, "is that should the course of recent history have been slightly different from what it was, I can easily imagine a congressional committee being extremely critical of the Agency for not having done investigations of this nature." The implication being, of course, if Congress or America had survived.

Understanding the cold war now is almost impossible: it seems a bad metaphor, blatant and simplistic, a national mobilizing of unnecessary fear. It was as if defeating one huge evil had left such a vacuum that another more unimaginable evil had to be created to take its place. At Yalta, Germany and Japan became almost side issues as the Allies divided up the world into spheres of Soviet and American influence; the lines of a new global conflict were the direct heritage of the victory. Soon, no eyes could penetrate the Iron Curtain or the mysteries of Chinese Communism—anything you could imagine could be happening there, committed by the brain- and body-snatchers, the necessary enemy in a world defined by war.

That the good guys and not the bad guys had brought the one new thing into the world—the technological possibility of total annihilation—was not yet grounds for ambivalence. Not in public, anyway, and not among the warriors. In fact, the scope of the Second World War, its global threat, had given the warriors licence to use any means to get to victory, including the bomb. That is perhaps what Sid Gottlieb wanted to remind the senators of. Most of them were old enough to remember or to have participated in the war in which war itself burst all old military boundaries, in which it was waged by whole nations and not just the boys chosen to carry the guns and the old men who told them what to do with them.

It does not even matter, to the Gottliebs of the world, that the perception of Soviet threat that laid the groundwork for the cold war was stage-managed by key members of the OSS: that Allen Dulles, a deeply conservative man who was to become director of the CIA in the fifties, was in Switzerland and Germany recruiting Fascist intelligence agents for the new war against Communism before the old war was even over. Out of fear, ambition, and who knows what else, the rise of the CIA was intimately tied to cold-war terms: fear-mongering and empire-building were one and the same thing.

Here, for instance, is Dulles, as the new CIA director, addressing a Princeton alumni conference on April 10, 1953, on "how sinister the battle for men's minds had become in Soviet hands". Some of the Russian "brain perversion techniques", he said, "were so subtle and abhorrent to our way of life that we have recoiled from facing up to them. The minds of selected individuals who are subjected to such treatment...are deprived of the ability to state their own thoughts. Parrot-like, the individuals so conditioned can merely repeat the thoughts which have been implanted in their minds by suggestion from outside. In effect the brain...becomes a phonograph playing a disc put on its spindle by an outside genius over which it had no control." In essence, Dulles was doing what Stansfield Turner said an ethical CIA director should do—making sure that he could justify in public what the agency was planning to do in secret. Three days after that speech, Dulles authorized MKULTRA, a sweeping program urged on him by Richard Helms, to be run by Sidney Gottlieb, and dedicated to acquiring all the techniques he feared the Communists already had, abhorrent as they were to the American way of life.

To understand the origins of the CIA's mind-control quest, you have to venture not so much into the minds of the cold warriors as into those of the soldiers, the generals, the Allied and Axis leaders of the Second World War. Winston Churchill called it "the wizard war"—and indeed it was the first technological war, won by scientific advances, by an unprecedented union of scientists and soldiers. "One reason that Hitler failed," jokes a historian, "is that he was out of date." But it isn't really a joke: massively prepared for war though Germany was, it was prepared for a short war. Ahead of the Allies at the start in crucial technologies such as radar and missile development, Germany failed to keep pouring money into research. Sulfa drugs, penicillin, DDT (which killed malarial mosquitoes to make tropical campaigns possible); operational research in which scientists strategized along with the soldiers; bazookas and the A-bomb: all were the winning contributions of the hard sciences to the war.

The soft sciences, too, had a huge part to play. The growth and development, the respectability and advancement, of psychiatry and psychology are intimately linked to the two world wars. Psychoanalysts had their first successes *d'estime* treating war neuroses that had defied the ministrations of psychiatrists—who at that time dealt with madness largely by diagnosing it and confining it, and whose biological ideas (a search for the physical lesions that resulted in mental disease) had not yet given way to a psychological understanding of behaviour. The common attitude to war-induced neurosis in 1914-18 was to call it shell-shock, to believe it was actual physical damage to the brain caused by the concussive effects of heavy artillery fire. That fear and anxiety produced by constant proximity to heavy artillery fire might be the cause was regarded as still conjectural. And even those who believed that the heavy rates of war neuroses were physically caused still somehow thought shell-shock happened only to the overly susceptible, to weaklings and cowards. War was for the strong, not for the weak.

In Germany, after that war, there was a convulsive effort to understand the great defeat. The consensus of psychologists and psychiatrists between the wars was that enemy propaganda must have broken the German spirit, because nothing could have broken the brave German body. Whether it was true or not (in that war, undoubtedly not), the term "psychological warfare" was coined in Germany in the 1930s. Hitler was the only national leader to write knowingly (in *Mein Kampf*)—cynically and horrifyingly—on the uses of propaganda, the only head of state then to understand the possibilities of mass communications and the developing advertising arts, and to attempt to practise conscious mass manipulation as a standard part of governing. The Nazis believed that a war against minds might be even deadlier than a war waged solely against the bodies of enemy soldiers; Germany was the only nation to go into the war with a full-scale psychological-warfare strategy, mapped out by Joseph Goebbels and his Ministry of

People's Enlightenment and Propaganda. It was not the only nation to come out of the war with one.

Winston Churchill, whose consciousness was forged in the First World War, didn't care much for the greys of psychological warfare (except for deception, which he understood as the faking-out ploy of a good chess player or general). The British called it political warfare instead, and—under the policy that the best propaganda was the truth selectively applied—they excelled at it. George Orwell worked as a propagandist at the BBC, broadcasting to India, and noted in his diary a dark thought that was an obvious precursor to *Nineteen Eighty-four*, his novel of mind control: "All propaganda is lies, even when one is telling the truth." It's not that cynicism had never reared its head before 1940—it was more that men of stout morals were persuaded, in the face of the Nazi threat, that anything and everything had to go in order to win. They were encouraged, and none so much as the American OSS, to adopt the trickster amorality of boys. The final impact of the psychological war is impossible to gauge: the important thing here is that, in the crucible of the Second World War, Allied governments gained the insight that minds and thoughts were as important a target as bodies, and that scientifically planned assaults could be made on the spirit's citadel.

Ideas about the psychological balance of ordinary men also underwent a sizeable reworking in the war. On the basis of psychiatric screening, the American Army alone rejected 1.6 million men as mentally unfit for war, only to find that it still lost 504,000 soldiers to psychiatric collapse, a higher rate than in the First World War.

Psychiatrists were crucial, and moderately successful, in the radical and quick treatment of war neuroses brought on by the stress of battle or (what turned out to be worse) the stress of waiting for battle. Psychiatrists worked behind the lines in the invasion of Normandy, treating mental wounds on an emergency basis just as the surgeons and medical doctors treated the bodily ones. Heavy sedation—several days of chemical sleep induced as soon after the traumatic shock as possible—often did the trick. Those for whom that didn't work were shipped quickly back to England to neurosis centres where narco-analysis and other abreactive therapies were used with great success. To a certain degree, it was madness and the mind demystified—anyone could become mad if the stress was great enough. The crucial realization in the treatment of war neurosis in the Second World War was that every man had his breaking point: no amount of moral fibre or courage could hold a soldier together if forces conspired to break him to pieces. That realization was radical for the healers, but it was also radical for the generals, because it suddenly made the idea of a truth drug or technique for breaking into someone's mind seem a tangible, achievable goal—especially if you could enlist the people with the insight, the healers, in the quest.

William Sargant, a British psychiatrist who had his first tastes of therapeutic success with war neurotics, was quick to realize that "World War II provided medicine with rare opportunities for studying the breakdown of normal persons subjected to intense stress," and that early in the war "the value of certain drugs had become obvious in helping patients to discharge their pent-up emotions about the terrifying experiences which had caused their mental breakdown." The goal that soon intrigued the secret warriors, of course, was how to harness the same psychological forces to break a person down in order to reap the naked truth, the real dope, the pearl of hidden information, from among the personal debris. The methods used to heal psychic breaks on the beaches of Normandy might hold the key to perfect interrogation.

John Marks called the OSS, established in 1942, "the first American agency set up to wage secret, unlimited war". Its birth was contentious; U.S. military intelligence didn't want a bunch of civilians muddying the waters and didn't believe that a bunch of "amateurs" could do much to help win the war. The mandate given it by President Roosevelt attempted to clarify matters: under the control of the Joint Chiefs of Staff, the OSS was to undertake "the planning, development, co-ordination, and execution of the military programme for psychological warfare" and the compiling of "such political, psychological, sociological and economic information as may be required by military operations".

Its director, General William "Wild Bill" Donovan, knew what his own goals were: to throw notions of fair play out the window, to fight dirty, to create and deploy "every subtle device and every underhanded trick…against the Germans and the Japanese". Donovan, a First World War hero with a *Boy's Own Annual* notion of the heroic death-defying spy, recruited the cream of the East Coast WASP élite to play spy with him behind enemy lines (quite often to the horror or amusement of older hands at the covert action game); he was strong on action, not analysis, and generally made mischief, not war.

Gadgetry, gimmickry, cloak and dagger: how better to gain the psychological edge on the enemy than through the new behaviour sciences—or, rather, through the ignoble hearts of the scientists? Stanley Lovell, Donovan's head of research and development, saw his job as transforming Dr. Jekylls into Mr. Hydes: he wanted "to stimulate the Peck's Bad Boy beneath the surface of every American scientist and to say to him 'Throw all your normal law-abiding concepts out the window. Here's a chance to raise merry hell!' "

Lovell's own mind was fertile and devious; his wild ideas flew far ahead of, sometimes obliterated, sensible operational goals. Eager to get the psychological edge on Hitler, Lovell enlisted Cambridge psychoanalyst Walter Langer to do a case history of the German leader in an attempt to predict his behaviour. Langer was dubious, but did gain enough insight through Hitler's writings and speeches to forecast that a losing tide of war would drive the Führer into increasing mental and physical isolation. But what Lovell and the OSS-recruited scientists made of the insight was something else altogether. They hatched schemes to infiltrate Hitler's entourage in order to put female sex hormones into his food, blind him with mustard gas, drug him to set off his suspected epilepsy and perhaps poison him—never seeming to realize that if they did manage to invade the Nazi leader's inner circle the direct action of a gun might prove of supreme propaganda value. In retrospect, the flavour of the OSS is more Maxwell Smart than James Bond (the good guys won but they looked like fools doing it, and were often booby-trapped by their own gadgets).

And, in fact, Lovell's Peck's Bad Boys operated from a rather limited understanding of sin. One of Lovell's first acts was to appoint Winfred Overholser, superintendent of St. Elizabeth's Hospital in Washington, D.C., chairman of a six-person committee that included the then president of the American Psychiatric Association, Dr. Edward Strecker, to look for a truth drug. After considering such candidates as barbiturates, cocaine, and scopolamine (a drug that induced what obstetricians called a twilight sleep, in which many an American female had yelled, cursed, and sweated her way towards birth, remembering nothing of the experience afterwards), the committee hit on marijuana as the most likely loosener of reluctant tongues. In scientific fashion, they produced an odourless and tasteless liquid preparation of the drug; the only trouble was that you couldn't deliver it orally because it made people sick. The solution they dreamed up? Cigarettes injected with the drug by hypodermic needle; the technological joint. And who were the drug's first test subjects—a drug that was meant to winkle out the secrets of the enemy? Workers on the Manhattan Project, the American top secret research effort to develop an atomic bomb.

It's hard not to see the whole project as some kind of cosmic joke; but it's only possible to see it that way because none of the Overholser committee's inventions and devices achieved its aim. And, despite the fact that no one came up with a truth drug during the war, several new ideas were implanted in both scientific and military brains. Out of the ambitious attempt to psychoanalyse Hitler and other leading Nazis from afar, and out of the more straightforward psychological testing of soldiers and intelligence recruits, came the notion that there was (or should be) a scientific way to predict how people would behave in certain situations. What followed inexorably was the temptation to try to *make* people behave in certain ways, based though it was on a simple-minded idea of the complex relations among brain, mind, behaviour, personality, and circumstance. After their war success, it was felt that the soft sciences *should* have hard techniques and hard applications—that they soon would provide the means of eliminating that most difficult aspect of human relations, the human element itself.

Dr. William Sargant, an old friend of D. Ewen Cameron's, recognized an unprecedented congruence of post-war aims in his 1957 book *Battle for the Mind*:

> Politicians, priests and psychiatrists often face the same problem: how to find the most rapid and permanent means of changing a man's beliefs. When, towards the end of World War II, I first became interested in the similarity of methods which have, from time to time, been used by the political, religious and psychiatric disciplines, I failed to foresee the enormous importance now attaching to the problem—because of an ideological struggle that seems fated to decide the course of civilization for centuries to come. The problem of the doctor and his nervously ill patient, and that of the religious leader who sets out to gain and hold new converts, has now become the problem of whole groups of nations, who wish not only to confirm certain political beliefs within their boundaries, but to proselytize the outside world.

Disclaiming politics, and with a moral rider condemning false prophets and politicians, Sargant went on in the book explicitly to examine the mechanisms that he imagined worked in sudden conversions and to invoke their use for therapeutic ends. With hindsight (and standing outside his profession) it's easy to see how seduced the doctor was by the idea of mind control for the good of mankind—that is, mind control in his hands.

Having sought a drug to make interrogation easy, having wished for useful amnesias and thought control, it was easy for the Western powers to believe that the Soviets had sought the same things. Confronting the alien, Communist cultures of the post-war world, whose masses seemed to them will-less, mindless, soulless, it was easy for the technology-minded Western governments to believe that the U.S.S.R. and China had made some kind of scientific breakthrough to achieve thought control. When it seemed that the Communists could work their will on American prisoners of war and on entrenched opponents of Communist regimes, it was easy to see it as confirmation that a technique called brainwashing did exist. And, worst threat of all, that the Communists had got to the battlefield of the mind first. That there was, in fact, a mind-control gap that the West had to rush to close, or face a takeover more insidious than literal invasion.

CHAPTER FOUR

Good Science, Bad Science

In *Against Interpretation*, Susan Sontag spun an essay called "The Imagination of Disaster" out of a fascination with the science-fiction films of the fifties and sixties. Recent events (the bomb, the war) had enlarged the scope of imaginable disasters, wrote Sontag; where vampires or Frankenstein monsters had stalked a community, alien invaders threatened global destruction or, like mental neutron bombs, kept human bodies intact but infused them with zombie minds. More interesting to Sontag was how the new scale of threat or destruction acted on the heroes of the sci-fi films. Though the task was superficially the same as in the oldest of fairy tales (to defeat evil, to protect the human community), "the protagonists—perhaps by the very nature of what is visited upon them—no longer seem wholly innocent."

It was no longer a hero's strong arm and steadfast morality that defeated the invader, but his mobilization of science and technology— dangerous things, the very tools of the conqueror. "The science fiction films are strongly moralistic," Sontag wrote. "The standard message is the one about the proper, or humane, use of science, versus the mad, obsessional use of science.... Generally, for a scientific enterprise to be treated entirely sympathetically in these films, it needs the certificate of utility. Science, viewed without ambivalence, meant an efficacious response to danger." Pure science—divorced from obvious utility—appeared as "a maniacal dementia that cuts one off from normal human relations." Good science was team-work and technology, and a fitting of science's purposes to clear social and political ends; bad science was one man's intellect running away with him and endangering society.

Sontag rarely found science viewed without ambivalence in the science-fiction movies. Hope for world peace was embodied in enlightened scientific practice (all the good scientists of formerly warring nations band together to defeat the alien threat and thereafter establish a world-wide utopia of sweet-reasoned consensus). But science also threatened to enforce consensus, to dehumanize. In the old vampire legends, an ordinary man was made monstrous by the deep hungers of his animal nature. In the sci-fi films of the fifties and sixties, invasions of body-snatching aliens produced human monsters free of pain, hate, lust, fear, and love: man "has simply become far more efficient—the very model of technocratic man, purged of emotions, volitionless, tranquil, obedient to all orders." Normal humans viewed the body-snatched with absolute horror: the horror of modern life, argued Sontag, is that we will not go mad but be turned into machines.

The catch is that the good guys, the saviour-scientists, were more akin to the zombies than to normal humans, in such qualities as "the ascendency of reason over feelings, the idealization of teamwork and the consensus-creating activities of science, [and] a marked degree of moral simplification". Arguing backwards from pop culture into the death at the heart of modern life, Sontag saw the imagination broken into numbed fantasy or useless moralizing in the face of the threats of technological annihilation and depersonalization. The sci-fi films, she wrote, were an "inadequate response" to modern-style apocalypse, functioning "to normalize what is psychologically unbearable, thereby inuring us to it". Their central effect was to engage their audiences "in complicity with the abhorrent".

One wonders what Sontag could have written had she been arguing not from pop culture but from a knowledge of what scientists and governments were actually doing during the cold war. "Haunted" and "depressed" by a failure of popular imagination, she might have been pushed into an inarticulate, defeated sense of doom had she known what both the bad scientists and the good scientists were up to in the face of the alien (Chinese, Russian) threat—how they were meeting in committee with military and political leaders, just as scientists did in the movie scenarios she outlined. Some of them were even comfortable talking in the melodramatic, inappropriately humorous dialogue of B-grade science fiction: "Gee whiz, boys, they're washing brains over there. We've got to do something about it!" And the thing they perceived as so threatening—some kind of Communist mind-control machine—was their own nightmare, a creature from the twilight zone of scientific imagination.

Worse, in order to save the free world from the monster they themselves had dreamed into being, many of them were quite ready to trespass on the values that made the free world worth saving. Heck, in the science-fiction movies of those times, they would have been the bad guys.

There was no pressing ethical reason to end the partnership between science and the military created by the Second World War when the war was over. Not only were both professions by then in the habit of partnership, it was profitable for both scientific inquiry (i.e., there was money there) and aggression in the new cold war. In Canada, the Defence Research Board was established in the spring of 1947 precisely to co-ordinate "facilities" that had operated under different branches of the services during the war. A small board with a relatively small budget ($14.5 million in its first year), the DRB also wanted to maintain its collaboration with its wartime allies. A memo prepared to send on to the United States in 1950 was pragmatic about it: "Due to the relatively limited resources of Canada, considerable thought has had to be given to preventing duplication of effort with other democratic countries. Any Canadian research program must therefore be integrated very closely with that of the United States, and it is Canadian policy to make Canadian facilities available to the United States if called upon, in furtherance of the common aim." One example of co-operation was a program of experimentation in chemical and bacterial warfare based at the Field Experimental Station in Suffield, Alberta. In the post-war scientific effort, Canadians built a bit of an empire in that area.

Common aims, as far as the DRB went, seemed to be shared more often with the United States, even though the bureaucrats who ran the board were well aware that the exchange between the two countries was unequal. Canada, hardly a huge target in the cold war, had intelligence and military establishments just as concerned with destabilization and Communist fifth-columnists; Soviet cipher clerk Igor Gouzenko, who defected into the arms of reluctant Canadian officials in September 1945, bearing information about Soviet spy rings in the West and subversion in the intelligence community itself, had destroyed any complacency on the subject. Liaison was judged to be good with the United States (better than with Britain), and information flowed not only to the U.S. military but also to the CIA. The chairman of the DRB at the time, Dr. Omond Solandt, says that the CIA had an agent at the U.S. Embassy in Ottawa in the 1950s who was publicly introduced as being from the CIA and who was free to attend staff and committee meetings of the board.

A relatively small proportion of DRB money went to funding psychological and psychiatric research, but when the thought of a mind-control gap loomed, the Canadians were eager to do their bit to help. In fact, while many of the American intelligence documents of the era couch the quest for mind control in defensive terms (rhetorical or not), the minutes of a tripartite meeting held at the Ritz-Carlton Hotel in Montreal on June 1, 1951, are blunt about cold-war objectives. Representatives of the CIA, the DRB, and the British scientific establishment concurred that "present methods of offence had moved over into the psychological field and that the whole area of the change of public opinion and individual attitude was assuming rapidly increasing importance".

The meeting had been called to discuss research into "the general phenomena indicated by such terms as—'confession,' 'menticide,' 'intervention in the individual mind'—together with methods concerned in psychological coercion, change of opinions and attitude, etc." From the record, neither of the two CIA representatives at the meeting, Dr. Caryl Haskins or Commander R.J. Williams, was particularly forthcoming on research the United States was already engaged in. Sir Henry Tizard, the eminent British physicist who was arguably the most influential scientific adviser to his government in the war, arrived with Solandt. His sole contribution, according to the minutes, was to announce that the British were doing *no* research in the area. Worried by reports coming from behind the Iron Curtain, they had already submitted the problem to a scientific advisory group, which "had pointed out that the phenomenon of confession itself had precedent in the inquisitional confessions and that apart from any physical methods involved, the methods of psychological coercion and argument had been well developed by the Inquisition at that time. The general phenomenon was apparently felt to be little different except in time and place."

It was left to the psychologists and psychiatrists present, all DRB committee members, to differ: Dr. Travis Dancey, head of psychiatry at Montreal's Queen Mary Veteran's Hospital, Dr. James Tyhurst, who was funded through the Allan Memorial Institute and the DRB to study civilian reactions to disaster, and the brilliant McGill University chairman of psychology, Donald Hebb. The old inquisitors had used not just psychological argument but the rack to induce confession: what fascinated Hebb was that obvious physical duress did not seem to figure in the confessions and conversions being put down to brainwashing. The relation between physical duress, fear, and confession seemed easy to figure, though sometimes obvious fear wasn't the predominant result of duress. He recalled the story of a female chimpanzee at the Yerkes Laboratories of Primate Biology in Florida (where he had worked) who was friendly and affectionate towards one male researcher and consistently tried to bite another. In a cage one day with the man she didn't like she attacked him; "he seized a length of rubber hose and proceeded to beat her." After the beating, the chimp was obedient and affectionate towards the man she had previously tried to bite and became quite dependent on him. What little bit of neurophysiology caused that reaction, wondered Hebb.

The thing that most preoccupied Hebb was the study of how people think. As a scientist he felt he had to start from what was provable: "All that we can know about another's feelings and awareness is an inference from what he does—from his muscular contractions and glandular secretions." He was already engrossed in an effort to understand the relationships between experience and the development of intelligence, and the connections between mammals (specifically dogs and humans) and their perceptual environment; he and his research associates and graduate students were rearing Scotch terriers in various levels of isolation, and from those studies Hebb had come to believe that learning was fundamental to all but the most primitive of human perceptions. If a normal environment (that is, interaction with other dogs and experiences of the noisy sounds, smells, and action of the world around them) was vital to the development of personality (Hebb here made a leap from primate studies and his own dog studies to humans), what would happen to mature personalities suddenly deprived of normal levels of stimulus? Would they so crave sensory input that even ham-handed propaganda would sound good?

As noted in the minutes of the meeting, Hebb suggested an experiment "whereby an individual might be placed in a situation (translucent suit) in which, by means of cutting off all sensory stimulation save some minor proprioceptive sensations and by the use of 'white noise,' the individual could be led into a situation whereby ideas, etc. might be implanted".

The idea could have been let drop, lost in the flow of a discussion that ranged rather vaguely through other approaches to the problem, even to considering the rumour that Cardinal Mindszenty's sister was living in Halifax and might shed some light on her brother's confession. But before the June 1 meeting Hebb had talked several times with DRB staff about the need for basic research into totalitarian methods of producing attitude change. And he followed the meeting up with a research proposal (in hand at the board by June 12) for $23,000 for two years' work. In a memo recommending the grant, Whit

Morton, director of the DRB's Operational Research Group, noted that the project "appears to me to be very much on the borderline between work which Dr. Hebb would be interested in doing anyway and work which he feels he is doing essentially on the Board's behalf".

What Hebb and his graduate students and research assistants found out soon had Hebb writing letters to Morton begging for permission to declassify the results, one complete with a little drawing of himself on bended knee beside his signature ("muzzle not the ox that treadeth out the corn. —Humbly yours, Don").

The basic McGill perceptual-isolation experiment was as follows: a volunteer, usually a grad student paid twenty dollars a day (or twice what he or she could normally earn in those years), was installed alone on a comfortable bed or couch in a quiet room. Volunteers' eyes were covered with goggles that allowed them to see diffused light but no pattern; their arms were covered to the tips of the fingers with cardboard tubes so that, though they still had some mobility, they didn't have much of a sense of touch. The room was miked so that if they hummed or talked or thrashed restlessly the researchers could hear them; subjects knew that if they yelled to be let out they would be let out immediately. They wore headphones that delivered either "white noise" or inane ditties like the sixteen-bar chorus of "Home on the Range" repeated several times, and stock-market figures, passages from a religious primer for six-year-olds, numbers, and nonsense syllables.

Six potential volunteers surprised the researchers by refusing to go on with the experiment after it had been described to them and before they had even got into the room; eleven of the twenty-two initial subjects could not stay for the twenty-four-hour minimum they had promised, four of them telling Hebb's group that "being in the apparatus was a form of torture". For most the experience went like this: at first alone in a quiet room they slept a little; for five or six hours, anyway, their thoughts were controlled, connected, and coherent. Then they began to feel thick-headed, unable to follow a train of thought for any length of time; as the isolation stretched on, they began to hallucinate visually and sometimes also to hear and feel things that weren't there.

Usually they first noticed spots before their eyes, then patterns, and then actual objects and scenes. One man saw squirrels with packsacks on their shoulders marching in single file over a snow field; another not only saw a space ship in the "sky" but felt projectiles fired from its guns hitting his arms. One of the experimental team, a clergyman who was in graduate psychology under Hebb, thought he was going crazy before he had passed even 24 hours: he hallucinated a whole scene that began with a stone sending ripples out over the surface of a woodland pool. Then naked boys dived in from above the trees, followed by naked women—at which point the researcher got himself let out. A subject who stayed in for five and a half days (the longest time any volunteer spent in perceptual isolation was 139 hours; the average person lasted just over 43 hours) felt as though another man was in the bed with him. Worse, he couldn't tell which body was the other and which was himself. He said, "My mind was like a ball of cotton floating in the air and looking down on my body."

Hebb and his co-workers had not anticipated that simple isolation would produce such intellectual, emotional, and perceptual confusion in their subjects—that to stay intact, adult personalities seemed to need steady interchange with a normal sensory environment. They also found it startling that it took up to twenty-four hours after leaving the isolation room for its effects to wear off: to some the world beyond the room looked flat (one almost had a car accident, which caused the researchers to warn volunteers not to drive for the first five or six hours of freedom); in general IQs were temporarily lowered and reaction times were slow.

Then came the brainwashing part of the experiment. The first fourteen volunteers showed that they preferred to listen to anything other than silence or white noise while in solitude, even things they found distasteful under normal circumstances; they became addicts of "Home on the Range". The researchers prepared passages of propaganda in favour of innocuous theories they thought university-educated science students would be fairly resistant to: a belief in ghosts and extra-sensory perception; and the anti-evolutionary point of view. As Hebb wrote in a summing-up paper he prepared on the research in 1958: "The effects of the propaganda were the only ones that showed signs of lasting beyond the experimental period. The groups tested two weeks later were too small to establish the point definitely, in a statistical sense, but the tentative conclusion was reinforced by incidental reports from the subjects. A number of the experimental subjects, unlike the controls, went to the library to borrow books on psychical...research, mind-reading and so forth; there were spontaneous reports of being afraid of ghosts late at night, for the first time in the subject's experience; and reports of trying to use ESP in card-playing."

Hebb completed the thought by saying that the research was "very unsettling to us": "It is one thing to hear that the Chinese are brainwashing their prisoners on the other side of the world; it is another to find, in your own laboratory, that merely taking away the usual sights, sounds, and bodily contacts from a healthy university student for a few days can shake him, right down to the base." What Hebb's work had, of course, done was open the scientific door not only to comprehending part of the mechanism of the dreaded brainwashing, but also to developing effective torture and interrogation techniques in which the damage was largely "self-inflicted". No bruises, no deaths—the Canadian contribution.

The irony of Donald Hebb's brainwashing work—shouldered, he implied in his dealings with the DRB, as the good scientist's burden in meeting the totalitarian threat—was that it was among the first experimentation to make scientifically explicit the "totalitarian advantage" in the cold war.

From the first alarms to the end strategies, the secret agencies and military organizations of the West had clear evidence that the Communists had not come up with any dreaded new technique or secret weapon to control men's minds. A report circulated as early as 1950 through the defence and intelligence communities described (relatively accurately) the Chinese method of thought control. Suspected anti-Communists were treated not to magic drugs but to intensive group dynamics. Teams of interrogators worked twenty hours a day on each prisoner, aiming to force them through the paces of confession, re-education, and then perpetual conformity to Communist thought. The questions asked were minutely personal and in the end political: "When did your father first meet your mother? What was your grandfather's nickname? What do you know about our Chairman Mao? What do you think is wrong about you that you should oppose Communism when it is so good for you? What faults in your own personality can you confess? You told us yesterday that your little cousin used to come over to play with you when you were five. Now you tell us that when you were five your family had no visitors. How do you explain that lie?"

The questions were asked over and over again. The answers were inspected for inconsistencies. Day followed day to the breaking-point, and then the written exercises began—prisoners had to compose autobiographies whose end was not just confession of sins against Communism but the reworking of an entire life history in correct Communist terms, from birth to death with Chairman Mao. Demands for revised confessions did not let up until the team decided that their target had reached a thorough acceptance of his or her guilt and was ready to be reborn a Communist. In some ways, Chinese brainwashing (a term invented, by the way, in 1950 by an American journalist and sometime CIA agent, Edward Hunter) reflected a total optimist's view of the adaptability and malleability of the human spirit—clay ready to be moulded into new shapes. Though there was plenty of killing in China, Stalin-style purges went against the grain. As Mao Tse-Tung wrote on thought control, "our object in exposing errors and criticizing shortcomings is like that of a doctor in curing a disease. The entire purpose is to save the person, not to cure him to death. If a man has appendicitis, a doctor performs an operation and the man is saved...we cannot adopt a brash attitude toward diseases in thought and politics, but [must have] an attitude of 'saving men by curing their diseases'." The interrogators felt as high-minded as the Catholic Inquisitors: their sense of their own correctness must have placed extra burdens of confusion and guilt on the people trying to resist them.

The process had what the report writer called a "high psychiatric effect"—not because the Chinese Communists were employing psychiatric principles to set the rules. Rather, they were old-fashioned inquisitors in the service of a secular church. If you can control their environment and their behaviour, it is a relatively straightforward matter to change people's thoughts. The totalitarian advantage. Whether enforced change proves lasting or deep is not even a question in totalitarian countries; the environment outside the prison walls is almost as controlled and information almost as tailored to government ends as inside. In China under Mao many waves of thought reform swept the country, culminating in the nihilistic Cultural Revolution, in which young Chinese learned that it was wise to have no personal thoughts, only state thoughts, or they'd be lost in the dialectical storm. The key to totalitarian thought control was not just getting the mechanics of conversion down but exerting perpetual control over the expressions of belief and the behaviour of citizens.

By the mid-fifties, not even the wild boys at the CIA were under any illusion that the Communists had a magic bullet they could fire at American brains. In late 1953, CIA Director Dulles had commissioned Cornell neurologist Harold Wolff (who was treating Dulles's son for brain damage from a head wound he had suffered in Korea) and Lawrence Hinkle, also of Cornell, to do an official study of Soviet and Chinese brainwashing techniques. What they came up with as a model (the report, says John Marks, is still pretty much "the best available description of extreme forms of political indoctrination") was not Pavlov-dog but police state, with the Soviets and Chinese adding national refinements. The Soviets pushed a prisoner to confession, broke him, sentenced him, and sent him off to labour camp. End of story. The Chinese viewed the confession as only the first step, and generally followed it not with punishment (*per se*) but with "re-education" in a group cell where cell-mates "struggled" the prisoner to the point that he seemed genuinely changed. Then the pressures were eased (though sometimes people were cured to death).

It might have been hard to perceive from some vantage points in the fifties, but the United States was not a police state. Neither of the Communist models of behaviour change was truly open to it, which is not to say that figuring out the scientific mechanism at the heart of heavy interrogation wasn't intriguing. Presumably, once you knew how it worked you would know what buttons to press in the isolated cases in which you thought you needed such a tool. In fact, as John Marks pointed out in his book on the MKULTRA experiments, the American response to the brainwashing scare was as American as it gets:

> Just because the Soviets and the Chinese had not invented a brainwashing machine...there was no reason to assume the task was impossible. If such a machine were even remotely feasible, one had to assume the communists might discover it. And in that case, national security required that the United States invent the machine first...the CIA built up its own elaborate brainwashing program...a tiny replica of the Manhattan Project, grounded in the conviction that the keys to brainwashing lay in technology. Agency officials hoped to use old-fashioned American know-how to produce shortcuts and scientific breakthroughs. Instead of turning to tough cops, whose methods repelled American sensibilities, or the gurus of mass motivation, whose ideology Americans lacked, the Agency's brainwashing experts gravitated to people more in the mold of the brilliant—and sometimes mad—scientist, obsessed by the wonders of the brain.

The key was to get scientists to work for them, pursuing a mind-control end in an officially undeclared war. Morse Allen, head of the agency's security office, had run a truth-drug search under the code names "Artichoke" and "Bluebird" in the late 1940s and early 1950s; but he had had trouble finding psychiatrists to travel with teams (field men and polygraph experts) to do sodium amytal and other drug-driven interrogations of hostile agents in Europe and of North Korean POWs. Partly, the CIA didn't pay very well; but also many doctors had moral difficulties with the goal of extracting information regardless of cost to the person who held it. "Terminal experiments", as Morse Allen called them. Potential truth drugs or amnesia-producing agents such as ECT, the mind-modifying effects of neurosurgery and hypnosis—Allen, and Gottlieb after him, felt that none of these could show their potential for covert operations if they were tested only on volunteer subjects, such as university students, or within the confines of a presumably therapeutic setting. Plenty of American doctors were willing to brainstorm with agency personnel on which drugs or techniques might have desirable intelligence applications; fewer were willing to do terminal experiments, and then only on people considered less than normal—drug addicts (mostly black), criminals and sex offenders, mental patients, prostitutes, and foreigners at the fringes of the spy world. The prospect of experimenting on a "normal" unwitting subject generally brought out the scruples of both the doctors and the agents—an attitude reminiscent of the Nazi doctors tried at Nuremburg.

The results of Hebb's sensory-deprivation work on normal subjects certainly unsettled the brilliant, brain-obsessed psychologist. The only safe ground for Hebb as a scientist (and he was an ethical scientist) was to view the perceptual-isolation results for what they told him about the human mind.

Hebb had been commissioned to do the work as a specific investigation of brainwashing by the military. Though full disclosure of his results might purify the process, at first Hebb did not want the circumstances of his commission known any more than did the DRB. But the students who had undergone the experiments were not under any obligation to keep their bizarre experiences secret; newspaper reporters caught a whiff of it and began speculating madly. Hebb eventually successfully argued that the DRB had to provide a false trail by releasing the essential research findings under a cover story—and without mentioning the startling results about attitude change. He suggested that they claim the work had been done to investigate pressures on people who had to maintain acute perceptions while doing boring jobs for long hours, those who had to stare at radar screens or pilot long aircraft flights. (The story did prevent the "real truth" from getting out for a couple of years.)

And even after the experiment's true colours appeared, Hebb still obfuscated. In his 1958 summing-up paper, he paints his entire military involvement in terms of self-defence: "For the problem of brain-washing we learned something of value, which should be known as widely as possible, since we do not know who will fall into Communist hands in the future and be subjected to this—appalling, indecent, choose your own adjective—this atrocious procedure: and knowing something about it might mitigate its effects."

Hebb was never approached directly by Gottlieb's researchers, but he did brief, in 1954 and 1955, two other scientists who were courted by the CIA. They worked down the hall from each other at the National Institutes of Health (NIH), and their reactions to the mind-control temptation were as day and night.

The first was John Lilly, whom Hebb talked to on the suggestion of Robert Morison. (Morison was Hebb's contact at the Rockefeller Foundation, which had funded Hebb's research program to the tune of $30,000 in the same years he was receiving money from the DRB.) Lilly was also engrossed in the mystery of thought, and had been working with depth electrodes implanted in animal brains, but felt that the electrodes caused too much physical damage for him to remain comfortable with the experimentation. As Morison wrote in his Rockefeller diary, on April 10, 1954: "Lilly...has been sufficiently excited by his visit to Donald Hebb...that he has undertaken to repeat the human isolation experiments with a somewhat different technique. In an effort to isolate the subject as completely as possible from all incoming stimuli, he has him lie in a tank of lukewarm water in a dark and soundproof room. He says that within two or three hours he can get almost all the effects Hebb has reported in 48." Lilly viewed the tank as a pathway into the transcendental, and combined the sensory-isolation experiments with investigations of mescaline and LSD. Morison wrote: "L. has acted as subject in many of the experiments and has experienced many bizarre physiological changes. His impression is, however, that the fact that he has had a complete psychoanalysis makes him able to support these changes without undue anxiety. One of the other members of the team has had a pretty bad time." The CIA, of course, was interested in the possibilities of bad times, but when they approached Lilly directly he showed not the slightest interest in collaborating with them.

The second was Maitland Baldwin, a former student both of Hebb and of Montreal neurosurgeon Wilder Penfield. Baldwin also worked with perceptual isolation at the NIH and had a different point of view. In 1955 he had taken secret work for the U.S. Army, using army volunteers, as far as he could take it; he himself thought that perceptual-isolation techniques might be more appropriately sponsored by the CIA; and he was willing to donate a month or so of his time if the agency would find subjects and arrange cover for "terminal type" experiments. Baldwin had worked under Hebb on animal isolation, but said he did not think Hebb had fully understood the interrogation possibilities. Yet he had asked Hebb to vet his own set-up, which was (according to a CIA description) "a padded box, approximately 8 x 3 x 3. Sound is piped into the box through the walls and food is passed in a more or less liquid state to the subject." And Hebb had told him that "results are entirely possible just as effectively in our apparatus as his."

Baldwin had in fact run out of willing subjects for his box experiments and was hoping that the agency would allow him to push them further. What's interesting is that with Dr. Baldwin it was actually people at the agency who held back. A group set up to study the value of isolation had concluded that with it they were on to something the Communists didn't have: "For the record, we can find no evidence the technique is being used anywhere in the Communist countries in interrogation matters or in intelligence work. The somewhat parallel methods that were applied to GI POWs in Korea by the Chinese (small cells, cages, pits in the ground, solitary confinement) seem coincidental and not based on any scientific knowledge of isolation." Further it found that "apparently to date no effort has been made to use the total isolation techniques in intelligence work either in interrogation or the possible alteration of personality by either friendly or unfriendly states." The coast was clear to gain some sort of technological edge.

Baldwin pressed for an "antagonistic subject" he could force to a total breakdown in the box, allowing however "that he would not want any other agency to know anything about this experiment unless it proved to be successful". And also, that "anyone going through a complete breakdown would come out with somewhat lowered mental faculties".

A memo from the CIA Isolation Group as of May 20, 1955, had a handwritten note added to the bottom: "Does (DO / CB) Project officer approve of these immoral and inhuman tests? I suggest that all who are in favor of the above-mentioned operation volunteer their heads for use in Dr. Baldwin's 'noble' project."

The Isolation Group decided in the end that they could get just as interesting results from workers using less drastic methods. Baldwin, who was also a neurosurgeon and who had lobotomized apes and then put them into his box—and who had tried the Dr. Frankenstein trick of transplanting one ape's head onto the body of another—was so much the mad scientist he made even the CIA men trying to recruit mad scientists wary of him.

In fact, the most effective collaborators the CIA attracted were not blatant Dr. Baldwins at all; their secret desires were more insidious, less black and white, more rooted in the aspirations of their profession. A comment from a Washington psychiatrist who took on close to 150 overseas assignments for the CIA from 1952 to 1966 is telling: CIA work called for "practicing psychiatry in an ideal way, which meant you didn't become involved with your patients. You weren't supposed to."

A chance to practise a pure psychiatry, stripped of the human element—it sounds like a contradiction in terms. But psychiatry viewed itself at the time as on the road to becoming a hard science; some believed that psychiatry had *already* become a hard science—as direct and to the point as surgery. Psychiatrists wanted to be rescued from the vagaries of madness, of the psychological understanding and psychological treatment of the mentally ill, which sometimes worked and sometimes didn't, for reasons they could never pin down but that always floated in the ether of the individual personality and the relationship that existed between doctors and their patients. All psychiatrists were trained first as medical doctors; and many longed for an equivalent "germ theory" of mental illness, for a mental penicillin. Specialists in the manifestations of personality and mind, they hungered for the reality of disease rooted in the biology of the brain that they could straightforwardly and swiftly heal. With pills, with operations—just like real doctors.

The shared goal of both the psychiatrists and the spies was to effect changes in human behaviour—rational, predictable changes. Or to control human behaviour, trim the sails of the manic, eliminate the depths of the depressed, or program the spy. The more cynical of the psychiatrists of the MKULTRA era may have been just as interested in truth drugs as the CIA, sharing a similar attitude towards what comes out of mouths—a distrust of what people say about themselves, a desire to get at the real truth, a discounting of what people say about their own experience because they might be lying. For them the brain was a black box in which people hid their true selves; a box that had to be forced open in order to effect a cure. It's an attitude that could justify serious invasions of other people's lives in the service of an abstract cause—mental health or the cold war. The spymasters distrusted physical torture because, while it could coerce, it didn't necessarily give them any truth except the thing that might stop the torture. Tactics and techniques culled from psychology and psychiatry were regarded as more effective, more subtle, more able to get at the things kept hidden, and more scientific—the boys running MKULTRA were in some ways giving themselves an advanced seminar on the brain, tinged though it was by a desire to use whatever knowledge was gained for covert ends.

Robert Jay Lifton, an American psychiatrist who studied Chinese thought reform for a good part of the 1950s under the auspices of the U.S. Air Force, knew the temptations that the cold war and the covert mentality put in the path of people like himself. In the introduction to his book, *Thought Reform and the Psychology of Totalism: A Study of "Brainwashing" in China*, he wrote: "And who during this era can pretend to be uninvolved in the issues of psychological coercion, of identity and ideology? Certainly not the one who has felt impelled to study them at such great length."

Lifton outlined the effectiveness and the failings of the Chinese thought-reform system and, from his interviews of both Western and Chinese internees who had escaped to Hong Kong, made a good stab at understanding the individual psychological forces that made a person either a convert or a resister of the process. But throughout his book he expresses a basic horror and disgust at methods of enforcing human change (the "closed" as opposed to the "open" approach, in his terminology). Partly this is pragmatic—all of his survivors experienced lasting psychological effects from the treatment, but none of them, free of the totalitarian setting, maintained the attitudes the Chinese had hoped to program in.

Another part is philosophic: "Are not men presumptuous to appoint themselves the dispensers of human existence? Surely this is a flagrant expression of what the Greeks called hubris, of arrogant man making himself God.... Behind ideological totalism lies the ever-present human quest for the omnipotent guide—for the supernatural force, political party, philosophical idea, great leader, or precise science—that will bring ultimate solidarity to all men and eliminate the terror of death and nothingness."

Another large part of Lifton's horror, however, seemed to stem from a personal fear and recognition that the possibility of thought reform played on the temptations to which his own profession was prone. An important part of his book explored the moral and ethical ramifications for psychotherapy of enforcing change, of assuming doctor knows best. The flavour is introspective: an inspection of the power of the therapist and the flattering light cast by the current trend, both inside and outside the professions, to thrust the behavioural sciences up onto the pedestal of pure science. "Accompanying this deification," Lifton wrote,

is the expectation that science will supply a complete and absolutely accurate mechanistic theory of a closed and totally predictable universe. Modern physics has long disowned this idea, but it persists in the human sciences—biological, psychological, and social—and is particularly damaging there. Thought reform is its ultimate expression—a mechanized image of man within a closed society, and a claim to scientific method in the remaking of man in this image.

There is the assumption that science...can liberate men from the encumbrances of all past institutions, family ties, social loyalties, professional affiliations, and religious and philosophical commitments: first by exposing these as "unscientific", then by demonstrating that they are no longer necessary in a truly "scientific" environment.

Lifton had a warning, too: "While this god-pole of science seems now to predominate almost everywhere, it is possible that there lurks beneath it more of the devil-pole than might be suspected."

Which brings us, at last, to Ewen Cameron, whose story intersects with the CIA mind-control quest exactly at that juncture of temptation—to effect human change and to thrust psychiatry into the pantheon of science.

Some who worked with him or who were trained by him suspect that in Cameron there may lurk the traces of a folk-hero of psychiatry. Even those who were wounded by him, like Val Orlikow, do not hesitate to talk about him as though he walked with giant steps.

It takes an outsider to recognize fully the contradictions—that the feet usually moved one step forward, two steps back. That Cameron championed the ethical heights of his profession but trespassed on the rights to treatment of his patients. That Cameron revered research above all and launched several glorious research careers at the Allan Memorial Institute but was too impatient and scattered to do good research himself. That though Cameron wanted to help in a big way, he often hurt—sometimes beyond belief—on a personal level.

Cameron was an American citizen who spoke out against McCarthyism at a time when it was definitely a professional risk to do so. He addressed the American Psychiatric Association on the dangers of mind control as outgoing president in 1953: "Nothing that has thus far transpired is likely to be more serious than for humanity to learn how to control the development of personality and how to master the forces of group dynamics before we have developed a value system capable of dealing with such a situation.... As psychiatrists we are physicians having an immemorial responsibility for the well-being of our patients.... Our knowledge of human nature, our techniques for the exploration of motive and memory, if torn from their framework of professional integrity and proper concern for the individual and for the community may, their use perverted, become the most deadly weapons yet directed against the dignity and serenity of human life." Cameron understood that some of the new tools of psychiatry would be dangerous if they fell into the wrong hands, but he never doubted for a moment that his own were the right ones.

The man who spoke out, who said he revered freedom and memory above all else, was the same man who systematically attempted to apply the mechanisms of brainwashing to the treatment of his patients; who wanted to win the Nobel Prize and whose memory has been popularly vilified.

Ewen Cameron's character was cut large enough that one can apply the word "hubris" to him without embarrassment. He was enough a man of his times—one of the creators of the currents of mainstream psychiatry—that his fellow doctors can legitimately look on him as some kind of folk-hero. He manifested hubris in large measure—and maybe also the devil-pole.

CHAPTER FIVE

The Elusive Cure

Ewen Cameron was an intensely private man. Those who worked with him for the almost twenty years he was in charge of the Allan Memorial Institute in Montreal thought of him almost exclusively as "the Chief", the physical embodiment of the place. He was usually there before any other doctor arrived, and he did his last set of rounds in the evening, long after most of them had left. He had an apartment near the institute that people thought was apocryphal (did he ever sleep?); for most of those years his family lived over the American border in Lake Placid, N.Y., and Montreal associates were not encouraged to visit them there. Cameron didn't give or go to parties, make small talk, or tell many anecdotes about his past. He loved mechanical gadgets—anything modern, from tape machines to the latest-model Cadillac—but such tastes didn't necessarily bring anyone humanly close to him. His small extracurricular pleasures—climbing the mountains around Lake Placid with his children, long-distance running, and then swimming—he kept largely to himself.

Even his wife, Jean Rankine Cameron, whom he married in 1933 and brought out to live with him in Brandon, Manitoba, while he pursued his first not-very-well-paying job as the reception-unit doctor at the provincial mental hospital there, does not know with any certainty why Ewen Cameron became a psychiatrist. Born on Christmas Eve, 1901, in Bridge of Allan, Scotland, a small town a few miles north of Glasgow, Cameron grew up trying to see over the hills that surrounded him—"a mile to the south, a line of low hills across which ran Hadrian's Wall and, a little over a mile to the north…another range of slightly higher hills on which stood an old Pictish fort which, two thousand years earlier, kept watch on the enemy to the south", as he once wrote. Cameron took note of the past but it didn't draw him; he wanted the future to be here yesterday. And he wanted to move in a much wider world than that of a child born in a Scottish manse.

The folk-wisdom about psychiatrists is that they are wounded healers, drawn to the study of human nature by a recognition of the dark forces in their own. Among those who have had to think a lot about Cameron are the man who succeeded him at the Allan Memorial, Dr. Robert Cleghorn, and the present director, Dr. Brian Robertson (who finds himself in the position of having to defend Cameron without ever having met the man). Both speculate a lot about Cameron's relationship with his father, Duncan, a handsome Presbyterian minister of great eloquence and ambition, who for much of his career had his eye on attaining the appointment at St. Giles Cathedral in Glasgow. Cleghorn tells two anecdotes that hint at the rigours of the relationship between Duncan Cameron and his eldest son. Knowing the Chief was leaving on a holiday to Scotland, Cleghorn idly asked him if he was going to play any golf. "Hell no, Doc," said Cameron. "I had my belly full as a boy. I used to caddy for my father and after eighteen holes, at one PM, he would say, 'Now, Ewen, we will go another nine holes.' And you know what a pre-teenager's stomach is like when hungry, rubbing up against his spine." Cleghorn, with the psychiatrist's habit of driving the psychological point home, adds, "This small vignette says something about an inconsiderate, powerful father—to be later avoided at all costs, though having provided a pretty solid ego."

Throughout his Montreal years Cameron certainly avoided the two other giants of the scene—Wilder Penfield, who was instrumental in getting Cameron the job of founding a department of psychiatry at McGill in the first place, and Donald Hebb. The three men were a trinity that put McGill on the brain/behaviour map in the fifties and early sixties; but they did not pull together. Penfield had his eye on annexing the psychiatry department to his own rather shakily funded though world-famous Montreal Neurological Institute (MNI); Cameron violently resisted being annexed by anyone and proceeded to build a psychiatric network (some would say empire) among Montreal's English-speaking hospitals and institutions that made the MNI look almost marginal. As far as psychology went, Cameron hired his own department, including the prominent researcher R.B. Malmo, and largely kept out of the way of Hebb. Cleghorn says that men like Penfield and Hebb made the Chief nervous and anxious, over-competitive. He recalls a passing comment made by Sir David Henderson, the eminent British psychiatrist who was Cameron's own first chief at the Royal Mental Hospital in Glasgow. At a lunch put on for him in Montreal by Cameron, Henderson leaned over to Cleghorn and said, in the loud voice of a deaf old man, "He's done very well for a man who hasn't overcome his adolescent difficulties." Cleghorn believes that both Cameron's strengths and weaknesses arose from his inability to tolerate strong father figures: he could chart a course through new territory without having to rely on anyone but himself, a necessary trait of an adventurer. But because he could not regard any man as wiser than himself, not even the greats of his own field, he suffered no checks on his judgement—from either father figures or peers—and that had unfortunate consequences.

Brian Robertson puts forward the cultural hypothesis that Cameron—like so many bright young men who were teenagers in the First World War—replaced the God of his father with the God of science in an elaborate act of generational rebellion. There is considerable confirmation of this in Cameron's own writings and actions, his railings against religious traditions and cultural suffocation, and his hope that psychiatry would become sole and proper owner of the turf once occupied exclusively by religion. But Cameron's own eldest son, Duncan, says that though his grandfather insisted that Ewen attend church on Sundays he did not force religion down his throat and supported his son's interest in medicine, a career that others in the family had pursued.

As a teenager, Cameron read deeply in psychology, religion, and philosophy, and his widow, Jean, says it was that reading that made him jump the rails from medicine to psychiatry. His father supported him in that choice, too—and Cameron's postgraduate education, with Adolf Meyer at the Phipps Clinic in Baltimore, and at the Burghoelzli Clinic in Zurich, was an expensive proposition. The only thing that stopped Ewen Cameron's wanderings to the various centres of the psychiatric universe was his father's untimely death from cancer: the oldest son had to start earning a living to help his younger siblings finish their own schooling.

In fact, Ewen Cameron didn't set out to be a therapist or healer at all; he wanted to be a research scientist. In the 1920s, viewing psychiatry as a science of any sort was more of a vision than a real goal. There's a strong argument to be made that Cameron identified primarily with the aspirations of his profession, not the sufferings of his patients. An ambitious man, like his father, and a clinically insightful but not empathetic doctor, Cameron and his progress can be seen as a kind of bellwether of twentieth-century psychiatry—beginning with his job at the Brandon, Manitoba, mental hospital, the job he had to take when his father died.

Cameron had studied with the cream of the profession; he had imbibed the intellectually respectable theories of Meyer, whose notion—psychobiology—seemed the only option capable of bringing together the two poles between which the profession always swung: that mental disorders were either of the psyche, and approachable only by psychological treatment, or of the soma, the body, and open to physical (or somatic) cure. Meyer, a Swiss-born neurologist who became the most eminent psychiatrist in post-1900 North America, did not fall between those stools so much as plant himself firmly on both: he argued that even if a mental disorder resulted from an actual physiological disease one could not ignore the psychological factor. He felt that individual psychology, biology, the person's social position, and stresses in the community at large were all wound together in the genesis of mental disorder—that treatment had to recognize and admit all these factors. He also believed that mental disturbance did not knock a person out of the human running altogether and that successful treatment depended on rooting out and mobilizing the functional assets the person still had. This was impeccable thinking on the face of it, but very hard to put into practice: most people with such trouble were immediately locked into huge, understaffed custodial institutions far away from the communities in which they had functioned—or ceased to function. Still, Meyer's analysis suggested to the bright young men who were his residents that there were things they could actually undertake to alleviate the condition of their patients (an inspirational value Cameron himself was later to provide for many of his own bright young residents). If you couldn't truly fix the disordered mind there were other fronts for activism.

Cameron had the rhetoric and some of the concerns of the psychobiologist. He was always intensely interested in the social impact of his profession—eager to collaborate with industry, as just one instance, in social engineering of the workplace. But at heart what stirred him most was the pathfinding role of the research scientist—the first (and only) psychiatrist to win the Nobel prize for medicine was Julius Wagner von Jauregg of Vienna, for the malarial-fever cure of general paresis, in 1927. A physical, biological intervention in the course of what, around the turn of the century, had at last been perceived as the terminal stage of syphilis, the point at which spirochetes cut loose in the brain causing all kinds of psychotic symptoms. Cameron, late in his life, wrote that Wagner-Jauregg's discovery marked the beginning of "the great upward surge" in psychiatry: that it was "amazing alike for its success and for the unflinching courage of its discoverer".

That courage consisted of taking the clinical opportunity and the hunch as they arose: Wagner-Jauregg had noted and done some brief work on the notion that psychotic patients who suffered a high fever seemed to be better—in their minds—after the fever had run its course, but his early publications to that effect attracted little notice. Then, when he was already in his sixties and chief of the Psychiatric Clinic in Vienna during the First World War, he encountered a shell-shocked soldier running a high malarial fever and took it as a "sign of destiny". Wagner-Jauregg took blood from the sick soldier and injected it in three paretics; when they in turn developed fevers he took blood from them and injected six more. Of the nine patients so treated, he reported that six improved substantially, the six who were the least far gone to begin with. Further work produced an improvement rate, he reported, of 44 per cent—pretty impressive, his peers thought—in the combat of a condition that was the archetype of hopeless madness and that in the 1920s and 1930s burdened mental hospitals everywhere with soldiers who'd been infected with syphilis in the First World War.

The young Dr. Cameron, fired with the socially freeing ideas of Meyer and the therapeutic optimism that a breakthrough like Wagner-Jauregg's inspired in the field of formerly bleak prospect, looked like just the kind of bright young man Alvin Mathers—provincial psychiatrist for Manitoba—was looking for in 1929 to recruit to the staff of the Brandon Mental Hospital, an institution that had ambitions to be in the forefront of mental-health care in the western provinces.

The seven years Cameron spent at the mental hospital at Brandon, at the height of the Depression when the prairie farms were blowing away and all their social supports with them, were as formative as the years he'd spent among psychiatry's blue-bloods. His peers there were generally ill-trained young fellows passing through, his lifelines a membership in the American Psychiatric Association and a drive to read all the literature and publish as much as he could. But his nose was rubbed thoroughly in the real world of a large custodial hospital for the insane: a powerful spur to change the things, he wrote, "that appalled those of us who entered psychiatry in the early 20s…the ingeniously depraving restraints, the slow destruction of personality through years of institutionalization, the hopelessness, the night and fog of misery which enveloped patients and staff alike, the long lines of men and women passing three times a day, seven days a week, month after month, down to their meals in the dining room and back up to the wards again." Twenty years later, Cameron would be president of his lifeline professional organization, the APA; he would have helped to found the Canadian Psychiatric Association to guarantee that no young doctor would ever be quite as isolated as he was. Thirty years later, he would found a World Psychiatric Association as a culmination of his organization of networks for himself. And he would look back just before he died and write (seeing with the eyes of one who hoped it was true) that all the things he had despised in his youth had changed, because of the efforts of men willing "to risk challenging authority and dogma to bring in new methods of treatment and [ceaselessly] search for every and all means of relieving the suffering of their patients."

Diving into psychiatry in the 1930s is like arriving in the middle of a novel and not quite being able to pick up all the strings of the plot. Psychiatrists everywhere are in action, treating and (they claim) curing what they now call mental illness (not madness), with physical (not psychological) methods, as if they'd finally established the connections between brain physiology, mental function, and behaviour. It does not take much hindsight to see that they hadn't: the fifty years of brain/mind investigation done since still amount to baby steps towards the understanding of those connections. It takes even less hindsight to know that the somatic treatments that were developed in the thirties—insulin coma, various kinds of shock, of which electro-shock is the survivor, and lobotomy—were not the cures they claimed to be.

The invasion of an instrument shaped like an ice-pick or an apple corer into the frontal lobes of the brain may be a crude action, but at least it's an action. More important, psychiatrists perceived it as a medical action, a thing that a doctor might do. To understand the emergence of the somatic treatments you have to understand that by the 1930s psychiatry as a profession was in such dubious straits—despite brave talk from its young men—that the doctors who adhered to it were desperate for treatments that made them look like real doctors. For many psychiatrists the imperative to treat, arising out of the profession's impotence at treating, far outweighed the basic ethical principle of *primum non nocere*—first of all, do no harm. To rest content with doing no harm seemed to be the attitude of a coward.

Cameron had his MD, and he had patients in pain in front of his eyes; he wanted nothing more than to be able to do what he was supposed to do, which was cure them. In the introduction to his first book, a bit of wishful thinking published in 1935 and called *Objective and Experimental Psychology*, he made both his desire to treat and his inability to find scientific or medical ways to do so absolutely clear. Cameron wrote, "Whether we recognize it or not, the influence which most strongly beat upon those of us who passed into psychiatry...was the humanitarian. Sympathy, patience, insight, rapport—these were the magic words. They must remain so, but as a means to an end and not an end in themselves. The more skeptical, 'tough minded' worker, thrusting out from these enshrouding curtains to the harder realities of active treatment found himself at once in a sad dilemma, where to find solid ground?"

He saw himself and all his colleagues as "fatally entrapped by words and by logic". Psychoanalytic theory was intellectually satisfying but was not much use to an asylum psychiatrist faced with huge numbers of chronic psychotic patients rather than a private practice of neurotic ones. Cameron longed to apply the rationalism of the scientific method to the study of behaviour and was sure that psychoanalytic theory didn't fit the bill; a rational scientific mind looking at the major mental disorders couldn't help feeling there was a somatic base that could be satisfyingly, actively, medically attacked, if psychiatrists would only get scientific enough. "An increasing number of us," wrote Cameron, "experience a feeling of growing distrust of purely descriptive and intuitive concepts of human behavior and find it more and more difficult to content ourselves with facts or assertions save where they will withstand experimentation and will not fail us on prediction."

But words were all they had, and even the somatic treatments that first rescued Cameron and his generation from a helpless passivity and pessimism were only words made flesh, not effective therapy.

Cure. A word implying relief for sufferers, achievement for healers, and the distinct possibility that they will each define it to their own ends. It first reared its head in relation to mental disorders as a result of the philosophizing of the Enlightenment. If (as John Locke and Rousseau and others argued) man was born a blank slate upon which experience wrote a lifetime's knowledge, there was no such thing as innate madness. Or hopeless madness. If experience and environment drove people mad then new experience and a changed environment might possibly undo it. In essence it was a dream of social control, a dream that human beings could take their destinies in hand—that human nature was a workable, fixable thing somewhat like the automata that so fascinated the eighteenth-century mind. (The French physician La Mettrie called his book on human behaviour, published in 1747, *L'Homme-machine*, and in it argued that essential man was matter in motion, like everything else in the universe.) From such thinking came the waves of revolution and social reform (sometimes viewed as social control) of the late eighteenth and nineteenth centuries.

Modern psychiatry is founded not in a growing body of medical knowledge or in a particular philosophy of healing, but in the optimistic belief that there was no such thing as the incurably insane (no possession by demons, or original sin, or God's mysterious way)—and in the humanitarian reform of the treatment of lunatics, symbolized by the French physician Pinel's act of striking the chains off the inmates of the Bicêtre in 1793. From such Enlightenment roots it seems that psychiatry should have developed as a form of social engineering (some, of course, argue that it has) rather than as a profession that views itself as a logical extension of medicine—but therein lies a good chunk of psychiatry's almost continuous crisis of confidence. In the persistent absence of cures (as opposed to treatments) for the major psychotic disorders, it's easy for psychiatry to seem, in sociologist Andrew Scull's words, like "a metaphysical wager that has yet to pan out".

At the end of the eighteenth century, public attention was drawn to madness and its therapies for the simple reason that a king was mad—George III of England. For him the mad-doctors of the day brought out what were considered the most efficacious treatments, and were found wanting. In the Countess Harcourt's words, "the unhappy patient...was no longer treated as a human being. His body was immediately encased in a machine which left it no liberty of motion. He was sometimes chained to a stake. He was frequently beaten and starved, and at best he was kept in subjection by menacing and violent language." As well as being, in effect, tortured, the royal body was bled and blistered, purged and dosed with drugs such as digitalis, according to a medical practice fixated on the proper flow and balance of bodily fluids.

Pre-eminent mad-doctors at the turn of the eighteenth century, such as the American Benjamin Rush, viewed themselves as compassionately and scientifically in search of weapons to use against madness. The mechanical contraptions into which madmen were strapped by the mad doctors were extraordinary. Rush devised a chair with a box on top that fitted over the head, chest and arm restraints, and ankle shackles; in an illustration of it there is a comfy cushion on the seat. He wrote proudly to his son:

> It binds and confines every part of the body. By keeping the trunk erect, it lessens the impetus of the blood toward the brain. By preventing the muscles from acting, it reduces the force and frequency of the pulse, and by the position of the head and feet favors the easy application of cold water or ice to the former, and warm water to the latter. Its effects have been truly delightful to me. It acts as a sedative to the tongue and temper as well as to the blood vessels. In 24, 12, 6, and in some cases in 4 hours, the most refractory patients have been composed. I have called it a Tranquilizer.

Others swung patients in a rotary machine, round and round, like astronauts in training to withstand motion sickness. The nausea and heavy vomiting so induced were supposed to be calming and healing, though any quietening of behaviour should largely be put down to fear of being placed in the machine again. German mad-doctors harked back to the folk-wisdom that the insane, if shocked to the existential heart by a near death, seemed to gain a certain clarity of mind—just as fright cured the hiccups. The contemporary German device was a coffin with holes drilled in the lid into which the lunatic was placed. The coffin was then hoisted into the air and lowered into a pool of water until it was submerged. When bubbles stopped rising from the holes in the lid, the coffin was hauled out and the lunatic examined for salutary effects. Some were no doubt cured to death, which at least gained them a kind of peace. (Andrew Scull says this method was later adopted in some American prisons as a punishment for recalcitrant criminals.)

It was hard for a lay person to make much distinction between the treatments of the mad doctors and the garden-variety abuses suffered by the insane in the lock-ups and workhouses and attics of the time; rescuing the insane from physical coercion and mechanical restraint became one of the first great social crusades of the nineteenth century in France (after Pinel), in England, and in North America. A treatment called "moral therapy" was the shining hope for cure, the fruit of Enlightenment thinking on human nature. Take lunatics out of the environment that caused the madness—away from the family or the stresses of the new industrial city—and place them in a garden, an Eden, a new and beautiful environment miles from urban life. Treat them kindly; lodge them in the care of attendants carefully trained and uniformly concerned with their individual well-being. Give them useful work to do, so that they feel like accomplished members of a community. Appeal to and strengthen their reason, their will, and their sense of responsibility for their actions. Organize the asylum so that it rewards their progress towards reason in literal movement from Cottage D to Cottage A and, at last, out into the world again—changed and cured. The physician Pinel abandoned medical methods entirely in favour of moral therapy, finding the results highly satisfactory; the cure rate at the famous York Retreat in England, where lay people attended to the care of the insane in a setting that was regarded as therapeutic in itself, was also viewed as exemplary.

Out of the principles of moral therapy came the broad-scale reform—the asylum movement that did revolutionize (or, perhaps more accurately, institutionalize) care of the insane. Nothing in moral therapy called for medical input, but mad-doctors kept a tight grip on their right to treat lunatics; kindness, good nutrition, and useful work became medical prescriptions, with the asylum building itself regarded as a scientifically calculated therapeutic tool. The mad-doctor (now called an alienist or asylum superintendent) bent his efforts at securing a recognized expertise in the practice of a healing architecture—lauding the curative rather than the confining powers of his building in an attempt to secure paying, private patients (not the usual load of paupers) to guarantee psychiatry's professional legitimacy.

The trouble was that cure was still elusive: moral therapy's social reprogramming rested upon the intense, dedicated efforts of the entire asylum staff. Applied on a wide scale as a state-sponsored solution to the harsh lot of lunatics of all classes, asylums inexorably descended into overcrowded holding bins and alienists into custodians looked at askance by both the communities they served and colleagues in other branches of medicine. To the general public, a loony-bin, no matter how bucolic the setting, was still a loony-bin.

And the wheel went round again; by mid-century, psychological methods had fallen into great disrepute. Any approach to cure, even ones that were blatantly psychological, like American neurologist S. Weir Mitchell's rest cure for diseases of the nervous system, had to be painted as somatic to achieve any kind of scientific respectability. Mitchell prescribed rest, diet, massage, relief from all responsibility, and isolation from the family for his patients—yet believed that the fundamental mechanism of the cure was not its impact on their minds but on the building up of their fat and blood. In fact, neurologists, riding high on knowledge gained out of the observation of brain damage inflicted on soldiers by the American Civil War, made a good stab at gaining control of the field of brain and nervous diseases (as they defined madness) from the alienists. They were brought up short only by the fact that while they could describe and define obvious organic brain syndromes—and even take a flying leap at creating a condition called neurasthenia, a depletion of the nervous system, they claimed, that accounted for all kinds of psychological nervous disorders from sick headaches to uterine irritability to claustrophobia—they couldn't treat them either.

The turn of the century found an uneasy truce prevailing between neurology and psychiatry, both professions certain of only one thing—that medical men such as they should somehow prevail scientifically

against the charlatan hypnotists and quacks and the religious healing movements like Christian Science that were drawing more and
more troubled people away from doctors' offices. Andrew Scull describes the situation of psychiatrists in deliberately Gothic but still
accurate terms: "Presiding over a ramshackle and decaying empire of
ever-more-overcrowded and run-down institutions, and swamped by
legions of the poor, the aged, and the chronically disabled, institutional
psychiatrists could do little more for their charges than provide a dubious haven from a heartless world." Cure was an impossibility; at best
they could keep the inmates relatively clean, and fed, and clothed.

The prevailing scientific mode was a kind of botany of madness:
the giant of the time was the German Emil Kraepelin, who developed
careful, individual case studies into elaborately worked out—and essentially pessimistic—diagnostic categories. The conditions he called
manic-depression and dementia praecox (later renamed schizophrenia
by another great categorizer, the Swiss doctor Eugen Bleuler) were
viewed as diseases of progressive, inevitable deterioration. To have
diagnostic guides and prognoses was at least to set the discipline in
a scientific framework, and did justify the changing terminology of
the profession. The nineteenth century had seen the mad-doctor transformed into first the alienist and then the psychiatrist. The madhouse
became the asylum and then the mental hospital. Madmen and mad-
women, the lunatics of the loony-bins and bedlams, became mental
patients.

The medical profession had once been as fractured and ineffectual
as psychiatry; but now, through Pasteur and Lister's demonstration
of the germ theory and the recent development of anaesthesia and
antiseptic techniques, the discipline had risen to great heights of
prestige and therapeutic optimism. Gazing into the mirror held up
by medicine, psychiatrists could only wring their hands. C.G. Hill,
giving the president's address to the American Medico-Psychological
Association in 1907, said bluntly, "Our therapeutics is a pile of
rubbish." And even the profession's elaborate artful categories of
disease, while clinically demonstrable (at least when doctors shared

the same clinical apprenticeship), were not biologically self-evident—they could define mental disease only by its impact on behaviour. No pathologist had yet been able to find any organic evidence in the brain that the disease process, say, of manic-depression clearly existed.

In the early years of the twentieth century, psychiatrists were ripe for either of two things: the sheer intellectual thrill and satisfaction of Freud's psychoanalysis, a comprehensive theory of the psychological action, causation, and cure of functional mental disorders in which one did not have to prove that lesions existed in the brain to be either a scientist or a healer; or a closer connection and affiliation with an already powerful profession—regular medicine. To act like a doctor and therefore be a doctor.

American sociologist Andrew Scull has spent a fair amount of time in the last couple of years in the basement archives of the Trenton State Hospital in New Jersey, reading the correspondence, the hospital records, and the publications and self-promotions of Henry A. Cotton—the superintendent in charge there from 1907 to 1933 and in whose memory every year thereafter an outstanding staff member was honoured by the Cotton Award for Kindness. The story that follows is about a man who was so eager to make a therapeutic breakthrough, to find an easy one-stop solution to the problem of insanity, that he could not see anything but the perfect neatness of his theory—certainly not the suffering it caused his patients.

Henry Cotton intended to do his best by the inmates of the Trenton State Hospital. He came by the job of superintendent at the young age of thirty-one, through the influence of his mentor, the dean of American psychiatry, Adolf Meyer and through the pedigree Meyer had helped him to obtain: two years of study in Europe with Kraepelin and Alzheimer. Trenton was a mess; as Cotton wrote to Meyer, "Such a deplorable condition of affairs one would not believe could exist in an insane hospital today.... Patients had been restrained for years, and no-one knows why."

In short order Cotton ordered ninety-six patients out of shackles and threw out more than seven hundred restraining devices. He reorganized wards and, borrowing a leaf out of Meyer's book, looked to providing social workers for patient after-care, instituted occupational therapy, started a training program for nurses, and reorganized the administration of the hospital. But even more crucial to Cotton, a definite somaticist, was to give his so-called mental hospital the trappings and atmosphere of a real hospital. Through some able manoeuvring of the board and state politicians, Cotton got for Trenton a clinical laboratory, an infirmary, a TB isolation ward, and an operating room—in which he tried out every medical, physical treatment he could think of that might have an impact on mental illness.

Nine years of hectic effort passed—and Cotton had to admit he had gotten nowhere. The cure rate at his by now exemplary institution was no better than it had been when he arrived; he was not famous and he had not achieved a therapeutic breakthrough. But then, in 1916, Cotton began to pull teeth, literally to extract teeth out of patients' mouths, so that soon the locals knew exactly who had been in the state hospital by the number of teeth they had left. By 1917 Cotton had escalated to tonsils and thought he was onto something—the bacteriological or focal-infection theory of mental illness.

Cotton was not an innovator here. There had been a brief fad for the pulling of decayed teeth as a treatment for mental illness in the mid-nineteenth century; it didn't really gel into theory, though, and soon stopped. Since then, the medical profession had finally accepted that bacteria caused diseases, and some physicians had been trying to pin chronic conditions they didn't yet understand, such as arthritis, on toxin-producing, long-standing, low-grade infections. A long-term systemic poisoning seemed to Cotton like the perfect analogy to explain mental "illness". Sustained by Meyer, whose psychobiological approach allowed any form of treatment if it "worked", and his own blithe attitude to the usefulness of various body parts, Cotton launched a surgical campaign to stamp out mental "disease".

Teeth were the line of first assault, followed by tonsils, the stomach ("for all the world like a cement mixer" and about as useful, according to Cotton), the duodenum, the small intestine, the bladder, the gall-bladder, the appendix, the colon ("for storage, and we can dispense with it as freely as with the stomach"), and the sexual organs. Eighty per cent of the females treated by Cotton lost their cervixes; 25 to 40 per cent of the males underwent "resection" of their seminal vesicles. Cotton wrote, "If we wish to eradicate focal infections, we must bear in mind that it is only by being persistent, often against the wishes of the patient...[that we can] expect our efforts to be successful. Failure in these cases at once casts discredit upon the theory, when the reason lies in the fact that we have not been radical enough." Anyone who died from the surgery—and Cotton himself admitted a death rate of 25 per cent—was simply believed to have been too debilitated by disease to withstand the operative shock.

Cotton believed that he had finally stumbled on the vaunted synthesis of medicine and psychiatry. The concurrent legitimate medical realization that general paresis was in fact the brain-infected end of syphilis—that a specific disease could cause psychotic symptoms—was fuel for Cotton's optimism. By the 1920s, Cotton was claiming an 85 per cent recovery rate among patients who were aggressively treated, and was chirruping: "More in truth than in jest may it be said that psychoanalysis will in time be superseded by gastric analysis."

Cotton gave lectures at Princeton on his results and had them published with a laudatory introduction by Meyer; he carefully orchestrated a public-relations blitz in which his cure rates were swallowed whole by the reporters. Desperate families flocked to Trenton with their disordered members for the surgical cure. Cotton also operated at the local reformatory on juvenile delinquents, at local prisons, and on children not institutionalized for anything at all. Cotton's reasoning was that things like a propensity to crime or masturbation were signs of incipient infection; in order to prevent the impending psychosis you had to perform preventive surgery. With his own hands he removed portions of the colons of a six- and an eight-year-old, on grounds that their chronic constipation was the forerunner of madness.

While many of Cotton's American contemporaries were horrified at the carnage, his own hospital board was reluctant to argue with success—paying patients at Trenton had increased 45 per cent since Cotton had started to operate. Still, by 1924 they were worried enough by professional criticism to ask Adolf Meyer to conduct an investigation into the rates of cure claimed by their hospital superintendent. Meyer sent another protégée, Dr. Phyllis Greenacre, to look into Cotton's methods, and what she found horrified her. By then, Cotton was claiming an 87 per cent cure rate and saying that the best results came from cutting out the most. Greenacre found only a 20 per cent cure rate (a standard recovery rule of thumb in psychiatry is that roughly a third of all patients get better without any treatment at all). And she found the best results among patients who had suffered the least from the knife. As her report read, "the most thorough treatment" had been utilized in "the unimproved and dead groups"—Greenacre's calculation of the death rate approached 42 per cent.

But all this was kept from Cotton by Meyer for some time, and in fact, kept by Meyer from the world at large because Cotton was already undergoing a public hearing in front of a New Jersey state commission on financial waste and mismanagement. Hearing about the elaborate surgical set-up at Trenton, investigators thought they might be on to the lavishing of the public purse on that lost cause, the insane. Cotton paraded his cure rates before the commissioners, claiming that he actually saved the state money by rescuing it from the long-term carrying costs of the chronically insane. Then followed a two-month parade of the toothless, wombless, and mutilated, the families of non-survivors, and ex-staff members, telling tales about the surgical cure.

As Scull writes, "During this recital, Cotton's behaviour became increasingly erratic. He interrupted witnesses, attempted to prevent their testimony, and berated them privately after they had testified."

Before he could take the stand in rebuttal, Cotton himself had a breakdown. The Trenton hospital board went on the offensive in Cotton's stead—summoning eminent men to testify to the progressive nature of the hospital, and hospital managers to paint the ex-patients as still deluded. Without too much difficulty the board won over the commission members and the matter was dropped.

Taking his own breakdown in hand, Cotton had three "dead and badly infected teeth" removed and felt much better, as he wrote to Meyer in the fall of 1925. Recovered shortly after the state commission stopped its investigation, Cotton resumed his duties at Trenton with the full support of his board—who all the time were also aware of Greenacre's scandalous findings. Two years went by while a series of negotiations was held to try to communicate Greenacre's results to Cotton and get him to modify his treatment—with no result. Meyer and the board finally let the matter drop. Let it drop so entirely, in fact, that when Meyer attended a special meeting of the British Medical Association and the Royal Medico-Psychological Association in Edinburgh, Scotland, in 1927—an event devoted to praising Cotton's focal-infection theory of mental disease and explaining British elaborations on his techniques—Meyer did not say a word against the theory. The meeting was a great mental boost to Cotton, who returned home feeling entirely vindicated and ready to battle on against the American nay-sayers.

When Cotton suddenly died, still ensconced at Trenton, in May 1933, Meyer wrote his obituary for the *American Journal of Psychiatry*. Bending a knee a little to the fact that the focal-infection theory was controversial in the United States, Meyer for the most part let the trumpets blow: work he knew to have been over 40 per cent fatal he described as "a most remarkable achievement of the pioneer spirit...an extraordinary record of achievement [by] one of the most stimulating figures of our generation".

Digging further through the hospital archives and newspaper clippings, Andrew Scull discovered that the dental surgeon Cotton had hired, Ferdearle Fischer, did not retire from active service at Trenton until 1960; and that as late as 1955, according to the hospital's annual report, "Sepsis [was] carefully searched for and eliminated in all cases." By then, of course, Trenton was into a surgical assault on the ultimate in infected organs—the brain—via lobotomy, an operation invented in the 1930s on as ridiculous a theoretical basis as Cotton's by a Portuguese neurologist who had heard that frontal-lobe damage had modified the behaviour of a single laboratory monkey. The fellow who invented lobotomy, Egaz Moniz, didn't work at the Trenton State Hospital so he wasn't in line for the Cotton Award for Kindness. Instead, he won the Nobel prize.

CHAPTER SIX

The Imperative to Treat

If Ewen Cameron had been a different kind of man, less active and more reflective, being consigned so early in his career to the Brandon Mental Hospital might have put paid to his professional hopes. Brandon itself was a shock for one accustomed even to the minor capitals of Europe. A city of roughly twenty-seven thousand, with no major industry, its fate was tied to serving the needs of Manitoba farmers going bankrupt in the face of drought and depression, and its international reputation was based on a single fact—Brandon was the place the railway added an extra engine in the long transcontinental haul.

Jean Cameron, who bore their first child there, remembers that for recreation she and Dr. Cameron (which is what she calls him still) went to the local hockey games and on Sundays took drives out into the country "until we got stuck". Wandering pregnant through the winter landscape she was brought up short by the realization that she was walking on top of the hedgerows. For tennis (she had been ladies' champion back home) she resorted to taking the two-hour drive to Winnipeg to find her competition; there were staff courts on the grounds of the hospital, but it bothered her husband a little that the doctor's wife should display herself in brief tennis whites. As far as social gatherings went, Jean Cameron remembers vividly going to a luncheon for doctors' wives shortly after she arrived in Manitoba to find the discussion entirely taken up with how to can a turkey. "There are lots of ways," she recalls. "It was 1933 and there wasn't much money to pay doctors so they got paid in produce. One woman there had a hundred and ten turkeys."

Jean Cameron's version of her courtship—how as a bride she ended up living in an apartment in a mental hospital in the Canadian prairies—is rather laconic. She says she first noticed Ewen Cameron because he was the only player on the University of Glasgow rugby team wearing the wrong colour socks; that he kept going away to America and Europe, but that he always came back. When he finally proposed to her, she had herself graduated and was the first female tutor in the university's mathematics department. Cameron's own version (a family joke, says Jean) was that he first noticed her during the annual game between the ladies' field-hockey and men's rugby teams when she committed a foul on him. In fact, their families were acquainted, and whatever the origins of their union the couple proved to be well matched; soon after arriving in Brandon, the doctor's wife took two courses in statistics at the local college so that she could help her husband in his research. She was binding the manuscript of his first book to mail off to his New York publisher the day she went into labour with Duncan, the eldest of a family that extended to three boys and a girl; at the time Dr. Cameron was away in the States at the annual APA meeting, delivering a research paper.

Research and trying to communicate the results of his research were all Ewen Cameron had to sustain his remarkable ambition. His job was to admit patients to the hospital, to categorize them, and to assign them either to the Reception Unit, where he worked and where the staff did its best to provide treatment for acute cases, or to the chronic wards. It was neither a high-level nor a high-paying job, and it brought him into constant irritating contact with the atavistic view the local community had of the hospital. In his view, admissions were rarely timed for the benefit of the patient: families either used the hospital as a dumping ground for unwanted members (the senile or seizure-ridden, the recalcitrant spouse) or regarded it as a horrible place of last resort, bringing their afflicted far too late in the progression of their illness, Cameron judged, for doctors to do them any good.

The institution's proper name was the Brandon Hospital for Mental Diseases, but to the locals it was still "the hill"—the forbidding collection of stone buildings on the bluff above the river north of town where the crazy people were sent, the dread "funny farm". When the original buildings burned down in 1910, the local paper had noted with amazement the miracle that 643 "raving maniacs and imbeciles" had gotten out alive. "There were people in all parts of the city in great dread lest some of the inmates of the asylum might wander around, and on the streets outside of the well-lighted portions of the city, not a woman could be seen. From all over Brandon people were telephoning for information and in almost every instance inquiries were made as to whether many of the lunatics had got away from the guards," reported the *Brandon Sun*. Local attitudes had changed not a whit by 1929, when Cameron arrived. Though "the hill" employed more than 250 people (among them eight doctors) and took care of close to 1,200 inmates, not even families living through the Depression on the earnings of hospital attendants could understand why anyone risked working there. The stigma of being committed was enormous.

The largest proportion of patients were the neurosyphilitics, the soldiers who had come home infected from the European War; for them at least, thanks to Wagner-Jauregg (in Cameron's view), something could be done. Treatments at Brandon included the malarial-fever cure and dosing with variations of arsenic, bismuth, and mercury. (Most of these patients remained in the hospital, however, dying of their disease in the early forties). But the epileptics, schizophrenics, catatonics, manic-depressives, and those patients classified as stuporous, who lay or wandered in a daze—for them there was still no standard treatment, no hope of cure.

So the young Dr. Cameron tried things: things he'd read about or put together for himself, working late in the laboratory just a few steps from his apartment, through a room where visiting doctors were billeted. A male nurse who worked with Cameron briefly in the thirties describes him in terms his Allan colleagues would easily recognize: "He was inclined to be a bit hyper. He didn't just walk—he was on the move. I could see him being a little tough to work with. He always had to be doing something and going somewhere." Sometimes the nursing staff threw a spanner in the works. One of Cameron's ideas was that epileptics drank more than ordinary people, and he decided to try to control their liquid intake ("The Dehydration Method in Epilepsy", as the paper he later published in *Archives in General Psychiatry* was titled). "He had the staff trying to measure and regulate the liquids of their patients," says William Willey, a nurse who worked at the hospital from 1926 until he retired in 1971. "But this was hard to do, because the wards were open and the water taps had to be available all the time." The effort soon proved too much for both epileptics and staff. "It was a guessing game more than anything else," says Willey, "but that didn't matter. Cameron was determined."

Willey, now in his eighties and with memories of hundreds of doctors who stopped briefly at Brandon on their way to getting ahead, remembers few with as strong a drive as Cameron's. "If he saw a problem, he would just walk right into it," he says. Willey admired him and describes him as a "pretty fair man" who "got along with most people"; but he didn't warm up to Cameron. "He was climbing the ladder fast, and he was brilliant," Willey says, but "he saw his co-workers and the patients as a means to an end. Through them he could do the research to make a name for himself. There weren't too many other psychiatrists or nurses who maintained that attitude."

Reasoning as others before him had reasoned—if heat from a fever helped neurosyphilis, heat might also do something to schizophrenia—Cameron tried using an external source of heat, described in one of his articles as "an electric cage", to warm a test group up; however, he couldn't raise the patients' temperatures above 102 degrees Fahrenheit without their pulse rates rising "unduly", and he soon abandoned that idea as unworkable.

Nothing seemed to work with schizophrenia; anything was (therefore) worth a try. In his last couple of years at the hospital Cameron had read how red light promoted the growth of both laboratory rats and plants, and seemed also to increase both male and female fertility (or so the literature claimed). "Since it has been well known for a considerable time," he wrote, "that schizophrenia is often accompanied by an endocrine hypofunction, particularly as far as the sex glands are concerned," he decided to try bathing catatonic and paranoid male schizophrenics in light of "a transmission spectrum similar to that of blood". He rigged up a red-light cage carrying fifteen 200-watt lamps, filtered by an inch of running water and then a layer of "sodium salt of ditolyldisazo-bis-naphthylanine S sulphuric acid...impregnated into cellophane", which transmitted light of the right wave length. (Cameron loved the challenge of gadget-making; he once even tried to rig up with intravenous tubing a self-feeding unit for his infant children—no muss, no fuss, no bother.)

He got patients to lie naked a foot below the filters for eight hours a day for as long as eight months, supplementing their diet with cod liver oil just in case their production of vitamin D suffered. In his paper, he reported that, of fourteen patients treated, five were discharged, one showed marked improvement, one showed moderate improvement, and four showed slight improvement; only three showed no change. He documented his judgement with clinical notes on each case, because he had nothing else to measure with. Cameron didn't know why it worked. (He failed to note, for instance, that the patients he was able to discharge weren't chronic, but had been in the hospital only a short time before he singled them out for special attention.) He had only his own observations to prove that it did work, but on the basis of fourteen cases he was ready to recommend the red-light treatment to the readers of *The British Journal of Physical Medicine* "as a therapeutic agent probably of unspecific nature and of as yet definitely limited potency". Such was his desire to keep his name in professional view.

Still, Cameron suffered no delusions by the end of his years in Brandon about the state of both his art and his science. With his wife's statistical assistance he looked at the records of patient care on one of the hospital's ten-bed acute wards over the four years from 1930 to 1933. Ward West 1, he wrote, was "a good example of the modern planning of acute wards. It is small, containing only ten beds, seven of these being located in single rooms. The ward itself is designed to furnish good sound breaks. There is a battery of three continuous tubs, two large sun balconies, the lighting is exceptionally good, and the protection of the windows is not obvious. There is ready access to the occupation rooms next door, and the ward has, of course, recourse to the laboratories, operating room, dental clinic and X-ray unit."

What Cameron found was encouraging for a person in charge of the care of mental patients, but depressing for a doctor trying to cure them. He and his colleagues, over those years, had treated their charges more responsibly, allowing them more liberal parole into the community, unlocking several of the wards, and getting rid of "protective" devices. They'd learned to intervene in "excitatory" states as quickly as possible, winding the unruly into wet packs of cold sheets, which lowered their body temperatures and cooled them into slumber. They'd learned that keeping all their patients well nourished, using tube and spoon feedings with the unwilling or unable, lowered the incidence of such excitements.

But as far as treatment went, Cameron had to concede that basket-weaving or making wooden lawn ornaments and trunks in the hospital shop or working on the farm—the plain therapy of work done in a setting that encouraged independence—was by far the best treatment the hospital could offer. Shades of moral therapy. Toilet-training the incontinent was far more therapeutic than any drug or medical technique he could dream up. In his report he listed all the medical attempts: thyroid extracts seemed to work a little for depressives and schizophrenics "complicated by endocrine imbalance". Otherwise gland extracts were "unsatisfactory". The sleep cure—putting patients to sleep using barbiturates for a period of weeks, a technique Cameron had been taught in Europe after it was publicized by Klaesi in the early twenties—was complicated by risk of bladder and lung infections. "From our experiences elsewhere...," he wrote, "we have felt that, in that it is usually patients who, in any case, have the most favorable prognosis that are selected, this form of treatment results in a deceptively high recovery rate."

Cameron lists other things tried—carbon-dioxide and oxygen treatment, acidosis, hyperventilation, ketogenic diet, his own heat and dehydration efforts—and concludes that none of them served any useful end at all. He lauds the hospital, and particularly the Reception Unit where he worked, for its "general hospital atmosphere" but hints that atmosphere is all there is: "We still feel considerable doubt [about] whether most modern treatments of the psychoses could not be entered under the headings of palliative and humanitarian." How could a doctor rest easy with that? "In considering these gains which have been achieved, it has to be kept in mind that we can ameliorate the 'explicit' behavior of the patient by filling his time with occupation, raising his weight by diets, and securing his sleep with sedatives, without altering his true condition." More than anything, Cameron wanted to alter his patients' true condition. Instead he found himself no better off than the asylum doctors of the nineteenth century with their healing architectures and work cures.

Cameron's energies at Brandon found many outlets. He dreamed up training schemes to remedy what he thought was an appalling lack of education on the part of Canadian asylum doctors. He proposed, too, that in each hospital a new post of director of clinical investigations be created, with salary commensurate with at least an assistant asylum superintendent's, so that doctors like him would have something to aspire to to keep them busy at their research. Following the Meyerian lead—and reacting to the widespread social stress of the poverty-struck prairies—he established travelling mental-health clinics in nine local towns, so that if the stigma was too great for people to come to the "hill", the "hill" would go to them. In his book manuscript and incidental papers, he wrote of the ways things soon should be in psychiatry: that psychology would stand to psychiatry in the way that pathology stood to general medicine, so that there would be something more than bare clinical judgement to bolster the lesionless world of the psychiatric doctor. There *had* to be laws of behaviour to discover, he was certain: "There is no reason to think other than that the present almost inextricable confusion of attempted social evolution, social regression, disappearance of age-old beliefs and abandonments of former folk ways and culture, is actually a response to ascertainable causes, and is as precisely governed by laws as the reactions in the fields of physics or physiology." Cameron was a scientific positivist who brooked no despair.

It was, however, a rather slight bit of research that finally sprung him from Brandon and into the mainstream post of director of research at Worcester State Hospital in Massachusetts in 1936. Cameron established, on a shoe-string budget, that guinea pigs that had one leg tied down got depressed and lost weight; as soon they were let loose, they gained weight again and (presumably) their spirits rose. "I used to help him some evenings by holding the guinea pigs down," says Jean Cameron. "He gave a paper at the APA on that experiment, and the director of Worcester heard it. He had [already] received a similar research proposal costing a lot of money. So he had an appreciation of this economical Scotsman and hired Dr. Cameron. Dr. Meyer had done that job, before he went to Baltimore, and here was Dr. Cameron doing the job of his eminent teacher."

And not too soon, either, for after seven years Cameron was truly chafing at the ceiling put on his activities by the provincial mental-hospital bureaucracy and by the absolute dearth of professional associates in that part of Canada. How was he to do anything if there were no challenging colleagues to spur him on? A memo on record at the Brandon hospital, from Dr. Alvin Mathers, the man who recruited him, reminds Cameron that the proper protocol was to have his research reports approved by Mathers before publication and to okay all press interviews with the hospital superintendent, the ex-missionary Thomas Pincock, before he gave them. Though Mathers himself agreed with most of what Dr. Cameron had to say on the state of Manitoba mental-health care, the government had been embarrassed by a few of his comments. Cameron was a bit too eager to push himself forward, and the hospital didn't want to bear the consequences.

In those years the discoveries of regular medicine set the pace. Psychiatry was the perpetual follower, sometimes so close it stepped on medicine's heels in its haste to apply great medical breakthroughs to the treatment of its own hopeless cases. Insulin, for instance. At first, institutional psychiatrists were content to use small doses of insulin to improve the appetites of their reluctant eaters: fattening them up seemed to have a calming effect. Then, in 1930, a Polish-born psychiatrist named Manfred Sakel reported the results of an accident he had had while tending to a famous German actress in a Berlin sanitorium. The actress was diabetic and addicted to morphine; injecting her with insulin, Sakel overestimated the dose, and the actress fell into a light coma. When she woke, her craving for morphine seemed abated.

That was good enough for Sakel, who in grandiose moments (of which he had many) said he was directly descended from Moses Maimonides, the great twelfth-century rabbi and doctor. Sakel began to treat all his drug addicts with insulin, and reported great empirical successes; in his first report he claimed to have cured fifteen addicts, though he did not define "cure" or give any idea of how long-lasting it might be. Then, while further pursuing the empirical (if it works, don't fight it) treatment of addicts, Sakel had another accident. He gave one of his patients, who also happened to be psychotic, such a large dose of insulin that the man went beyond light sleep and into major coma.

The catastrophe (an insulin-produced coma can easily prove fatal) turned into a major development. On coming to, the fellow was lucid—just for a little while, but nevertheless relatively rational. Working on animals in his kitchen, Sakel got to the point where he could induce comas and then bring the animals round by using glucose to rectify their drastically reduced blood-sugar levels (which caused coma by lowering oxygen levels in the brain). Rough and ready research it was, but Sakel emerged from the kitchen confident that he could safely try the new technique on schizophrenics, the frustratingly untreatable bane of psychiatric existence. Between 1933 and 1935, he published a blizzard of papers trumpeting the news that he, Manfred Sakel, had created the first effective medical weapon against schizophrenia. In his hands—the induction of coma being a fairly complicated technique—Sakel claimed, insulin coma produced an improvement rate of 88 per cent.

Nowhere in those papers did Sakel present a half-way reasonable explanation of why taking patients to the edge of brain damage or death (and sometimes over the edge)—not just once but usually in the neighbourhood of fifty times—should cause a real "remission" of schizophrenic symptoms. He suggested that perhaps psychotic patients suffered from a superactivity of certain brain cells, and that insulin worked by selectively muffling the combustion process in those cells. He retreated to war metaphor—the convulsions sparked in some patients were the "artillery" needed for their particular battle, but the standard hypoglycaemic effect was the "infantry", and it was wave after wave of infantry that usually won the war. He quite blatantly threw up his hands: "I have high regard for strict scientific procedure and would be glad if we could follow the accustomed path in solving this special problem: it would have been preferable to have been able to trace the cause of the disease first, and then to follow the path by looking for a suitable treatment. But since it has so happened that we by chance hit upon the wrong end of the right path, shall we undertake to leave it before better alternatives present themselves?"

As Sakel understood, in the first flush of expectations, explanation didn't really matter. Sakel's cure rates beckoned institutional psychiatrists as the lights of Las Vegas lure gamblers hoping to win big. In early 1936, the New York State Commissioner for Mental Health, Dr. Frederick Parsons, paid Sakel's way to the United States to give a training course in the administration of insulin-coma therapy to twenty-five state-hospital psychiatrists at the Harlem Valley institution in Wingdale, New York; the treatment spread as quickly as a chain letter. By March 1936, Ewen Cameron had become one of the first psychiatrists in the United States to begin an experimental program of insulin-coma therapy at Worcester. At thirty-four, after his long prairie interregnum, he had finally got to the cutting edge of his profession, and this time not as a student or a doctor but as a research scientist.

Dr. Bill Holtz, retired head of the department of psychiatry at Albany Medical College, first worked with Cameron in 1938, when, in the last year of Holtz's training at Worcester, he got himself reassigned from the acute admissions ward to the research department. He remembers Cameron as "a tall, distinguished-looking doctor whom everyone regarded highly". Holtz says the research ward had "complete control of forty patients, and a staff of about five clinically trained psychiatrists". Its mandate was studies into schizophrenia, and specifically the new convulsive therapies being introduced from Europe. Insulin coma was regarded as the first of such therapies because convulsions were a common effect and, says Holtz, research seemed to indicate that the patients who had convulsions benefited most from the treatment. It was Cameron's special turf. But Ladislas von Meduna's metrazol-convulsion therapy (metrazol was an artificial form of camphor) and the brand-new electro-shock technique introduced by Ugo Cerletti of Italy were also under discussion. All the shock therapies, as they were called, were equally mysterious in their effects, and for their credibility in the treatment of schizophrenia relied on Meduna's observation (later proved false) that epileptics didn't seem to come down with schizophrenia, and vice versa.

Cameron, following the precepts of his teacher, Adolf Meyer, didn't hold with the notion that mental disorder could be described as "disease"; he scorned those (like Henry Cotton) who viewed it as a kind of "fungus" in the patient that could be cut out. He criticized psychoanalysts for being driven by what he regarded as a nineteenth-century image of mental illness as a homunculus at the heart of the patient—and for believing that a healer had to get at that root cause of the illness and eliminate it before a patient could be "cured". Yet weighed on the scale of his actions, Cameron's quibbling proved to be semantic: insulin-coma therapy was nothing if not disease-oriented treatment. It turned patients regarded as sick in mind and disordered in behaviour into patients lying on hospital beds sick in body and literally dependent on the ministrations of doctors and nurses for their survival.

It also took bold medical judgement to perform. "The big decision," says Holtz, "was whether to bring the unconscious patient around by intravenous glucose or by stomach tube." Intravenous was faster, and therefore necessary in emergencies. Much of the hands-on care was given by the nurses. The doctor could inject varying doses of insulin to all of a ward of twenty patients early in the morning and leave them sweating copiously, glassy-eyed, twitching, moaning, and convulsing, their limbs flailing the air. Nurses monitored pulse and respiration and coma depth, calling the doctor back only when it was time to bring their charges round. First-hand witnesses commonly liken the scene in a darkened insulin-coma ward to one from Dante's *Inferno*. Limbo was certainly close. "There was a one per cent mortality rate," says Holtz; "one hundred times greater than ECT mortality. The patients took a great interest in surviving and not dying."

In fact, those doctors looking for the psychological explanation of the treatment viewed the threat of death as therapeutic. Says Holtz, "By being brought near death the patient had a change of attitude. The person struggled hard to live, and formed a strong attachment to the doctor and the nurse helping them overcome the coma. The patients got very close hands-on contact, which fostered a kind of dependency, like a child, which made them struggle for a return to reality." (Doctors looking back on the treatment realized that the cures put down to insulin coma were largely the result of the disproportionate amount of attention lavished on the few objects of experiment picked out of the huge populations of the mental hospitals. It's a comment on normal hospital conditions of the time that one doctor could describe insulin-coma therapy as TLC—tender, loving care.)

The papers Cameron and his team published never went so far as to postulate a death cure (too vague and existential for Cameron's taste, one would suspect). The explanation they tried to develop was biological: the treatments heightened the "irritability" of the nervous system through the effort of the body to raise blood-sugar levels; the adrenal glands had a strong demand made on them, producing floods of adrenalin; and something was also going on with oxygen levels, affecting the biochemistry of the brain. Cameron was worried by not knowing how it all worked, but what troubled him most was that he couldn't get the improvement rate claimed by Sakel and some of the other European researchers.

Cameron's first series was on twenty schizophrenics at Worcester; he put them into two- to five-hour comas, which were ended with intravenous glucose or, if the patient was conscious, spoonfuls of Karo syrup. He repeated the comas daily for upwards of fifty days. He was successful in duplicating Sakel's lucid period, though he tended to view it as not utterly lucid: "The patient's condition immediately after interruption of the treatment is rather similar to that of mild alcoholic intoxication. He is usually friendly, often sentimental and flirtatious. Antagonism, refusal to talk, ideas of persecution and hallucinations are usually reduced. On the other hand, critical judgment is not good." But after weeks of comas, Cameron reported that only three of the twenty "are able to be home on a fairly stable basis". Seven had to be taken off the treatment for one reason or another, and ten were still undergoing coma in the hopes that something would happen if they were kept on it long enough.

It was puzzling. Cameron believed that some of the distance between his results and Sakel's was caused by his difficulty in finding the appropriate moment to terminate the coma, or even any rationale for choosing one phase over another. People roused while unconsciously agitated seemed to stay agitated; those roused from a deep calm tended to stay almost stupefied. All of it was frustratingly dependent on his own judgement of the individual case: "The technique is difficult," he wrote, "the more so since there is as yet no adequate explanation of the results obtained." And he wondered "to what extent the various changes in a psychosis that we have seen concomitant with the insulin treatment have been actually caused by it".

There's no doubt that Cameron understood all the questions and the limitations surrounding insulin-coma therapy. The papers he published show that he saw Sakel's theory and claims for cure with relatively clear eyes. After all, it wasn't his theory; he had nothing personally invested in it. He was just trying to duplicate results.

Doubts well in hand, he carried on—Cameron used insulin coma and its successor, sub-coma (a lighter version), into the late 1950s—largely because, before the discovery of psychoactive drugs, it was one of the few active things he could do to intervene in the course of an illness. He didn't have to sit and endlessly listen, or content himself with the care and feeding of people consigned to an institution for life. He could act.

There was another reason, too. At Brandon he had been maddened by the fact that being committed to the asylum was such a stigma that families postponed coming for help until (in his view) disorders were so ingrained there was little chance any treatment would work. At Worcester, as resident director of research, he did a study of the attitudes of the relatives and friends of a hundred psychotic patients. "The facts all indicate only too clearly that in the majority of cases people are generally unwilling to send their relatives to mental hospitals until it has become impossible to keep them at home," wrote Cameron. "In other words, it is still very much the case that patients do not come to hospital because they are mentally sick but because they are unmanageable."

The only thing to do was to complete the transformation of madness into physical sickness, to eliminate, finally, the distance between "real" doctors and "mad" doctors. If a general hospital had been in store for them rather than an asylum, Cameron's survey showed that all hundred patients would have sought help sooner. But the only way to transfer the care of mental illness to general hospital wards was to find quicker ways to treat it. Wrote Cameron, "If the claims of the more recently introduced [somatic] therapies can be substantiated, even in part, it would appear to be quite practical to consider carrying out these procedures which usually call for a hospitalization period of a little more than six weeks…in psychopathic wards and even in certain instances on the general medical wards [of ordinary hospitals]."

Those were Ewen Cameron's goals. Get to the disorder fast; the sooner you treat, the more chance you have of returning a workable human being to society. Get to it even before it happens—in the deep heart of families, in the tensions of modern life, in the workplace, and eradicate the conditions that cause it. That's what the mental-health movement should be for—to persuade the powers that be that the modern world required some personality engineering. Treat mental disorders as acute illnesses, a matter of intensive therapy over weeks, not hour-a-week psychologizing stretching fruitlessly over years. Be pragmatic enough to treat symptoms. Avoid being trapped by a search for the elusive root of the disorder—get the person functional again, not "cured". Cure was an illusion anyway. No one was ever cured in Ewen Cameron's view, because you couldn't restore anyone to the mythic "way they were before".

You had to help them change to meet new circumstances, not restore their souls. Healthy people seemed to be able to adapt almost infinitely; their childhood fitted them with mechanisms for taking things in stride. It was sick people who got stuck in bad patterns, sick people who couldn't adapt and ended up dysfunctional and distressing to themselves and others. Change was the answer; but change was also especially hard on them. You had to sandbag them into changing, you had to push—and they had to trust that you, the doctor, could at least see where health was.

Pragmatic, progressive, modern: Cameron was all of these things. It was Ewen Cameron, young Turk, who rose to lead the discussion of Cornell University psychiatrist Oskar Diethelm's paper on the somatic therapies at the APA's annual meeting in San Francisco in June of 1938, the first discussion of the ethics of the new aggressive treatments recorded by that professional body. Diethelm dove back into psychiatric history, producing reams of grotesque examples of psychiatry that had trespassed against both patients and pretensions of scientific method out of a desire to treat. From the nausea-producing gyrations of the mad-doctors' rotary machines to focal-infection theory to insulin-coma treatment, Diethelm pointed out the same avidity on the psychiatrists' part to reach "for the therapeutically stirring discoveries in the general field of medicine". He judged that thoughtless eagerness harshly as "an expression of therapeutic hopelessness in a naively hopeful physician".

Too much of the new psychobiological approach, he said, was merely the age-old mind-body dualism dressed up in new clothes. The new assaults on the physical body, he implied, were not great breakthroughs but the result of perpetual therapeutic frustration. He warned: "There is too strong an enthusiastic drive to help where others have failed, or to find an answer to what had been an unsolved riddle."

The profession needed pioneers and pathfinders, yes, said Diethelm, but it needed ones who understood their responsibilities "to those who follow voluntarily, that is physicians; to those who follow blindly, that is lay people; and to those who are forced to follow, that is patients". The trouble with treatments that are not understood, said Diethelm, is that it is impossible "to predict possible damage".

Cameron listened hard, but was not impressed. Yes, he conceded, it was possible to view all the physical treatments that had come before as grotesque and unjustified, but that was missing the point: "we must recognize that these attempts to utilize general medical procedures were healthy evidence of a determination to see psychiatry as one of the medical sciences. Indeed it is not hard to imagine that without this bond with the rapidly developing field of general medicine, psychiatry might have remained for an even longer period under the domination of moral and philosophical considerations."

Insulin coma, he insisted, was truly psychobiological—if you read Sakel, he told his peers, you'll find he urged "that all possible attention should be paid to the psychic management of the case".

Further, said Cameron, it had at long last begun to make genuine scientific sense to attack the body as a way to the mind: substances like alcohol and benzedrine changed behaviour; scientists were in the midst of discovering the great impact of hormones on behaviour. It was impossible for him to imagine behaviour, disordered or otherwise, taking place without an underlying "matrix" in the body—this was the essence of psychobiology, wasn't it? Somatic treatments, even if not fully understood, made sense because "somewhere or other the chain of events which goes to make up behavior must pass through a lower functional level which can be attacked...."

There is no record of who won the day, but Cameron ended his remarks with a crowd-pleaser: "I think that when the shouting and the tumult in regard to our more recent therapy subside and the captains and the kings who brought these on have departed, we shall find that probably our time will be conspicuous in the historical development of psychiatry as a period during which for the first time a real attempt at the development of a psychosomatic psychiatry was attempted and actually achieved."

Any general discussion of professional ethics was soon pushed to the side by the imperatives of the Second World War, and then by the great therapeutic optimism of the 1950s—the breakthrough decade, in which psychiatry first developed drugs of its own, moving at last (in its view) out of its lock-step at the heels of medicine. It is only hindsight that lends Oskar Diethelm's words oracular overtones as a failed attempt to barricade the road Cameron was compelled to travel. Even if Diethelm had managed to hold his barricade in place, Ewen Cameron still would have felt fully justified in leaping it to serve his own version of the greater good.

CHAPTER SEVEN

At Last, a Mover and a Shaker

Ewen Cameron had first encountered Oskar Diethelm in the glory days of his youthful idealism, at the Phipps in the mid-1920s, when they were both students of Adolf Meyer. "It was only when I came to Baltimore and started to work with Meyer," Cameron wrote, "that I felt that this was what I had always hoped psychiatry might be." Meyer suited Cameron very well because all he talked about was psychiatry. Even when he invited his young residents home (something Cameron never was to do) the talk was all professional. Meyer's wife was the first psychiatric social worker in the United States, and the couple's convivial impulses were largely confined to retiring to consult several huge encyclopedias in their domestic library when discussion got stumped for want of a fact. In a remembrance of Meyer, Cameron joked that it was no wonder their only child left the bosom of his family to pursue a career on the stage.

Meyer's writings were convoluted and his speech almost incomprehensibly abstract; but Meyer was a teacher, wrote Cameron, with "an extraordinary capacity to take some simple thing and, as it were, hold it out to you in his hand and say, 'Look,' and, as you did so, you could see...that it was something new and strange and that the vastly greater part of it was an undiscovered country." On rounds one day with Meyer, Diethelm, and Aubrey Lewis (later Sir Aubrey Lewis, distinguished director of England's Maudsley Hospital, and a great rival—in Cameron's eyes—of Cameron's), Meyer stopped in front of a woman who was crying. After considering her closely for some time he turned to his students and said, "You know, it is strange why water runs down one's face when one weeps. And what is the explanation of the particular contours which the face assumes in crying? Moreover, the sound which is made at such times has peculiarly compelling and disturbing qualities." Lewis and Diethelm ran off to the anatomy department and launched a study of the distribution of the muscle fibres that pull the human face into expressions of grief. Cameron did not record whether any of them tried to staunch the woman's tears.

In Cameron's view, both Diethelm and Lewis had kept on in that descriptive, conservative vein. Cameron had been cast out of the centre for a while by circumstance, but he had come back to take his rightful place and no stance of careful and correct passivity would suit him. Defending his own approach against Diethelm's in front of his peers at the APA must have been sweet. Even sweeter, however, was the realization that he had finally achieved a position where what he thought counted for something. Despite the prairie side-step, Cameron had managed to keep pace with his peers.

When a job offer came his way a little later in 1938 to move to Albany and take up the chair of psychiatry and neurology at the medical school there, Cameron was reluctant. The job would put the Mosher Memorial, the first psychopathic ward established in a general hospital in the United States, in his hands, but it wasn't pure research. It was teaching (which he hadn't done much of); administration (which he'd never tried); and clinical care (which he'd never really done either, except in experiments). His wife tipped the scales on that decision. Her children were growing up on the grounds of mental hospitals, and she was worried that Duncan, not even of public school age, was already able to recognize and classify a mentally deficient boy on the beach during a Cape Cod holiday. A little normalcy, please, Dr. Cameron. And though Jean Cameron hadn't considered the Albany job as any kind of backward step for him, she was astonished by the ease with which he took to administering and motivating groups of people. She knew him as a shy man whose heart palpitated at the thought of walking through a door into a social gathering; here he was dealing with academe and with groups of students and patients and speechifying and lobbying as if born to it.

So the Second World War found Ewen Cameron in Albany. He became an American citizen the year the United States joined the war. His service for his adopted country consisted in two parts. Unable to join the army proper because his second-in-command in the U.S. Reserve had already enlisted, Cameron turned his attention to running a very short-staffed hospital, drafting medical students to come in early in the mornings to administer insulin-coma treatments, and even his wife, to "hand round coffee and things", on one occasion. He also served on the APA's military mobilization committee and, once a month, would travel to New York City at the request of Columbia psychiatrist Nolan Lewis to meet with a group working up psychological profiles of the major Nazi leaders. But it was the war effort of another country that finally threw into Cameron's lap the biggest challenge of his career: creating, from scratch, on the side of Montreal's Mount Royal, a psychiatric training, research, and acute-care institute, a thorough test of his visionary and entrepreneurial powers.

Since the mid-1930s, when McGill University lost its first and only professor of psychiatry, various deans of medicine and McGill chancellors had been fussing away at the notion that McGill had better start something major in the psychiatric area or stop thinking of itself as a first-rate medical school. Not only was the overall education of future doctors suffering, but the entire English-speaking population of Montreal had only two options when seeking local psychiatric care—either consultations with the staff of the Mental Hygiene Institute, a downtown community clinic, or internment in the Verdun Protestant Hospital on the outskirts of the city, one of the large holding bins of the era.

McGill's dean of medicine, Grant Fleming, had approached the Rockefeller Foundation's medical-sciences director, Alan Gregg, for suggestions as to what they should do. The Montreal Neurological Institute, academically affiliated with McGill and located on the university's campus, had been endowed by Rockefeller money. The foundation was devoted to helping set up both research and training facilities in psychiatry all over the world. Its one stipulation was that it would only back a facility or department for so long. If the local community didn't pick up the tab eventually, the foundation would not carry it—it wanted to plant seeds, not nourish full-blown trees. Gregg told Fleming he was willing to sponsor a grant if McGill and the Royal Victoria (its main teaching hospital) would ensure that any person coming in to chair a department would have at least fifty psychiatric beds at his command, preferably in a separate building or wing. Otherwise, Gregg said, McGill wouldn't be able to attract a first-rate man.

McGill, after commissioning a report and canvassing support, let the matter drop; psychiatry proved not enough of a draw to command its own building. In 1939 Fleming, writing again to Gregg in hopes that at least he could hire himself a full professor, received a rather tart response: "Failing some Maecenas who may present you with building and maintenance there is little that you can do merely from within the school."

The Maecenas turned out to be the Allan family, who donated their home, Ravenscrag, to McGill and the Royal Victoria in 1940 with only one string attached, that whatever it was used for, it was to be called the Allan Memorial in honour of the three Allan children who died as a result of the First World War, two when the *Lusitania* was sunk, and one in combat. The mansion then sat empty for close to three years because no one could figure out what to do with it. Only the threat of the appropriation of its thirty-four bedrooms, library, ballroom, and drawing-rooms to house troops roused McGill to action again. This time it was the vice-chancellor and president, F. Cyril James, who corresponded with Gregg. The war effort threatened the Allan bequest, but it also provided a pressing need. "The Canadian

Army Medical Service is increasingly concerned at the number of psychiatric casualties in the early training periods in camps and in the war," wrote James. "Now that second choice recruits are coming in, this is becoming more serious, and Meakins [the current dean of medicine, seconded to the army] wants some action taken by McGill in the field of psychiatry."

Within a couple of months, the funding details of the new institute were worked out between McGill and the Royal Vic, the Rockefeller Foundation (which supplied an initial $30,000-a-year grant over five years to pay teaching and research salaries), and the province of Quebec (which agreed to provide a further $30,000 a year for twenty years to cover the shortfalls of clinical care). By May 1943, the list of candidates for the top job was down to five. Alan Gregg had no doubts as to who he thought would be the best man: Aubrey Lewis "was easily the most mature and competent" but not likely, he thought, to be wooed away from England to take a pioneering post in the psychiatric outback. Of Ewen Cameron, Gregg knew little "other than to say that his writings are of good quality". He was "not so sure on the personality side and its adjustment to McGill conditions. They will need a man who can talk the language of neurology and as much as possible of medicine and surgery." Wilder Penfield, whom Gregg respected and liked in equal measure, wanted a very close relationship between his MNI and any new psychiatric department.

It was Ewen Cameron who impressed in the final interview, and Ewen Cameron who arrived at the train station in Montreal in September 1943 to take on the job. It was Cameron, too, who rejected the first and the last pieces of advice the great Dr. Penfield gave him. If he was going to be a success in Montreal, Penfield told him, he should do as the formerly American Penfield had done—learn French and take out Canadian citizenship. Learning French was the last thing on Cameron's mind. His institute was after all to be the pinnacle of an English-speaking psychiatric network, and English was the language of science. And though Cameron often spoke out against the evils of petty nationalism, he clung hard to his American professional network and his recently attained American status, even to the point of moving his family across the border into upper New York State to maintain his citizenship.

Needless to say, the relationship between the two men cooled before it had a chance to develop into any kind of close co-operation, though Cameron did find his first two staff appointments working under the wing of the MNI. Miguel Prados, analytically inclined, had fled his native Spain after fighting for the Republican side in the civil war; Penfield had lobbied for him to get the chair of psychiatry, but Prados agreed both to teach and to run the Allan's projected out-patient department under Cameron. The other was Karl Stern, an excellent neuropathologist who had fled from Germany to England in the mid-1930s, and then on to Canada. Cameron recruited him to head his gerontology lab, obviously approving of Stern's scientific gifts. But Stern's passionate religious and artistic nature was a constant puzzle to Cameron, who tended to view people with strong spiritual needs as old-fashioned at best, if not ego-damaged. Stern, born a Jew, had been a Marxist, then had undergone a Jungian analysis, and had finally converted to Catholicism. By 1952 Stern had abandoned the Allan, disapproving of Cameron's relentless secularity and essential aloofness; Cameron, flummoxed by things like Stern's trips to New York City to sit at the feet of Jacques Maritain, couldn't understand what more he could do for him. "What does the guy want?" he asked another colleague plaintively, when it looked as though Stern was going to leave. Still, for eight years, Stern performed as a compelling teacher and did ground-breaking work for the Allan, setting up one of the first community-based old-age-counselling clinics.

On fall afternoons in 1943, Cameron and his wife—the children sent to play outside on a swing set left behind by the Allans—would wander through the empty house making plans for the renovations: the stables, a long low building to the right of the mansion, he thought would nicely hold his behaviour lab, in which he at last could explore film and the new sound-recording technology as instruments to measure behaviour. With his first two residents in tow—Lloyd Hisey, who had been sent to the Allan for training by the navy, and Cecil Mushatt, a non-combatant

Irishman—he started to care for patients that winter, in the midst of the renovating and planning.

By the Allan Memorial Institute's official opening day, July 12, 1944, Cameron had already fought and won a battle with the university, the hospital board, and the province. Nothing on earth was going to persuade him that any doors in a psychiatric institute of which he was the head were going to be locked; madness was not a condition to be feared but a disorder to be treated. It was crucial to his patients' recovery, he felt, that they come voluntarily for treatment, that at any time they could walk out and down the mountain to see a movie or visit friends, that they continued to feel responsible for themselves. As long as there was even one locked ward, Cameron believed, his institute would linger in some kind of dark age, people outside pointing to it as the booby-hatch and, worse, its staff able "to push their problems into a room, lock them up and go away and leave them", never "advancing our knowledge of the management of disturbed human behavior". To open up hospital doors was a humane gesture that assured the mentally disturbed that they still belonged to human society. Equally important to Cameron, it was a gesture of faith in his profession's ability to cope, a coming-of-age for psychiatry. In the face of such confidence, the province exempted the Allan from committal laws.

On a podium under the trees on opening day, conscious that just down the St. Lawrence River, in Quebec City, Churchill, Roosevelt, and Mackenzie King were meeting in one of the great strategy sessions of the war—and despite the fact that his research, teaching, and clinical facilities were all jammed into one old family mansion and that his staff was small and his students few—Ewen Cameron felt bold enough to speak in grand terms.

"Those who have conceived this institute and have labored to bring it into being, and those who work here may rightly feel that with it they take their part in an enterprise of great scope and moment. Under the threat and actuality of disastrous events men have not stood apart appalled spectators of their own fate, but have stoutly set about the building up of strong centres armed with all present knowledge so that through long search and effort they may learn to moderate their nature and to secure their destiny.

"And of this great work, we are now a part."

No slouch at the art of rhetoric himself, Wilder Penfield must have viewed the public comments of the new man on the scene with a trace of wry distaste. His institute, after all, was in the throes of beggaring itself for the war effort, having thrown itself into a total war all of its own. (The MNI's 1946-47 annual report reported it thus: "*War.* In 1941, while Britain alone stood in the path of the enemy, we conceived the idea of enlisting our laboratories in research-combat.") They had investigated fatigue in bomber crews, war neurosis, wound healing and scarring, and seasickness: "hundreds of sailors, soldiers and hardy volunteers were swung in swings erected in the nearby Field House, or were rolled and tossed in a giant seasickness cradle that was built in the Institute squash court...christened the H.M.S. *Mal de Mer.*" By the time the Allan opened, however, the research focus (the thrill and the glory) had been dropped, as the MNI concentrated all its energy on attempting to fix the damaged brains and skulls of the war wounded. Its reward? Financial crisis lasting well into the 1950s.

The war had provided Cameron, too, with a checklist of the things he wanted literally to conquer: first and second, stress and anxiety, made respectable objects of attention by the sheer numbers afflicted with both on the battlefields and in the hard-pressed war industries. Any research into those conditions was now a heavy bet for funding from both the military and the civilian authorities. The third was a more personal item, old age, of which Cameron was to write: "Growing old is an immemorial grief of mankind. To lose the striding joy of our racing feet, the fierce, sweet pride in the long swim, the lonely climb, no more to feel the longing and the fear of the young girl going to her early love, are the eternal sorrows of man....We mean to master this business of aging." This business of pain and this business of anxiety, too. The war was the impetus for Cameron's headlong leap into the future, where man's abilities, he was sure, would finally match what Cameron believed was the heart's ultimate desire, "our age-old objective...control over our world".

The Allan Memorial, crammed though its research labs were into converted cupboards and blocked-off stairways, attics, basements, and stables, was a true expression of Cameron's expansionist, optimistic, modern spirit. The exigencies of war gave him the means to take his best stab at turning the myth of social control into a modern reality. The end of that war, Germany's defeat, brought him the signal honour that lifted him securely into the public pantheon alongside Dr. Penfield: Nolan Lewis chose Cameron to go along with him as part of the American psychiatric team picked to judge whether Rudolf Hess was fit to stand trial at Nuremberg.

He became a witness to history in a big way, there in Nuremberg, as part of what he called "a clean wind to the prison house that was Germany". Hess was one of the first of the Nazi leaders brought to justice, in October 1945; his defence lawyer thought he might be able to forestall a trial altogether if he could get him ruled unfit. Hess, who undertook a solo flight to England in the latter days of the war to plead man to man (he hoped) with Churchill for an end to the blood-bath, had been unstable, neurotic, and hysterical in the months of British imprisonment following his self-imposed mercy mission. Among an array of physical aches and pains of mysterious origin, he suffered long bouts of amnesia and fits of paranoia in which he would save portions of his dinners to use as evidence that his jailers were poisoning him.

Instead of allowing the defence to hire its own psychiatrist, as was standard practice in legal circles, the war-crimes tribunal put together a panel of ten, representing the Soviet Union, Britain, France, and the United States, ordered to report directly to it. There is little doubt that the last thing the tribunal wanted was for its panel to judge Hess insane; the major purpose of the war-crimes trials was to bring German moral responsibility for the war home. But the tribunal had little cause for worry. Cameron, in his draft account of the affair, made it clear that the psychiatric rule of thumb applied to Hess's state of mind was whether he could consciously appreciate the nature of the charges brought against him and the mechanisms of the trial. On that score, all four psychiatric delegations found Hess resoundingly sane, though they danced rather delicately around the issue of his "hysterical amnesia" and were all relieved when, as the Russian psychiatrists had predicted, Hess announced that he had regained his memory during the course of the trial.

As he watched the trials, Cameron's interest was not so much in punishment, guilt, and retribution, as in thinking his way through what had happened in Germany and pondering how "to secure ourselves against a repetition of these things". No German could have committed such crimes against humanity, he thought, if all Germans hadn't ceded responsibility for their actions to the *Führerprinzip*. The rise of the Nazis, he wrote, was "a story of the mass manipulation of a disorganized continent": Hitler never would have got so far had it not been for the fact that he emerged as a leader during times "when man had lost confidence in a design of living which had seemed sufficient for decades, when there were vast areas of unemployment, when there was general frustration". The Holocaust was the result of a "psychological epidemic" that could certainly happen again; the revelations of the Nuremberg trials, Cameron concluded, were a call to arms for the psychiatric profession.

Some psychiatrists viewed the sanity decision made at Nuremberg as a major professional failure. The results of Rorschach tests done on the Nazis facing trial circulated like samizdat literature through the Western psychiatric community after the war; two of Cameron's own colleagues in Montreal, Heinz Lehmann of the Verdun Protestant Hospital, and Clifford Scott, a psychoanalyst hired by Cameron to teach at the Allan, believed Hess's Rorschach results showed evidence of schizophrenia. Scott, in an article entitled "The Psychiatric Tragedy of Rudolf Hess" (which he had the gall to send along to Cameron for comments), was vehement on the subject, condemning the Nuremberg psychiatrists for studying Hess, not treating him. They had committed, he wrote, "the sin of omission—they had omitted to treat the patient".

In a copy of Scott's article among Cameron's personal papers that charge is heavily underlined, but it's doubtful that Cameron took it to heart. For him, Nuremberg confirmed the absolute importance of psychiatry to the proper unfolding of human affairs. A mentally healthy society, in Cameron's view, would not have succumbed to the charisma of a Hitler; it was psychiatry's mission to break out of the medical-disease model that had confined it to the treatment of "sick" individuals and to reach into the community—using research as its guide—to ensure that society built personalities able to withstand the increasing stresses of modern life. It was time to treat society as a whole, so that no holocaust would find its starting point in any of the democracies.

Cameron did not witness the second round of trials at Nuremberg, in 1946 and 1947, in which doctors faced prosecution for acting on just such overarching ambitions, for undertaking medical experiments and "medical killing" devoted to healing society as a whole (the phrase is Robert Jay Lifton's, from his major study, *The Nazi Doctors*). Some members of the German psychiatric profession had been more than happy to take Nazi direction in the task of social engineering, prepared for Hitler's biomedical "vision" by a medical training that stressed objective detachment, not empathy, and the doctor's role as servant of the health of the state. The killing technology used in the death camps was designed in the mental hospitals; the beginning of genocide was called eugenics and euthanasia. Psychiatrists decided which of their inmates, whether mentally deficient children or "hopeless" schizophrenics, possessed genes dangerous to the state and decided either to sterilize them or to kill them. It seems almost a furbelow that, in addition to their duties of selecting who would go to the gas chambers or giving lethal injections with their own hands, some of the Nazi doctors bolstered their medical enterprise with experiments of a barbarous nature on human subjects. Perversion of the physician's Hippocratic oath was complete. It was just one more joke of world history, as a witness testified at Nuremberg, that Nazi medicine paid elaborate romantic homage to the great Hippocrates.

At the trials, it was the details of human experimentation that best expressed the doctors' degradation of science: ill-designed, wasteful, stupid, tainted thoroughly by the larger death-dealing. Dye injected into the brown eyes of little boys in hopes of turning them Aryan blue; prisoners dosed with various poisons who, if they didn't die of the drugs, were killed anyway so they could be autopsied to study the poisons' effects; prisoners killed and defleshed so as to provide a university with a skeleton collection; prisoners slowly chilled to death in vats of ice-water so that researchers could estimate how long downed German pilots might risk exposure to frigid seas; the testicles and ovaries of Jewish men and women irradiated and then removed for pathological examination to see if deep X-rays were an effective means of sterilization; and on and on. The chief prosecuting lawyer, Telford Taylor, summed up the case against the twenty-three men on trial in his opening statement when he said that as far as ethics went, "No refined questions confront us here."

The set of ten principles that came to be known as the Nuremberg Code, first set out by Leo Alexander, an American psychiatrist acting as a consultant to the prosecuting team, and then delivered as part of the final judgment, merely codified the previous fifty or so years of thinking of the best medical researchers on the ethics of human experimentation. In a way, the code warded off evil acts very few Allied doctors believed they could commit, despite evidence that to a lesser degree doctors who were also researchers had always been tempted to place the pursuit of knowledge in front of the more mundane task of patient care. Scientists had a great and necessary capacity to abstract themselves.

The first and most important point of the code read:

The voluntary consent of the human subject is absolutely essential.

This means that the person involved should have the legal capacity to give consent; should be so situated as to be able to exercise free power of choice, without the intervention of any element of force, fraud, deceit, duress, over-reaching or other ulterior form of constraint or coercion; and should have sufficient knowledge and comprehension of the elements of the subject matter involved as to enable him to make an understanding and enlightened decision. This latter element requires that before the acceptance of an affirmative decision by the experimental subject there should be made known to him the nature, duration, and purpose of the experiment; the method and means by which it is to be conducted; all inconveniences and hazards reasonably to be expected and the effects upon his health or person which may possibly come from the experiment.

The duty and responsibility for ascertaining the quality of the consent rests upon each individual who initiates, directs, or engages in the experiment. It is a personal duty and responsibility which may not be delegated to another with impunity.

One after another, medical professional bodies and health organizations promulgated various versions of the code. The American Medical Association's legal advisers pointed out in the 1950s that malpractice suits could be lost if doctors deviated from the principles of informed consent: a blanket consent would not do even for procedures recognized as strictly therapeutic—patients had to consent to the specific treatment or operation. The American government demanded that military research carried out for the navy, army, and air force, from 1953 on, had to abide by the spirit of the code.

Still, experimentation on human subjects escalated dramatically after the war and, though ethical codes proliferated, the only constraints truly felt by doctors well into the 1960s and 1970s were the same ones that had failed to prevent the Nazi medical barbarism—personal ethics, values, and conscience. In 1966, Harvard professor Dr. Henry Beecher published a litany of cases of current unethical research on human subjects in the *New England Journal of Medicine*. Informed consent wasn't enough, concluded Beecher, citing research in which the mother of a woman dying of melanoma volunteered to accept a transplant of a piece of one of her daughter's tumours "in the hope of gaining a little better understanding of cancer immunity and in the hopes that the production of tumor antibodies might be helpful in the treatment of the cancer patient". Vain hopes, since the daughter died the day after the transplant operation and the mother, a little over a year later, of melanoma. Beecher believed a "more reliable safeguard" for ethical human experimentation than informed consent alone was provided "by the presence of an intelligent, informed, conscientious, compassionate, responsible investigator".

The issues were even more personal for the soft sciences—sociology, psychology, and psychiatry—where no strong history of applied scientific method existed. One danger was that the search for objective truth did not marry well with the study of human nature. Informed consent depended on the patient's ability to reason through the risks and benefits of proposed treatment, and was hard to achieve (scientists felt) when the patient or experimental subject was not entirely rational. As at the Allan in the 1950s, the professional bias was that mental patients were not reliable witnesses of their own experience, let alone adequate judges of treatment.

The lesson Cameron took home from his days at Nuremberg was not that he should scrutinize his own attitudes and practices more carefully, but that psychiatry was a very important business indeed. As far as the Nuremberg Code went, he probably felt himself to be in agreement with it: no doors were locked at the Allan Memorial; each patient signed as complete a consent as any general hospital at the time required; patients came to the institute voluntarily and could leave when they wanted to. Cameron believed he was an ethical man. The times were such that his patients largely had to take his ethics on trust.

Arriving back in Quebec, Cameron found plenty of things to goad him into pursuing full force his larger professional goals: the old order, in all its damaging strength, clung to power in the rural byways of Quebec, where Catholic church and provincial state—or rather the autocracy of Premier Maurice Duplessis—colluded (to Cameron's disgust) in the social control of the Québécois. Except for the network Cameron was starting to build in Montreal, the care of the mad in Quebec was then largely in the hands of the Catholic church, part of its pastoral duty along with tending to the poor and the aged. In the big Catholic mental hospitals, the idea of treatment hardly entered the picture; they were places of desolation, lock-ups for the disordered and abandoned. Cameron called the whole set-up medieval: in his progressive vocabulary that was a term of considerable abuse.

Cameron resented the deep hooks organized religion had sunk into the psyches of his own patients: Montreal when not Catholic was Calvinist. The people he had treated in Albany came to him for the most part suffering from depression and frustration. In Montreal he saw far more anxiety and guilt. Having targeted problems of human adjustment to a rapidly changing world as his psychiatric mission, Cameron found himself in the perfect setting to study them. The city, despite the predominance of churches (or perhaps because of the predominance of churches), had a red-light district whose reputation was continent-wide. Rural Québécois, drawn to Montreal by dreams of jobs and easy money, were either attracted to "sin" or shocked to their bones by it. In short, a good proportion of the rural migrants broke down.

Quebec's social condition drove Cameron to heights of oratory that would have made his father proud, had his pronouncements not been so scornful of convention and so resoundingly secular. In a book written for lay people called *Life Is for Living* (which came out of a series of public lectures Cameron inaugurated on coming to Montreal), he damned all that was old:

There are pieces of discard and rubbish from practically every system of belief whereby men have lived. You can recognize the litter from every major battle that men have fought for freedom from the old and entrenched systems.

"The divine right of kings—and parents."

"You can't change human nature."

"In sin did thy mother conceive thee."

There are fragments of the stupefying doctrine of predestination and many pieces still actively ticking away from that formidable apparatus of beliefs in absolute evil and absolute good which once crushed out enquiry and intellectual enterprise through all Western civilization.

Had it not been for the occasional medical term that slipped through, Cameron could have passed as a political revolutionary. Perhaps, in a sense, he was.

The state was in the midst of picking up the reins of power from the hands of the outmoded church, Cameron preached. The only hope for human freedom from centuries of domination lay with a "new force"—"the sciences which are devoted to the study of human behavior". His eyes on the aftermath of a bloody war, Cameron spoke respectfully of the continuity of life on the planet but seemed bitterly to resent the continuity of human culture. The only way profitably to study man, he thought, was the new way, by "looking at behavior—that is, how does it work and how can it be controlled". Psychiatrists, "with their unique position between the medical and social sciences, have a special responsibility to act as leaders and guides in entering and opening up this new territory". They had to support "the new, the more liberal, the more effective" and drive out "the old, the harmful, and the entrenched".

The Allan, Cameron determined, was going to be an expression of the new way, from innovations in patient care to the broadest possible spectrum of research labs. The establishment of the pioneering Day Hospital at the Allan in 1946 was typically Cameron. Strapped for space and for beds, and longing in his expansionary fashion to draw in more patients, Cameron began to wonder whether a bed was at all necessary to treatment in the first place. A bed implied hospital—the place you went to lie down, to be cared for and cured. Many psychiatric patients, on the other hand, needed nothing more elaborate than a chair, at most a couch, in a doctor's office. Admitting them to hospital often cut them off from families and work and made it difficult for them to go home again. Re-entry pangs caused their disorders to flare up. The solution was a department of the Allan that mimicked working hours: patients would check in from nine to five, go home at nights, and have their weekends off. If they were undergoing either ECT or insulin treatment, that could be done during the day too, by borrowing a bed. The Allan also reached into family, social, and work lives as part of an effort to treat the whole patient (in homage to Adolf Meyer, who was certainly one of the few other "new" thinkers whose example Cameron was willing to follow). The day-hospital idea caught on and spread throughout Canada, the United States, and Britain.

Before the turn of the decade, Cameron had established research programs and training courses in areas from basic science to community psychiatry and had linked up a network of psychiatric facilities that ranged from local veterans' hospitals, to general hospital wards, to the Mental Hygiene Institute, to the Verdun Protestant Hospital, where patients finally judged chronic were sent. The one weak spot in the net in the 1940s was psychoanalysis. Though Cameron certainly paid lip-service to a psychodynamic approach to human behaviour, Freudian terminology made him laugh. "Oedipus complex", he told a young resident, was just plain old-fashioned sibling rivalry. Only the threat of losing his brightest students to schools in the States, where psychoanalysis was the intellectual rage, persuaded Cameron to bring strong analysts on staff. Even then he bided his time till the 1950s.

There were times when Ewen Cameron's administrative acts of creation seemed like pure legerdemain: for instance, in 1946, when he hired Dr. Robert Cleghorn, a biochemist with a long background in endocrine research, to come and head a lab Cameron airily named "Experimental Therapeutics". Cleghorn was never sure what the name was supposed to mean and found it especially high-faluting when he confronted the physical actuality of it—one room with benches, water, and gas, an office, another empty room, and a large empty hall, in what had been the servants' quarters of the Allan mansion. A good friend of Cleghorn's on the McGill medical faculty, J.B. Collip, secured him a technician and a grant of $5,000 from a local drug company to outfit the lab with a centrifuge and a refrigerator. Cameron made it clear that the Allan would pay him a salary, but the rest—securing funding, finding the right co-workers, the direction of the research—was up to him. In Cleghorn, Cameron backed a good one. Out of his labs for the next two decades came a steady stream of solid research on the endocrine system and the adrenals, on neurochemistry and psychopharmacology.

The Chief, Cleghorn wrote in his memoirs, had no time for hand-holding: "He was...a driven man, with too many ideas to express, too many projects to accomplish in too little time."

Dr. Charles A. Roberts, who for a good portion of the 1950s was the bureaucrat in charge of the federal funding of mental-health research under the Dominion-Provincial National Health Grant system, says that Cameron was alarmingly entrepreneurial: "He had an organizational chart and everything was a clinic, even if there was only a half-time staff person running it." In 1948, the year the mental-health grant was established, he says, "Cameron was all ready to jump the gun and go after that money. By the 1950s, we were dealing with $500,000 plus a year. A few examined it and told me Cameron was getting a third of it." His successful grantsmanship was embarrassing to officials looking for balance and even distribution of federal largess across the country: "We were always trying to keep the lid on him. But his people were name people and it was really hard not to give money to McGill. And at the time, no proposals were coming in from Laval University or the University of Montreal"—institutions where French was the language of science. "It wasn't that I couldn't say no to Cameron," says Roberts. "It was more his constant readiness state."

It was also that Canada was such a small pond and Cameron's acute organizational skills so much in demand. He was, more often than not, sitting on the government peer-review committee that okayed the grants. And, though he was adamantly Anglophone, that didn't prevent him from getting along well with Jean Grégoire, the provincial deputy minister of health, who channelled all requests for funding and all disbursements for English-speaking researchers in the province through Dr. Cameron. And, one after another, Cameron helped found or injected vigorous life into professional organizations—always moving on once he achieved his immediate goal, but leaving behind him members who knew that he would come out to bat for them in a crisis. His influence in Canadian circles was inestimable. Says Roberts: "He is now viewed so ambivalently, but at the time everybody wanted to *be* him."

The only government funding body in Canada that didn't fall to Cameron's charms was the Defence Research Board, under Omond Solandt. At first, simply because Solandt resented Cameron's empire-building. Cameron's big dream in the late 1940s was to corner the market on all psychiatric research in Canada in one big institute dedicated solely to that purpose and run by him in Montreal. Solandt did not solicit Cameron to sit on any of his grant committees, let alone fund Cameron's own work, arguing that Cameron was not a Canadian citizen and that the Allan was already getting enough money from American defence sources: the U.S. Army, for instance, was sponsoring work on stress and on the drug sodium amytal at the Allan. Solandt certainly wasn't going to let Cameron get away with a national research institute (though Cameron did manage over twenty years to lobby himself a research wing built onto the Allan). Later, Solandt had a more personal reason for not funding Cameron's research. He knew a woman sent to the Allan for treatment who was "depatterned" by Cameron. Solandt did not care for the results.

McGill's vice-chancellor, Cyril James, had watched a world-class institute blossom under his eyes through the efforts of the indefatigable Cameron. He had no doubts about the wisdom of his choice. Writing to the Rockefeller Foundation's Alan Gregg just before the first five-year grant ran out, James declared himself to be "personally delighted". Gregg himself was impressed, though he had one reservation: "[Cameron] is rather formal and forbidding in his bearing and if he had got rid of that formality I think he would be an almost unqualified success." The general consensus—as put forward by Robert S. Morison, the officer specifically in charge of the Allan's Rockefeller grant (after a series of interviews with Cameron's colleagues)—was that he "has done a very much better job" than anyone had expected.

In his notes after an interview with Cameron himself, Morison was more grudging: "C. is a good expositor, with what appears to be a critical and reasonably broad approach to his subject. On the other hand he seems a little tense and ill-at-ease. It may be this quality which contributes to his lack of interest and effectiveness in psychotherapy and failure to establish warm personal relations with other faculty members, both of which were mentioned repeatedly when I visited Montreal." Morison, himself a neurophysiologist, was a friend of Wilder Penfield's and later close to Donald Hebb: Cameron's entrepreneurial talents brought him into conflict with both and, worse in Morison's eyes, his science was not as good as either Penfield's or Hebb's.

Cameron himself admitted that his own research was not going well. He'd started a series of experiments in Albany based on a hunch that he could "desensitize" people suffering from non-stop anxiety by injecting them with increasing doses of adrenalin: "C. is obviously not happy with the results," wrote Morison, "but feels the work is worth continuing since the results of other forms of therapy in anxiety states is not very encouraging." But all the Scottish persistence in the world did not get him the results he wanted, and he finally abandoned the work.

The truth was that though Cameron could wield power and influence, be elected to the highest posts of professional organizations, hire excellent scientists to work for him, and hob-nob with the world's best psychiatrists, no laurels would crown his brow unless he made a great research breakthrough. The ultimate insult for a man who so highly valued the achievements of science was contained in a letter Morison wrote to an acquaintance who had been impressed with Cameron's book *Life Is for Living*—mistakenly impressed, implied Morison: "I think Ewen Cameron would be generally regarded as sound, and he is certainly an extremely sincere and conscientious person.... I do not believe, however, that Cameron is generally regarded as a creative thinker in the field of psychiatry."

In a definite sense, Cameron's work as a teacher, administrator, and professional organizer was invisible. He could put the pieces for an institute as grand as the Allan together and still not be given credit for being a creative man.

Many of his associates, and even his eldest son, Duncan, say that what Cameron really wanted as the ultimate symbol of accomplishment was the Nobel prize. And certainly other people who weren't great scientists—Canada's own Sir Frederick Banting, for one—had won it. The thing was to find something undeniably useful, as insulin was to diabetics. Something physical, as close to medicine as he could get, like Wagner-Jauregg's fever cure. Utility was all; it had to work.

Charles Roberts, who owes much to Cameron and holds at least two-thirds of his memory in high respect, says, "I wonder if Cameron's mistake wasn't to try to be a scientist. To wish to be a great researcher."

Schizophrenia was the big one, the painful, incomprehensible, ultimate madness. And Cameron, the researcher, decided he would go after it as he had gone after everything else. He'd use anything—in the book, or out of it—that might give him results.

CHAPTER EIGHT

The Automatic Cure

It was a bit of a joke around the Allan, how much its distinguished Chief was in love with new technology—from his professional passion for tape machines to his one apparent personal indulgence, new-model cars. It matched oddly with his appearance, which was strictly absent-minded professor. Cameron wore twenty-year-old suits, the jacket pockets stuffed with index cards on which he recorded a steady stream of thoughts; his shoes were scuffed and his socks often down around his ankles. In meetings he tended to hunch down in his chair and play with, even nibble on, the end of his tie. There was too little time in the world to spend much of it polishing the exterior. An occupational therapist who worked at the Allan in the 1950s, a woman of twenty-three whom Cameron had put in charge of her own department and who adored him for it, remembers leaning over to discreetly flick a long white hair off the back of her Chief's collar only to discover—to their mutual embarrassment—that it was attached.

The body itself was another matter, vigorous, always striding somewhere. Snatching five minutes of the Chief's undivided attention during the day was an impossibility; to catch him you had to work the kind of hours he worked and wait to talk to him after final rounds.

Motion and mastery: he viewed the loss of physical power as a tragic aspect of growing old. He kept himself fit to forestall it.

Cameron may have worn old clothes, but visions of the future attracted him the way shiny metal draws a crow. He read widely, both professional literature and popular press, in the fifties saturated with optimistic technological visions that were definitely to his taste. He kept a stack of science-fiction novels by his bed. "He called them his blood," said his son Duncan. "He read science fiction every night before he fell asleep." Cameron probably wished he could keep on reading—or doing something useful—after his eyes closed. In 1948, press reports on a fad for sleep teaching caught enough of his attention for him to set Lloyd Hisey, his one-time resident whom he had put in charge of the Allan's EEG lab, to exchanging letters with Max Sherover. Sherover was the American inventor of a device called the Cerebrophone, which he was sure was going to turn the inner-spring mattress into the university of tomorrow. Eight out of twenty chronic nail-biters, in an experiment at a New York summer camp in 1946, had quit the habit after Sherover's modified record-player had delivered six hundred repetitions a night of "My fingernails taste terribly bitter" into their sleeping ears all summer long. For $120, he claimed, you could learn languages, music, and Morse code painlessly while you slept. With the under-pillow speaker that came with the set you could do it all without disturbing (or even educating) your mate.

Hisey accumulated enough details about the machine to have one built at the Allan. He tried "a bit of this sleep learning but I gave it up"—as American consumers soon gave up the commercial version, having discovered that the sleeping human brain is not entirely a sponge. For Cameron, however, bits of the gadgetry of the Cerebrophone—its repeating messages, the speaker under the pillow, the subliminal approach to a supposedly defenceless human mind—came to figure prominently in a series of experiments he hoped would be the making of his research reputation. At first he called the treatment "psychic driving", then "accelerated psychotherapy", and finally "automated psychotherapy", which is what he was aiming for all along. He wanted to get rid of the long-drawn-out time-wasting elements of therapy, the endless, sometimes useless vistas of talk. He wanted to devise an automatic cure. If, one night before bed, Cameron hadn't read Aldous Huxley's 1932 science-fiction classic, *Brave New World*, he and Huxley were familiar with the same professional journals. In the novel, group dynamics, learning theory, and high technology (babies grown in bottles to the sound of piped-in messages) produce a modern utopia wherein every member has been genetically and psychologically programmed to fit. No stress, no fuss, no bother. Dr. Bill Stauble, who worked at the Allan as assistant to the Chief and who describes himself as one of Cameron's "blue-eyed boys", says that, whether the Chief admitted it or not, the idea for psychic driving was straight out of *Brave New World*.

Cameron, with the cold-war terminology of the 1950s floating around his own ears, subliminally and otherwise, was quite prepared to call it something else: brainwashing. A few eggs might have to be broken to get there, but he was equally sure that, once perfected, psychic driving would be nothing but beneficial to the patients. As the Allan's reputation grew, it attracted more and more people classified as hopeless cases, for whom nothing could be done. There was nothing Ewen Cameron hated worse than doing nothing.

Hopeless cases might be depressing to some, but to Cameron they were a true challenge—a test of just how much his profession had got under control. Also, they were excellent objects for clinical experiment: if everyone and everything else had failed and you succeeded, then it was your method and your method alone that had produced the change. Such was Cameron's proving ground. Any change at all was a victory because he had made it happen.

He first began to pay attention to the power of repetition in June 1953, during an hour of psychotherapy with a person he described as a "blond and sultry girl from Bermuda whom I roundly suspected of incestuous but carefully covered up feelings for her father". Not too hard to suspect, on both her and her father's parts, since they had regular encounters that Cameron summed up like this: "He would wait up for her, she would come home late. She would undress noisily.

He would come in. He would pour out angry accusations. She would become furious. He would hit her. She would grapple with him. Both would fall to the floor and there would engage in what was outwardly a furious—but I believed mutually enjoyed—scuffle from which both emerged exhausted." The trouble was, the girl would not agree with Cameron's interpretation.

He, by then, was routinely tape-recording his sessions, and had sometimes relied on instant replay to make a point to one of his patients. "One hot and sticky summer afternoon," Cameron got the Bermuda girl to make what he thought was some kind of admission, and he immediately played it back to her saying, "There!"

"There nothing!" she replied. Exasperating Cameron so much that he played her phrases back to her as quickly as he could operate the switches, as many as thirty times, to the point at which she jumped up, yelled, "You're a damned fool!"—and ran right out of the Allan. Cameron wrote, "[She] was retrieved with some difficulty."

The level of her upset totally intrigued him. Why should the repetitions have bothered her so much, when the initial saying of the thing had not seemed to affect her, or even reflect any real insight on her part? Furthermore, why should the process bother *him* so much? "There is a general feeling that this is something one is doing to the patient that one shouldn't," Cameron wrote six months after the incident. "There is a feeling of uncomfortableness, of minor guilt, a feeling of being unfair in some way, of this not being quite the right thing to do.... It was a little reminiscent to my mind of similar feelings I had years ago when, as a resident in the surgical service, I had to make an incision."

But just inside the queasy feeling was another: elation

I was immediately alerted to the fact that here was something new—something which was particularly appealing to me because it looked as though it might be possible to elicit this [response] regularly...most of us working in psychotherapy and psychodynamics look quite anxiously for phenomena which we can be sure of regularly producing. To do so gives us some reassurance, some sense of actually having the situation in our hands, of knowing where we are, of being able to control events.

He tried the same routine on all the other patients he had in psychotherapy and it did regularly produce in them the same results: "discomfort, embarrassment, aversion and resentment". For his part, he consistently felt that he was "being unkind, insensitive, and imperceptive". Cameron was convinced that within all this storm of uncomfortable emotion was a therapeutic insight stronger than anything in his experience.

Another patient took him the next step when he told him that he couldn't get the played-back sentences out of his head for the entire week between visits. Cameron surveyed the rest and found: "Indeed, for some people it was almost as though the topic we had lit up by repetition had started to blaze out like a fire blizzard, drawing in with greater and greater rapidity more and more recollections of a related nature."

The fire blizzard was in a fair way to consuming the girl from Bermuda. Shortly after the incident in Cameron's office she ran away across the border into the States with a man she said had promised to make her a movie star. When it turned out that the private drama was all he had to cast her in, she had a violent breakdown, which, Cameron wrote, "landed her back as an inpatient in the Institute. I did not think that the playback was completely responsible for this, but there was now no doubt, to my mind, that it was largely responsible. I now began to experience that pleasant anticipatory feeling of having got my hands on something that did something."

He got his new technician, Leonard Rubenstein, a recent *émigré* from England "who understands the mysterious workings of the most complicated recording machines with the greatest of ease", to work out a way of making a loop of the tape, and began to devote ten to twenty minutes at the end of a treatment hour to playing back to the patient twenty- to thirty-second-long repetitions of significant things they had said. Sometimes the impact was so powerful the patient would become obsessed with that area of his or her life, like a character in a bad novel come to the turning point—losing sleep, losing the ability to concentrate on anything else. Cameron would end up having to sedate such patients till the over-excitement passed. More often he was frustrated by their seemingly innate talent not to hear the message he was so insistently driving home, and even in their minds to flip the signal or cue, as Cameron soon began to call it, into its exact opposite. Worse were the patients who were not articulate enough or far enough along in their therapy to come up with any insight of therapeutic value whatsoever—cut and splice as he would he couldn't make a useful cue for them.

Meanwhile, the institutionalized girl from Bermuda was becoming progressively more childish. Cameron tried to sedate her, but she suffered a toxic reaction to the barbiturates. He tried ECT, but "her childlike behavior became more and more apparent. She had to be dressed and helped to eat." Any distinction between experiment and treatment was lost altogether as Cameron struggled to rectify her condition. A young Iranian doctor, Hassan Azima, had just come to the Allan from France where he had trained under the French psychiatrist Henri Ey. Ey and others were experimenting with the new psychoactive drugs produced as a side-product of antihistamine research—chlorpromazine was the first, which the Verdun's Heinz Lehmann was in the process of introducing in North America. One of the things the French tried was to resurrect the old Swiss sleep therapy of the 1920s that had proved so dangerous when achieved by barbiturates alone. Chlorpromazine combined with barbiturates, however, seemed to work; with careful nursing a patient could safely be kept in a chemical sleep for up to sixty-five days. Azima had brought the revamped sleep therapy with him to the Allan, and Cameron decided that his patient was a good candidate for the launch. With one refinement—he would make up a driving signal of his own to be played to her continuously while she slept.

It seemed like an innocuous and benevolent few sentences: her parents were fond of her, they wanted her to come home to Bermuda, she was fond of them, too, and she wanted to go home. The loop was broadcast from a speaker on the wall of the sleep room in a female and (he hoped) maternal voice. At first, she showed little response to the voice. Then, unexpectedly, she became as hostile as her condition would allow: "at moments when she roused slightly from her sleep,

[she] would crawl or stagger out of bed, and try to destroy the source of the voice." The hostility peaked in about six days. By the end of ten days, "she not only became quite undisturbed by the voice, but she slowly began to incorporate the content, saying, 'Yes, I want to go back to Bermuda; yes, my parents love me.' "

They roused her after twenty-five days. She flared up again, and they put her to sleep for three more days. When she was woken for the last time she was quiet—and eager to return home to Bermuda. Cameron, speaking of the case in 1954 as part of a lecture on "the hunch as a method of scientific thinking", wanted to give her story a happy ending but was undone by reality: "Actually, she blew up almost at once upon her return to Bermuda, became violently antagonistic to her father, and this time, also to her mother, whom she threatened to kill."

"We have lost sight of her since," he added, "but have continued to carry out this kind of study of the playback with other patients in sleep treatment." Cameron, who had just scaled the political heights of his profession by serving a term as president of the American Psychiatric Association, had at last got his hands on something that did something, and he was not about to put it down.

Schooled on the experiences of Wagner-Jauregg, of Sakel, Meduna, and the inventors of electro-shock therapy, the Italians Cerletti and Bini, Cameron did not even consider abandoning his new tool just because he couldn't yet control it well enough to predict results. He tried the sleep treatment combined with psychic driving on four more patients and found that, save for one (an epileptic who had severe post-sleep convulsions), the reaction pattern was the same. No matter how benign the signal, they at first resisted mightily and only later appeared to accept it. Cameron did not hesitate to take a further leap: he believed he saw definite if short-lived changes in the personalities of three of the five, though at first he would not attribute them directly to either the sleep treatment or the psychic driving.

One woman, an "anxiety hysteric" with an alcohol problem, was readmitted to the Allan after her bully of a husband reneged on a promise that they would move from the small village she hated into Montreal. Cameron's driving statement was all about how she should have the confidence to assert herself. She came out of the sleep room feeling quite happy to stay in the small town—not exactly the effect Cameron intended. She also said, "I have peace of mind now that I haven't had for years. I don't know what you did to me in treatment." A battery of neurological tests conducted after she was woken showed a slight functional deficit (as they say) on her right side: "she fell out of bed or crawled out of bed on several occasions," wrote Cameron, "and we felt she might have hit her head." He wondered whether her new serenity owed more to head trauma than to psychic driving.

Still, between 1953 and 1955, when he began to report on psychic driving at professional meetings, Cameron tried it on more than a hundred of the patients he treated at the Allan and claimed that it had caused only one "possible persisting trauma" (no doubt the girl from Bermuda). The major problem he believed he faced was patient resistance: if it was hard to get someone to sit still for something unpleasant said once in the reassuring presence of his or her therapist, it was even harder to get a patient to listen to hundreds of repetitions of the unpleasant in a room alone with a machine.

He and Rubenstein tried to overcome the resistance technologically, working on variations on delivering the voice. For a while patients wandered around in modified football helmets, but too many of the helmets got thrown across the room; headphones made the voice sound as if it was inside the head, but the phones too were prone to damage. Rubenstein concocted a mega-recorder with eight separate playback units and pillow speakers to feed into the sleep room and installed wall speakers above the patients' reach in the private rooms. He and Cameron discovered that if they made the driving statements sound like bad radio reception—varying the pitch and tone, and fading them in and out—people tended to listen more attentively. The trouble with the patients who weren't undergoing driving in concert with sleep therapy was that when all other forms of resistance failed they tended simply to get up and leave the room, and sometimes the institute.

So Cameron also tried to make his patients more receptive through chemistry. As well as drugged sleep, Cameron tried driving under the influence of "adjuvant" drugs. An amphetamine called desoxyn combined with sodium amytal—he called the mixture "talking-out capsules"—was the most common, but he also tried LSD.

Everyone who was adventurous in psychiatry in the 1950s was trying LSD, at first under the mistaken impression that it mimicked psychosis—on themselves, to gain insight into madness; on their patients, to see what happened; in the lab, to find an antidote to the drug that could also be an antidote to delusions.

Humphrey Osmond, a young British doctor working in Weyburn, Saskatchewan, was one of the first researchers to move on to study the drug's transcendental qualities, as an extension of earlier studies of mescaline, in which he had opened the doors of perception to Aldous Huxley, among others. (It was in correspondence with Huxley that Osmond created the term psychedelic—literally, mind-manifesting— in a rhyming couplet that ran, "To fathom hell or soar angelic/Just take a pinch of psychedelic.") He tried LSD in the treatment of alcoholics, hoping to flip them right out of their addiction by using the drug to bring on a massive case of delirium tremens; instead many patients, in Osmond's supportive setting, achieved highs of great spiritual and emotional beauty and underwent a kind of conversion to a life free of liquor: Osmond's reported success rate was as high as 50 per cent.

Cameron never took the drug himself and apparently had not much use for Osmond's work, voting while on the federal research committee to deny him funding. LSD ceased to be a respectable tool altogether once it had been liberated from academic circles into the hands of what became the counter-culture. None of Cameron's psychic-driving patients, given the drug with no warning of its effects and in a setting not the least bit spiritual, discovered its transcendental edge. Cameron, in the end, abandoned it as "considerably overrated" both as to its effects and its dangers.

But he would try anything that would give him direct access to the unconscious, a term he didn't like to use but that was nevertheless an apt description of his target. He used hypnosis, and he even prepared his patients for driving by putting them into sensory isolation—to the horror of Donald Hebb, who was worried that Cameron would report on sensory isolation before the government cleared Hebb to do so and was disgusted that he would use the technique on people as vulnerable as mental patients. But Cameron intended an all-out assault. In his first paper on the subject, "Psychic Driving", published in the *American Journal of Psychiatry* in 1956, he did not hesitate to state that the series of clinical experiments he was now billing as treatment was "analogous to...the breakdown of the individual under continuous interrogation".

For Cameron had strayed far from his initial hunch that instant playback and limited repetition of insights uttered by his patients themselves could speed the course of their therapy. "Seeing that the patient did change and for the better following repetition of his own statements, would he not change more decisively and in a more controllable way if we set up the statements ourselves?" To Cameron that sounded logical; also "clearly, if this thing worked after thirty repetitions, it was only common sense to see what would happen if the repetition was increased tenfold, a hundredfold or even more." To, in fact, twelve to sixteen hours a day, and up to half a million times.

Some kind of "switcher" mechanism in the brain, Cameron thought, prevented the organism from responding in an adaptive fashion to the repetitions. The only way to overcome that imagined switcher was totally to overwhelm the patients' old behaviour patterns, to "disorganize" them so entirely they had no defence against the new patterns Cameron wanted to implant. All of this, couched in Cameron's distinctive and inventive terminology (if he could find a name for something, it existed), boiled down to a very old way of regarding the mind—as a blank slate coloured in by experience. In Cameron's eyes, his patients' slates told limited, damaging tales. He began to believe that he had to wipe away those old stories to make way for the new, the ones he thought should be told.

There's no evidence in Cameron's surviving papers or in the recollections of his colleagues that he ever suffered a moment of self-doubt over the damage his indiscriminate slate-wiping could cause his patients. In the grip of rhetorical flight, Cameron knew the value of memory. He chose "The Process of Remembering" as his subject when he gave the prestigious Maudsley Lecture in 1962: "Memory is the bastion of [a person's] being. Without memory there is no personal identity, there is no continuity to the days of his life." For at least thirty years of his career, Cameron even struggled vainly to find ways to improve memory retention in the elderly. At the same time, without apparent qualm, he was prepared to sacrifice the memories of his patients in pursuit of an experimental premise he couldn't seem to make come true. Instead of abandoning psychic driving as unworkable when he didn't get the desired results, Cameron escalated the intensity of his interventions.

If chemical sleep alone would disorganize them, then fine; if that didn't work he would try perhaps first sensory deprivation and then chemical sleep. If they still were not in shape to be receptive there was a final weapon, one that he literally named "depatterning". When details of Cameron's work began to appear in the mass media following the MKULTRA revelations in 1977, the fact that seemed to horrify reporters most was that Cameron injected unwitting people with LSD. Far more horrible and damaging in its effects was his depatterning use of electro-shock.

Cameron had been following the electro-shock literature and had come across something termed "regressive" or "annihilation" ECT. The usual course of shock treatments was one every other day to a maximum of ten in a series, which doctors had found minimized ECT's recognized impact on memory. A handful of American and British researchers claimed that by escalating shock treatments to three or four a day for a month and even more, they could regress hard-core cases, usually schizophrenics, back to a childish level of consciousness, give them REST, as the acronym went. The challenge was then to bring them back to a delusion-free maturity.

Cameron was looking for something more effective than insulin-coma therapy to treat schizophrenics. Despite the fact that he believed electro-shock to be "crude, elementary, [and] empiric" and complained that doctors all over North America were busy pressing little buttons when they should be researching the causes of depression, ECT was no more crude or empiric than insulin coma. In fact, to Cameron its effect on memory—the varying degrees of amnesia it caused—seemed more to the point: "we have found it expedient to try to destroy pathological behavior patterns held in the memory storage systems."

After trying it a few times, Cameron found that the so-called regressive ECT didn't really regress patients in any controllable way. They might have two-year-old attitudes to toilet training but remember how to speak a second language learned when they were twelve. Cameron thought the term "depatterning" was more accurate. He took bits of methodology from here and there: the actual form of shock he used was Page-Russell (named after its British inventors). Instead of a single shock, a single press of the button, a doctor hit the button six times, one after the other, causing a many-peaked convulsion. Because Cameron found that patients feared ECT—and also because a long period of chemical sleep was in itself "disorganizing"—Cameron combined at least two Page-Russells a day for thirty days (in recalcitrant cases much longer) with sleep therapy. At the end he hoped to have achieved what he called the "third stage" of depatterning— where patients had lost all sense of "space-time image" and even the sense that they should have one ("He lives in the immediate present. All schizophrenic symptoms have disappeared. There is complete amnesia for all events of his life.") What that means is that patients were rendered incontinent in both bladder and bowel, unable to dress or feed themselves; they knew neither where they were or who they were and responded to stimulus with at most an infantile smile.

It was only a tiny step further for him to wonder what effect depatterning would have on psychoneurotics, chronic cases who had been unhappy for years, to see how it would work combined with psychic driving. Whatever else it did to people, it certainly got close to producing a blank slate for Cameron to write on.

There's no doubt that Cameron thought his psychic-driving and depatterning treatments were forms of brainwashing. His technical associate, Leonard Rubenstein, told the *New York Times* that among themselves Cameron and his co-researchers had called it brainwashing. Leonard Levy, recruited as a first-year resident in 1956 for the Cameron team, described the project as a series of experiments with brainwashing techniques. That Cameron should have used the word did not necessarily mean a secret agency was setting his pace: the reported Soviet and Chinese mind assaults, the state of the Korean POWs, the blank stare of Cardinal Mindszenty, had alarmed researchers in the social sciences but also fascinated many of them. Therapy, after all, was the art of catalysing personality change. Brainwashing was supposedly a method of changing personality in ways the brainwasher determined. The thought of wielding that kind of power was seductive for therapists constantly faced with patients who rarely seemed able to change their ways for themselves.

In the late forties and fifties, the depth probe of psychoanalysis was the form of psychotherapy most in vogue, the aim being to plunge deep into the patient's psyche and past to trace the permutations of infantile complexes. At the same time, B.F. Skinner and others were developing behaviourism (the theory that modifying the behaviour modifies the whole being or, alternately, that since behaviour is where being intersects with world, modifying behaviour is all that matters), but their work was based largely on animal studies. Only thinkers right out at the edge would go so far as to speak of human personality in terms of ongoing, reinforced patterns, but that was quickly to change. Cameron's colleague Heinz Lehmann has said that the fifties furore over brainwashing pushed the entire psychiatric profession towards the hard study of both behaviourism and Pavlovian learning theory: "In a sense it stimulated an advance in the psychiatric model of man."

Cameron himself was fascinated with the work his British friend, Dr. Will Sargant, was doing on conversion experiences—whether produced by religion, psychotherapy, or the machinations of the totalitarian state. Cameron had also thoroughly succumbed to the vision of the mind as the last frontier of human control, the absolutely crucial next territory to conquer. But the thing that thrilled him most about his brainwashing experiments was that they replaced the tantalizing, unachievable goal of cure with something more attainable: change. Such a substitution suited Cameron's philosophy: "we do not subscribe to the notion that anyone is ever cured in the sense of being restored to what he used to be. This is not true of life itself. The living organism, whether sick or well, is emergent." But what kind of change, and for whom was it supposed to prove beneficial?

Cameron's own feeling of release from the therapeutic burden of cure is palpable in a paper called "Effects of Repetition of Verbal Signals upon the Behavior of Chronic Psychoneurotic Patients", co-credited to himself, Levy, and Rubenstein, and delivered in July 1959 to a Glasgow meeting of the Royal Medico-Psychological Association. "It is clearly demonstrated that reorganization of the personality may be brought about without the necessity of solving of conflicts or abreaction or the reliving of past experiences," he wrote. "While these long-held therapeutic concepts have been useful, and continue to be, there is evidence that they have begun to reach their limits and, indeed, in recent years have shown only too plainly that they are beginning to act as a straitjacket to creative thinking." Repetition of verbal signals, he claimed, provided a tool "where direct, controlled changes in personality may be made", allowing for the "direct building of new personality traits" after putting the old ones "out of circuit".

No other paper Cameron published on the subject matches the bald-faced wishthink of the one he delivered on his old home ground. But then, in 1959, Cameron was at the apex of his confidence in his great idea. In the early fifties he had struggled along, unable to explore the power of repetition for lack of money to hire a proper research team. The federal government had paid for some of the work, piggy-backed on a general grant of $17,875 to his behavioural lab. Occasionally he had wangled a small donation from a private benefactor. It was common knowledge among researchers in human behaviour at the time that military money was available for work in the brainwashing area; but Cameron had alienated the chairman of the most likely Canadian funding source, the Defence Research Board.

In what must have been an effort at seeding the financial clouds, Cameron broke professional etiquette by publicizing his work in the mass media before a word of it had been printed in psychiatric journals. In 1955 the Canadian magazine *Weekend*, a large-size rotogravure publication that was distributed in the Saturday edition of newspapers across the country, had for all intents and purposes issued a press release for psychic driving under the headline "Canadian Psychiatrists Develop Beneficial Brain-washing". Though claiming he wasn't entirely comfortable with the term, Cameron was quoted to the effect that brainwashing and psychic driving were "first cousins". The story pulled no punches in the description of the technique, and didn't hesitate to compare "Canadian style" brainwashing to the scary cold-war sort in which people cracked under "cold, hunger, isolation, fear and increasing indoctrination". The major difference, it said, was in attitude: "The doctors at the Allan, of course, are doing the exact opposite of mental murder: they are making sick minds well again. But they face many of the same problems as the professional brainwashers. Prisoners of war resist attempts to indoctrinate them—and almost every patient tries to defend himself against the unpleasant impact of his own recorded voice by deliberately not listening to it, or by thinking of something else." The story accepted at face value Cameron's claims of success, but must not have flushed out a backer.

Finally, in 1956, shortly after the first academic report of his work appeared in the United States, Cameron was approached by Colonel James Monroe of the New York-based Society for the Investigation of Human Ecology (SIHE), apparently a private foundation dedicated to explorations on the pioneering edge of psychology, psychiatry, sociology, and anthropology. The eminent Cornell neurologist Harold Wolff was founder, chairman of the board, and society president. The catch-phrase "human ecology" was his own. Wolff believed that just as nineteenth-century biologists had realized that one couldn't study animals outside of their natural habitats, modern scientists had to study "man" in his own setting. To achieve this, one had to draw on "any body of knowledge that was pertinent....[Human ecology] requires no arbitrary distinction between the 'natural' sciences and the 'social' sciences." Furthermore, one couldn't be bound by old ways of doing things. "[Much] productive thought and energy have been lost through research based upon rigid protocol," read the introduction to the society's first annual report in 1957. It added: "the contributions of the individual scientist are sometimes lost in the task force approach to research."

The society was pretty nakedly recruiting maverick scientists. As well, its stated main objective—"studies of marked behavioral change and the conditions under which it occurs, including political indoctrination, psychotherapy and other forms of therapy, education and training"—scored a direct hit on the research ambitions of Ewen Cameron. Before the year was out, Monroe had guaranteed a first grant to Cameron of $38,090 to cover two years' budget for a fully staffed research project on psychic driving. Though Cameron's application reached the society's New York offices in January 1957, Monroe must have confirmed the funding at least six months earlier, as Cameron started looking for a full-time research psychiatrist in June 1956. The first person he approached was a favourite resident of his, Ed Levinson. Levinson turned Cameron down. He didn't like the looks of one of the procedures Cameron intended to try, which involved injecting patients with curare to immobilize them in the "area of repetition". Simply put, if they wouldn't sit still and listen to their tapes, he planned to paralyse them. Levinson's objection to the process was not so much ethical as self-protective. Injections of curare, a South American plant derivative used there as an arrow poison and in North American operating rooms as an anaesthetic, seemed to him an unreasonable risk. The money Cameron was offering, however, was terrific—$7,000 a year, only $500 less than a senior staff psychiatrist then made. Cameron's second choice, Leonard Levy, leaped at the chance, but not only because of the salary. Said Levinson, "For a first-year resident like Levy, having the Chief smile on you was a potent thing."

And the Chief was truly smiling. At last he could afford a research associate, buy all the technical gadgets he wanted, pay half of Rubenstein's salary, and have a few dollars left over to enlist the occasional psychologist or other consultant. He budgeted no salary for himself, or for Robert Malmo, the head of the Allan's psychology department, who was down on the grant application to conduct research into physiological changes produced by repetition. Cameron had to prove that repetition alone (not drugs, or ECT, or sensory deprivation) was the chief agent of change. Malmo had already done some measurements to show that signals directed at activating patients' arm muscles had significantly increased muscle tension in them. Now, Cameron had enlisted him to try to prove that involuntary body systems also could be influenced by verbal commands—he planned to play repeatedly into the ears of some of his psychic-driving patients the suggestion that one of their ear lobes was getting hotter than the other. Proving that, he believed, would really lend some scientific credibility to research that until then had relied solely on clinical observations.

In 1957 a close inspection of the gift horse would easily have revealed the enemy lurking inside. As well as backing the Cameron research, Wolff's society was singularly interested in the psychology of 235 air-force men captured by the North Koreans; in the effect of stress on human brain function; in the mentality of the Chinese, and particularly the impact of Communist ideology on the young; in the psychology of Hungarian *émigrés* who hated Communism (or at least the Soviets) enough to flee to the west after the 1956 uprising; and in LSD investigations, at an unknown facility called the Butler Health Centre, in which the researchers had become most adept at predicting "the type and severity of reaction" to the drug. Cameron had won a small grant for an eminent member of his staff, Eric Wittkower, to edit a newsletter called *Transcultural Research in Mental Health*, under the aegis of a board that included Margaret Mead. It was the only grant in the society's first years that couldn't directly be linked to research aimed at discovering how to enforce human change.

While some of the research sounded excellent, nearly all of it was out on a far limb—which is, of course, just where the CIA wanted it to be. In its annual reports SIHE thanked donors with coy names such as the Foresight Foundation, but all were figments of its overactive imagination. Entirely funded by the CIA, the society was simply the most open, elegant, and intellectual expression of the agency's search for a technology of mind control. It was conceived at a point when some of the boys from MKULTRA had worked themselves up to aspire to an even larger mission. John Gittinger, the psychologist and CIA agent who put all the pieces of SIHE in place, said, "We had the grandiose idea that one of our responsibilities was to try to find out as much as possible about all of the research being done related to human behavior.... It was not an intelligence operation in the ordinary meaning of the word."

In fact, in statements before U.S. government committees and in depositions taken for the current lawsuit (launched against the CIA by nine of Cameron's former patients), Gittinger, Sidney Gottlieb, et al, claim a ridiculous innocence of intention for the doings of the society. It was their chance to play with big ideas, they say, kept deliberately separate from MKULTRA operational research. On the one hand, Gottlieb and crew were okaying the testing of new knock-out drugs on elderly cancer patients and programs in which drug addicts incarcerated in a federal institution could trade the use of their bodies in secret drug research for quantities of their own drug of choice. On the other hand, if they are to be believed, they were supporting brilliant scientists at the forefront of a search devoted to comprehending the human essence.

David Rhodes, who took over from Monroe as executive director in 1961 (after SIHE had changed its name to the Human Ecology Fund), says the purpose of establishing the research foundation was so that they could move undercover in the scientific ether: "If we picked up a *Newsweek* one morning and discovered so and so was doing something exciting in such and such a field, I could get on the phone...and say, 'I'm a rep of the Human Ecology Fund, and I'm excited about what you're doing. Can I come by and have lunch with you?'—which at the time was a lot easier than saying, 'I'm from the CIA. Could I have lunch with you?' " Rhodes was the only one of the principals frank enough also to say in a deposition, "the possibility of creating a Manchurian candidate is a total psychological impossibility, but it is intriguing; it is a lot of fun."

The CIA funded Cameron's research from January 1957 until September 1960. As sub-project 68 of the 149 (known) MKULTRA projects, it received $64,242.54 (U.S.) To hear Gittinger and his boss, Sidney Gottlieb, tell it, sub-project 68 was authorized only to lend a touch of class—and cover—to the fledgeling society. "[Cameron] was considered a status researcher at that time," said Gittinger, "and it looked good."

Gittinger also said that he authorized Monroe to approach Cameron after he had read the 1956 article "Psychic Driving" because he was interested in a technique of voice-stress analysis described therein: "I never thought that [psychic driving] was a particularly interesting or useful kind of therapeutic technique." But Cameron didn't mention voice-stress experiments at all in that first paper; it wasn't till the late fifties that he and Rubenstein got going on that particular technological vision, wherein they hoped to devise an elaborated tape-recorder that would measure levels of stress and emotional reaction in a patient's voice. Staff at the SIHE offices in New York actually worked on the statistical analysis required by some of that research, which Cameron described as the study of "ultraconceptual communication". It seems probable that Gittinger is dissembling about the initial lure of Cameron's work, which was surely its claim to have found an effective, if limited, way to brainwash mental patients.

John Marks in *The Search for the "Manchurian Candidate"* claims that in Cameron the CIA had found a "terminal" researcher, a man willing to push his patients far beyond their own good for his own— and the agency's—experimental ends. Gittinger, who was Cameron's project officer, claims that the SIHE never suggested lines of research to the scientists it funded. All it did was pour fuel on an already kindled fire. There is no direct evidence that Cameron knew the ultimate source of his lucky break; unlike those of other MKULTRA-funded researchers, Cameron's grant was stamped with the specific rider that he was to be kept unaware of CIA involvement.

In the end whether Cameron was witting or not is of little importance—CIA interests in no way shaped the direction of his research. He had already tried every variation of technique described in his 1957 grant application, save for the curare injections. He himself admitted that he made no big theoretical breakthroughs between 1957 and 1960; in those years he and his team were concerned with "refining" the procedure. Yet there is also no doubt that the grant from the Society for the Investigation of Human Ecology both reassured Cameron that someone out there in the larger "scientific" world was interested and empowered him to escalate his experimental program. There is absolutely no doubt that without the funding fewer of Cameron's patients would have been put to sleep, shocked out of their wits, and hooked up to tape machines. As Cameron wrote to Harold Wolff shortly before his grant expired, "the help which we have received from your Society during the last several years has been invaluable, and all of us who are engaged in this investigation have a considerable sense of indebtedness to your organization."

As a funding body, the SIHE certainly wasn't about to police Cameron's research ethics or censure him if he caused a few mental casualties on the way towards a perfected brainwashing technique. The only thing that would dry up its funds was if he couldn't get psychic driving to work. For the CIA, too, utility was all.

Some of his colleagues believe that Cameron figured out who the society stood for; others are adamant that a man like Cameron would never have allowed a covert relationship with the CIA to exist. All of them say that, CIA or not, Cameron was following his own agenda, and that, beyond self-interest, he had the interests of his own profession—not an intelligence agency—at heart.

Scratch Cameron's own writings on the subject and he would say that his new treatments were crucial. The structure of mental-health care was shifting from mental institutions to wards in general hospitals, just as he had hoped it would all those years ago in Brandon. Someone had to work on speeding therapy up, to cut the patients' cloth a little to make it fit the shape of the future.

Scratch a little deeper and one discovers a plaintive and honest question addressed to his own research file under the heading "Playback": "Why is it easier to listen to a tape than it is to listen to the patient? Could it be that listening to the live patient, the patient immediately evokes a negative response or better said, an inhibitory response?"

Cameron could travel with dispatch through revelations it took his patients, working with their driving tapes, hours to uncover. In that sense his treatments were efficient. But it was also true that, by either listening to them on tape or reading their reflections, memories, and accusations on paper, he turned his patients into abstractions—persons at least an arm's length away, whom the intellect alone could deal with.

Many of Cameron's residents remember how acute the Chief's snap judgements on patients were. Bill Stauble, for one, says Cameron was "really intuitive, really tuned into the unconscious"—then quickly adds, "but impatient." A man of deep insight but driven temperament, Cameron did not feel he had the time to slog with his patients through the miles of psychotherapeutic mud. His mind was quick, and he suffered the stupid (or stupefied) badly; he hated passivity possibly more than any other quality. Stauble remembers as a resident trying always to look as if he was taking an active course with a patient so that the Chief wouldn't be tempted to leap into the fray.

Cameron's preferred methods were such that when his judgement was wrong, he harmed where his intention was to treat. And his position at the Allan Memorial Institute was such that few could question that judgement.

CHAPTER NINE

Mary Morrow, MD

Dr. Mary Matilda Morrow was surely a hopeless case when she went to see Ewen Cameron in December 1959, but it was her career, not her mental health, she was most worried about. At age twelve, she had vowed to become a doctor, to follow in the footsteps of a father she could hardly remember, a cardiologist and McGill professor who had died when Mary was three. At age twenty, with not enough money for college, she opted for the closest thing to medicine she could get, nursing school. On placement at St. Mary's Hospital in Montreal, doing "slave labour, like sometimes twenty-four hours a day, you know, you washed the bedpans as part of training", Mary noticed that "the area of expertise which was most obscure to the physicians was neurology"—so obscure in fact that St. Mary's didn't have any staff neurologists of its own, relying instead on consultants brought in from the Montreal Neurological Institute. Mary's mother had hoped that nursing school would knock some sense into Mary; it offended Clare Morrow's sense of propriety that a woman should aspire to become a doctor—specifically, that Mary should aspire to the status of her father. Nursing school, however, did not humble her daughter, but carved the specific contours of her life plan. Not only would she, Nurse Morrow, become a neurologist, she would one day open her own department of neurology at St. Mary's and treat patients at the citadel of her dreams, the Montreal Neurological Institute.

In the entrance hall of the MNI, the names of great neurologists and neurosurgeons were painted on the walls, and a statue of a woman unveiling one breast, copied from the original in the Louvre, bore the legend, *"La Nature se dévoilant devant La Science"*—Nature revealing her mysteries to the great men of science. Mary hid her feminine mysteries to pursue the revelations of science, and in twenty years of single-minded effort came awfully close to joining the MNI fraternity. Her course had been almost as fraught with obstacles as that of the physician Paracelsus in the Robert Browning poem she loved to quote: "—And though I go through hail and blinding firestorms, in His time, His good time, I shall arrive."

Then, in 1958 and 1959, every door she had so laboriously pried open slammed shut in her face. A mentor had retired, putting an end to her plans for St. Mary's; she had failed to pass her licensing exams, which meant she could not treat patients at the MNI; and then, in a depression that took the form of violent anger against anyone she perceived as standing in her way, she had alienated anyone who might have helped her. In October 1959, the neurologist with eight years of postgraduate training and an MA in neuroanatomy found herself donning her nursing cap again to work in a convalescent hospital in east-end Montreal where no one would know her, in order that she could eat. Not that she had much will to do so: there was nothing in her life to balance her failure. At forty-two she was a vestal virgin of medicine—she had had no marriage, no children, not even a lover to lighten her isolation.

To keep going Mary Morrow took dexedrine during the day and barbiturates at night, self-prescribed. The cycle of drugs compounded the outbursts of tears and desk-pounding rages: "I was just in a bottomless pit. I was just in a hole." She wrote alternately demanding and pleading notes to her former colleagues and teachers. To Francis McNaughton, who had finally barred her from work at the MNI: "I am sorry I was hostile today, but it was only better than tears." But they would not let her back, not even to teach her courses in neuroanatomy to the medical students. Even if she tried her licensing exams again and passed, it was unlikely they'd ever let her onto the wards of the MNI. They said she had no interpersonal skills, and should not be closely involved with the care of patients.

Finally, in her desperation, she thought of Ewen Cameron. In 1956, as part of her neurology training, she had done a six-month course at the Allan. That same Francis McNaughton had then recommended her to Cameron, writing, "I am certain she will become an excellent clinical neurologist. She lacks confidence, and needs a good deal of moral support, but behind this apparent uncertainty is a very determined person with a capacity for sustained hard work." She had been assigned to Robert Cleghorn's service, but had encountered the Chief in the electro-shock room where she had worked two days a week. He would administer the anaesthetic himself when he sent a private patient for shock; Mary's job was to press the button for him. Other doctors asked her to press it only once. Cameron's standard request was for six. They were called Page-Russell treatments, she learned, and Cameron ordered them for in-patients and out-patients, schizophrenics, alcoholics, neurotics, and depressives, without, as far as Mary the psychiatric neophyte could see, much differentiation among the types of ailments.

To the young Dr. Morrow it seemed that Cameron moved in an aura of power and mystery. A nurse had warned Mary to stay out of Cameron's special treatment room in the ward called South 2; the only time she entered was when no other physician was available and a patient fell too deeply into an insulin coma—Mary rushed in to administer intravenous glucose. She wanted to know what was going on in that room, and also what his psychic-driving experiments were all about; she had encountered only one of those subjects, a young woman whose tape told her over and over that she was a good girl, and she wondered whether such an approach could be effective. Cleghorn was nice, but Cameron was where the action was. She eventually asked Cameron if she could transfer to his service, but he turned her

down. She wasn't heartbroken—her soul still belonged to the MNI—
and she emerged from the Allan with an excellent report, Cameron or
no Cameron.

Three years later, with her twenty-year dream shattered, she went
to him again, hoping that he could help her maintain at least her
professional status—rescue her from having to ride on the bus an hour
into the suburbs to the place where she was only an anonymous nurse.
Reminding him that she had done well before, she asked if she could
begin training as a psychiatrist in earnest at the Allan. But: "I had been
up all night. I was on dexedrine. I had no money, and I must have been
one awful mess. Cameron said I seemed nervous—I didn't explain
anything to him—and that before he'd take me on as a resident he
would like me to be medically inspected."

The doctor in Mary bridled at such a suggestion, and she stalled,
but each time she approached Cameron over the next few months he
insisted that it was the only way he would consider her seriously. In
April of 1960, she finally checked into the Royal Victoria Hospital for
a physical examination that ended up lasting four weeks. Diagnosed as
anxious and malnourished—Mary had lost roughly thirty-five pounds
in the year since she was barred from the MNI, enough to emaciate
her—her own doctor got her onto one of the new antidepressant drugs.

Once a week, Ewen Cameron would drop by. A social visit, he said.
He'd take a chair across the room from the one in which Mary sat and
they'd make desultory conversation, the bulk of the bed rising between
them. Mary was flattered; to her it felt like a courtship for the residency.
In her own opinion she had a level of anatomical knowledge of the
brain exceedingly rare in a candidate for psychiatric training. To one of
the most powerful medical men in Montreal (Cameron was chairman
of the medical board of the Royal Vic among his other honours), Mary
confided nothing of her failures. And Cameron didn't ask what had
brought her so low. She told neither Cameron nor her own doctor that
she had been taking dexedrine and downers. Pride could choke her
before she let on how lost she'd been. As a tactic, her closed lips failed
her. When the month was up, instead of accepting her as a resident,

Cameron raised the stakes: if she wanted to train under him she should check herself into the Allan.

Without benefit of a formal psychiatric interview, Cameron had made a diagnosis. During one of his social visits he had persuaded Mary to go over to the Allan to take a battery of psychological tests. She thought they were stupid; she felt humiliated and too depressed to bother responding to the questions the psychologist put to her. The Rorschach blots reminded her exclusively of what she had been studying—they all looked like distorted spinal columns. Down on her file went "nonresponse", considered a sign of schizophrenic withdrawal. Her anatomical descriptions of the blots were interpreted as the mark of paranoia. Cameron knew little of her background and nothing of her amphetamine use (amphetamines can cause psychotic reactions whose only difference from those of schizophrenia is that they go away when one stops taking the drug). He jumped to the obvious conclusion, that Mary Morrow was a paranoid schizophrenic.

Having delivered the ultimatum—the Allan or professional oblivion—Cameron stopped coming to see her. Her mother and sister were mortified at the thought of a Morrow in a mental institution, but Mary felt she had no choice. Believing that at the end of it all she still had a chance at a residency, she entered the Allan Memorial Institute on May 6, 1960. Cameron wasn't there to greet her. She was assigned to a junior resident, a Dr. Tan, who she believed had trouble understanding English. She was less than forthcoming during his attempts to take a case history, resisting giving him even the most minimal information—which was seen as evidence of negativity and withdrawal. She smiled when the notion that she might be schizophrenic was raised—which the doctors saw as "inappropriate affect" (the wrong emotional response). To them inappropriate affect was further evidence of schizophrenia.

A week passed, and she still had not seen Cameron. Finally she heard his voice in the hall, but he did not look in, and she understood that the courtship was over. The next day she heard his voice again, outside her door, apparently speaking to his residents: "I heard him saying...'We'll give her shock treatments.' And I screamed, 'What?

What?' He did not come near me. He did not enter the room. He discussed nothing." The nurse's note on Mary's chart, dated May 16, reads, "Expresses fear of ECT. Patient also said 'if I didn't know about them it would be different; I don't think I need them.'" On May 18, a further nurse's note: "Expressing fear of treatment but admits she cannot function the way she is so has no alternative."

On May 18, Mary finally saw Dr. Cameron in the flesh, bending over her to give her a needle that put her to sleep. Accepting sleep therapy, she hoped she was protected from ECT; no one had approached her with the specific consent forms she remembered having to fill out for patients in 1956. But ECT had become such a routine treatment that the consent she signed on entering the Allan was considered sufficient authorization. In her chart was another note: "We intend to depattern her and then…assess her at the end of this time." As a reward for her beleaguered compliance, Cameron was ready to strip her not just of the supposed schizophrenia but of the harvest of years of study. He told her mother that Mary Morrow, after treatment at the Allan, would never be able to practise medicine.

In a life that was mostly hard labour and even harder disappointment, Mary Morrow had one Cinderella moment. It was in June 1956, just after she had scraped every penny together to travel to Ann Arbor, Michigan, to take her oral for her masters of neuroanatomy. She loathed Ann Arbor, where she had spent a bitter year studying, so poor that even though she worked as a nurse in off hours she had to pawn her fur coat for food. Not even good food, but a supply of Cheez Whiz and bread ("I never liked Cheez Whiz").

Great odds had never daunted her. Her father, twenty-five years her mother's elder, left the family without money; Mrs. Morrow had transformed the family home into a boarding house after his death, and in the even tougher years of the Depression sent the children away from her to live with a maiden aunt outside Montreal while she held down a job. At sixteen, Mary had had rheumatic fever and missed graduating from high school; she suffered a bout of Sydenham's chorea—fits of irregular trembling—as a result, which may have left her with slight brain damage. She finished high school at seventeen and wanted to enter university. Her mother insisted that she earn money instead and sent her to business college for five months. Afterwards Mary took a job as a stenographer but squandered pennies at night school; over two years she managed to gain the equivalent of a first year at college. At nineteen she had a fierce confrontation with her mother over the despised career, ending up for ten days in the Royal Victoria Hospital from nerves and anorexia. She viewed it straightforwardly: "I wanted to be a doctor. My mother wanted me to be a stenographer. We were fighting and I won."

The fruit of the victory was nursing school, which led to a position as a nursing lieutenant overseas during the Second World War, and more importantly as far as Mary was concerned, to twenty-five months of veteran's benefits that finally allowed her to enter pre-med in 1947. It's a sign of the degree of her medical obsession that Mary, who stopped menstruating during her teenage war with her mother, only started again when she was accepted into medical school.

Through it all she nursed to make a living, at St. Mary's and at the MNI, sometimes assisting the great Dr. Penfield, sometimes working the night shift. Her family background gained her some access to the leading lights of the Montreal medical community, and Mary confided her plans to the MNI's Dr. MacEachern ("a very good, sweet man"). He encouraged her. She came to hope that when she was ready for a neurological residency the MNI would take her in. But MacEachern himself died of a serious neurological ailment in 1951, and when Mary applied in 1952 the man who replaced him, Dr. Francis McNaughton, turned her down. She realized that her medical school grades weren't great (the lower third of the class in fact) and, for the hot-tempered and bossy Mary Morrow, was philosophic, writing to McNaughton, "I wish to thank you for your kind personal answer to my application. I realize quite well that there is only myself to blame for its negativity, and that there was little chance for an alternative [answer]. Now, 'I shall lie me down and bleed awhile,' but perhaps I'll rise again."

So she studied instead for two years in the United States, first in Boston and then in Ann Arbor, in isolation and poverty. In 1955 she reapplied and got her wish: McNaughton accepted her as a third-year resident at the MNI. He had no money to pay her fellowship, but he offered her a half-day a week working for him in his epilepsy clinic at $150 a month and St. Mary's Hospital came up with another $150 for her services as a neurology consultant. So Mary in rather cut-rate triumph came home. With the full encouragement of Dr. Gordon Cassidy, St. Mary's chief of medical services, she began to plan for her neurology department. "She was a very competent neurologist," he said, "and we were very pleased with her services and glad to have her." It seemed as though she could go ahead and do anything, Mary sometimes bitterly thought, as long as they didn't have to pay her for it. Still, she continued working twenty-hour days in service of her dream.

Then came the Cinderella moment. Having scraped all her ready cash together to get back to Michigan to do her oral (which she passed), in June 1956 she decided to travel up to Quebec City to attend the annual Canadian Neurological Association meetings, a professional among other professionals. She went by bus in old clothes, carefully carrying her one beautiful dress with her in a suitcase, with just enough money to cover the hotel bill. Feeling transformed by her finery, she joined her peers for cocktails and was promptly invited by Herbert Jasper, one of the co-founders with Penfield of the MNI, to be his guest at head table at the opening-night dinner. It was glory and humiliation all in one; Jasper had to fly out of town after dinner and left her to make her way back to her hotel by taxi, which cost her ten dollars and "stripped" her of money. Worse: "McNaughton had seen me in my gorgeous raiment and invited me to go to the other dinner dance the next night as his guest.... But I couldn't pay the hotel bill if I stayed." Instead of confiding her predicament to anyone, Mary "got on my old clothes, took a bus and beat it out"—a Cinderella who was forced to go home before the ball had even started and whose prince did not bother chasing after her with a slipper.

Instead, Mary confronted McNaughton. He had offered her more advanced work at the MNI; after the events at Quebec City, she said she wouldn't do it without a salary. "Later on, I said it was acute physiological need that made me do it, but he didn't understand what

I meant. I was starving, literally starving. I had no money for food. I had a master's degree, I had been at the head table.... I had no food." Considerably upset, she took a summer job at a children's camp (largely because it offered three solid meals a day and a chance to cool off) and applied to take the necessary psychiatric training at the Allan Memorial a few months early. McNaughton wrote her a good recommendation to Dr. Cameron, but Mary was sure she had permanently alienated him. Turning him down, she said, "was a mistake of my entire life, and all else resulted from his hostility. I mean he'd forgiven me for my bad grades because I was a pretty good neurologist." It's doubtful that McNaughton felt hostile either because she'd stood him up in Quebec or because she had asked for a real salary. But over the course of three years, in the face of her outraged pride, he came to behave that way.

At the heart of it all was not so much her poverty as something Mary considered a grave insult to her skills as a neurologist. At St. Mary's she saw patients who thought of her as fully qualified, as *their* doctor. But when she had to refer them for more intricate tests to the MNI, as she almost always had to do, she could not continue as their doctor. At the MNI she was a resident who had to bow to other judgements; the only way that McNaughton, senior neurologist Theodore Rasmussen, and Wilder Penfield himself would allow her to follow her patients to the MNI, quite correctly, was for her to become officially licensed to practise as a neurologist under Quebec regulations. Her letters appealing to them to take her unlicensed self on staff were considered importunate at best: "As you both say that I am qualified now to be on the staff, then let me be on the staff, and stop this killing struggle and isolation from the work I love. It would make up for everything, I could feel on an equal footing, and in a capacity consistent with my training for the first time in many years....I could be friendly with everybody, if I could take my position in society that I have been trained for— instead of going around like a slinking animal, which is the way I feel, especially at night."

The strain she was under was enormous, and a good part self-imposed. Mary, being ambitious, wanted to go for the highest rank—fellowship—rather than the lower-level certification procedure. She tried the fellowship exam in October 1957 and failed it, which was not such a big deal, as many other working neurologists had never tried it let alone passed. She decided "to come down a peg" and go for certification.

But in the meantime, Cassidy, her mentor at St. Mary's, who had her working on architectural plans for the proposed department and studying EEG with Herbert Jasper so that they could offer that service as well, decided to retire. The man who replaced him, Dr. John Howlett, had not much patience for the driven spinster Mary Morrow. In the spring of 1958, she "was getting very tired.... My resistance was very low and I was up day and night, anyhow. I got a terrible pansinusitis and I landed in the Royal Victoria Hospital, really sick. At that time, Preston Robb, who was a senior [MNI] neurologist came to me and said, 'Mary, we're going to be bedfellows; we might as well be friends.'" Howlett had given Robb the job Mary had worked towards for twenty years—the director of neurology at St. Mary's.

"It was pretty tough. But I just went on, got out of the hospital, studied all summer...passed the writtens in neuro, both the Royal College and the Quebec certifying exam, took the oral of the Quebec certifying exam and passed it. By November I was scheduled for the oral in the Royal College certifying exam. The patient presented had what we call a bruit [an unusual noise in the chest]. I listened with my scope, couldn't hear it, got in a panic and failed the oral. And that was the end of my life."

The sinus infection had invaded her ears and deafened one of them, a disability Mary had not known about until she listened for the bruit. Once she had failed her exam, the powers that be at St. Mary's decided she wasn't qualified to have private patients of her own; all private patients from then on were to be referred to Dr. Robb.

No political manoeuvre she tried changed her situation. In January 1959 she wrote to Robb suggesting that he and she rotate hours of service in the St. Mary's neurology out-patient clinic. She had been on twenty-four-hour call there for roughly four years and couldn't afford to continue those hours when she could treat only public, not paying, patients. Robb wrote to Howlett that "Dr. Morrow had been reluctant to carry the complete load of public consultations", and, since the demands on his time made it impossible for him to do rotation, he suggested that St. Mary's hire a Dr. Donna Venecek, who had been trained at the MNI and was certified by the appropriate bodies. He would refer his own private patients to Venecek for tests, rather than to the overburdened Dr. Morrow. Advised of this plan, Mary angrily responded, "I will keep my clinic at least for the time being. St. Mary's is not big enuf for *one* neurologist."

Robb made gestures he may have viewed as conciliatory but that Mary found patronizing. He bought her a Coke one day along with a group of his interns. Mary accepted it and was then consumed with second thoughts. "Dear Dr. Robb," she wrote. "Thank you kindly for treating me to the 'Coke' on Thursday as one of your 'Internes'. As, in spite of the fact that you consistently see all the new patients in the clinic, I am not actually your 'Interne'....I am hereby returning the 10 cents."

Such missives quite simply made her either a person to be avoided at all costs or a laughing-stock. It seemed that only her old mentor, Dr. Cassidy, now unable to do anything tangible for her, made any effort at all to empathize. Of her troubles he simply said, "She spent most of her time improving her knowledge of neurology practically to the exclusion of everything else, and that made her a little different from the rest of us." That difference was generally not appreciated—people behaved cruelly, as if she were a species apart. When she finally felt forced to resign from her neurology clinic in early May 1959, John Howlett sent a copy of her resignation along to Robb with a little note: "Dear Prestie: Enclosed is a copy of a letter from Dr. Mary Morrow for your delectation."

By then all the professional income and the only professional association she had to survive on was $150 a month from the epilepsy clinic at the MNI. But in June, McNaughton, fed up with being the butt of Mary's blistering rages and tears, delivered another blow. The MNI would not take her on staff, licensed or not, until she became chief of neurology of St. Mary's Hospital—the position, of course, that Preston Robb had just filled. He offered her the income from the epilepsy clinic for a further year so she could straighten herself out (he suggested several times in 1958-59 that she needed psychiatric help to control her emotions). But Mary was made so irate by his act of charity that McNaughton dropped her from the clinic by July. She made her first suicide attempt later that summer. By fall she was forced to go back to nursing to earn a living. By December she was willing to abandon her life plan if Ewen Cameron would help her to remain at least a doctor.

Mary Morrow remembers nothing of the ten days of treatment following Cameron's injection. Only the evidence of her chart and the memories of her younger sister, Margaret, and her mother have helped her piece together what happened to her. In Cameron's scheme of things she underwent only a moderate depatterning: one Page-Russell a day for nine days, and on the tenth and last day, two. That time, the first six-pronged shock had failed to convulse her, so they upped the voltage and gave her 95-pound body another six presses of the button.

Her mother, confined at home as a result of a stroke, had ordered Margaret up to the hospital to see what was going on—called her back from New York City, in fact, where she had fled to avoid the issue of having a sister in a mental hospital. On the eleventh day, Margaret found Mary, her face and eyes a little swollen, sitting in a corner of her room. "I have to go out on the lawn to help with the other patients," Mary said. Margaret replied, "Mommy is going to have the treatments stopped." Mary said, "What treatments?"

But it was hard to get the treatments stopped immediately because Dr. Cameron was away in Lake Placid. Clare Morrow appealed first to Dr. Tan, then to the chief resident, Eddie Kingstone, and finally to Dr. Cleghorn, who said he hadn't known Mary was at the Allan but could do nothing about it. Finally Mrs. Morrow reached Dr. Cameron at home at eight o'clock on Sunday morning: "And he said that [Mary] was a hopeless case, that...there was nothing he could do for her but to treat her and send her to a foster home....That she would never doctor again." Mary's mother, who had implacably resisted her desire to become a doctor, thought it was outrageous that anyone should try to take Mary's hard-won MD away from her. As far as she was concerned the treatment was destroying her daughter. That Sunday she telephoned every department and person she could reach at the Allan and told them not to give any more treatments of any kind to Mary Morrow.

Margaret, a nurse, simply moved in and took over Mary's care. "The next day I found her lying on the bed and her clothes were all on her wrong. Her underwear was over her dress. I didn't know what I was supposed to do, but I put them on right and I started to bring her memory back. I told her who I was....

"She didn't know where her mouth was. That is what I remember most.... She was trying to put on her make-up, and she had her eyebrow pencil down at her mouth. And the next time I went, she was trying to wash her hair. She was always a bit vain. She didn't know how to wash her hair."

Mary's first memory, post-treatment, was "being in a deep, dark, pitch-black hole with no sense of appendages, like a worm. But...I didn't know I should have appendages. There was no sense of solidity, like I was not on ground and I was not in water....There must have been something of what we call the neocortex left, because there was an awareness, not of human identity, but an awareness of being.... I was also aware that there had been no beginning, that this seemed to have been going on forever." Within three days she had regained enough of her memory to know that "I was a human being, a physician, myself and a neurologist", but also to realize that a blanket of amnesia covered much of her life prior to the depatterning.

Cameron did not seek her out; her mother had stopped treatment, and he believed there was nothing more he could do for her. Mary says she confronted him twice, uninvited, in one of the Allan's dictaphone rooms. The first time she told him she was worried about the extent of her memory loss. He asked her what a Babinski response was. Mary was insulted: "You know that when you're in pre-med. He said: 'Oh, your memory's fine.' This to a 10-year [*sic*] postgraduate neurologist."

The second time she trapped him at the dictaphone she said, "I want to know, man-to-man, what you've done to me. Man-to-man, my own words." Cameron laughed, and made a feeble joke: "I can't discuss it with you; you're a woman." Mary did not see him again.

She was to have one more nasty episode at the Allan Memorial Institute. Though her mother had demanded that all treatment be stopped, Mary's junior resident, Dr. Tan, kept on prescribing chlorpromazine. His patient became itchy and restless, both effects of the drug: on June 11, Tan doubled the dose. Within a week Mary was covered in a rash and, with her larynx swollen, felt herself to be in such respiratory distress that she demanded and got both adrenalin and a consultation with a skin doctor, who transferred her to the Royal Victoria. Before she was allowed to leave, the chief resident, Eddie Kingstone, asked that she sign a refusal-of-treatment form. She wouldn't. Dealing with the doctors, Margaret thought Mary had sounded like her old domineering self. Then at 5:00 on a Saturday afternoon in the pouring rain she and Mary got in a taxi to go to the Royal Vic. Margaret was shocked to see that Mary, her older sister, the one who had always been strong, whose family nickname was "the policeman", was afraid of the male taxi-driver.

Cameron rather fleetingly mentioned, in one of his papers on depatterning, that after the treatment was over amnesia sometimes extended for as much as five years into the patient's past life. He even suggested, in the case of schizophrenics, that depatterning created a condition he called "differential amnesia" in which patients would recall healthy behaviour but forget all their bad, delusional symptoms. A comforting idea, indeed, but one that bore no relationship to the effects of depatterning on memory. For those who considered lost years upsetting, he advised that their families could work to erect a "scaffold of memories" to fill in the gap. Mary's family took her home, and for the next thirty days her mother and sister each did eight-hour shifts answering her obsessive questions about her childhood. The scaffold lacked planks for her adult personal life; and nothing they could do made up the damage to her professional knowledge. In that field all Mary was still sure of was that Dr. Cameron's treatment was like nothing she had ever read about. By late summer she was looking for a lawyer to take action against him—not such an easy thing to find considering Cameron's status in Montreal and the stigma she now bore as an ex-mental patient.

If the gods had been against her before the treatment, they were now pelting her with more of the fabled firestorms. To claim her health-insurance money for her stay at the Allan, she needed a doctor to sign the claim—which also required him to append a diagnosis. She went to Dr. Jacques Beaubien, with whom she had briefly shared offices and who had prescribed tranquillizers for her in the horrible summer of 1959. Beaubien, who worked at the Allan and did depatterning himself, had tried to encourage her to go back to Cameron to complete the treatment, and on the health form wrote down a diagnosis of paranoid schizophrenia. That she could not accept, and she went to Dr. Karl Stern, no fan of Cameron's and a friend of hers since medical school, who diagnosed her as suffering from a reactive depression.

Her family was dutiful but viewed her as a stranger. Margaret didn't particularly like the obsessive survivor and her mother found her changed even to her facial expression, which she claimed never again resembled the old Mary's. They did all they could to help, but sometimes blundered hopelessly into Mary's wounds. Advised by a doctor they trusted that Mary would never be able to live on her own again, Margaret and Clare Morrow went into Mary's apartment and packed up her things. Mary viewed it as the final invasion of her privacy: she didn't want them to see the detritus of her personal life, the "bills, loans, love affairs, romances, all kinds of things". It caused a breach; but it also propelled Mary into taking her damaged self and looking for a job.

She had been studying from ground zero again, but she did manage to find a position in Louisville, Kentucky, as a neurological consultant to at first one and then six state hospitals. Her nights were filled with the effort of recovering lost knowledge and with bad dreams. Something else was bothering her: coming home at Christmas, 1960, she couldn't find her way from the Montreal airport to her mother's house, couldn't remember the street or the number. She constantly got physically lost, but even more confusing was that she seemed to have no memory left for faces. Or rather, she could remember someone only if she saw the person in the same setting. If she met her secretary in church, she did not recognize her. She could remember patients only if they had some outstanding abstract protuberance, like a wart on the nose, or a missing limb or other disfigurement. Usually she could put face and case together only if each patient came with his or her file.

Mary the neurologist was beginning to realize that somewhere in the process she had suffered brain damage; she began a round of consultations with eminent neurologists to confirm her suspicions. Her double Page-Russell had caused her breathing to stop, and her contention was that it had caused brain damage. Lasting damage, because the confusion of faces and places didn't go away; all she could do was find systems for coping with it.

Then her eye doctor delivered a final symbolic blow. During a regular check-up he pointed out to her that in the intervening year something had caused her to develop arcus senilis, the white rings in the iris of advanced old age. Mary was only forty-three.

Pursuing Cameron through the courts also seemed to be an exercise in tilting against fate. Never a character to encourage sympathy from others, Mary could not seem to enlist a lawyer who would seriously pursue her claim—or even believe that what had happened to her was out of the ordinary. Portions of her discharge summary, finally released with the rest of her medical records in the late fall of 1960, were exceedingly unflattering. Wrote Cameron: "This 38-year-old single woman [Mary was actually forty-two] was admitted to the AMI on May 6, 1960, for the first time, with a history of growing interpersonal difficulties, a tendency to misinterpret, hostility, and actual misconceptions concerning the motivations of others. She denied any change in her personality but had apparently written letters to a number of colleagues which were so hostile and unsupported by facts that she became increasingly recognized as a potentially dangerous person."

While Mary's reactions may have been beyond the pale of polite professionalism, they were grounded in harsh fact. But Cameron wrote the summary not at the time of her discharge but in October 1960, after she had informed his office that she intended to sue. By then, having heard of her blaming and damning letters to other medical men, and faced with a possible suit himself, Cameron must have regarded her as a little dangerous.

Bleeding all the while, Mary Morrow was determined to rise yet again, far away from home. In 1963, she was accepted as a resident in psychiatry at the Missouri Institute of Psychiatry in St. Louis. Then, after three years' training, the American Board of Psychiatry and Neurology would not allow her to take the certifying exam, citing unsatisfactory references from Montreal. The letter in question, from McNaughton and Rasmussen to the board's Dr. David Boyd, was indeed black: "Her clinical ability was very average in quality. Her relationship with members of our staff was most unsatisfactory throughout her association with this Institute, and led to many personal difficulties, so that we were all very relieved when she finally left Montreal. Dr. Morrow had severe psychiatric difficulties and was treated as an inpatient in the Psychiatric Department of the Royal Victoria Hospital at one time. Following this admission she threatened to sue the Director, Dr. E. Cameron, and showed many evidences of a dangerous paranoid tendency. On the basis of our knowledge of Dr. Morrow we cannot recommend her to the Board."

McNaughton, it seemed, had a more vivid memory of Mary Morrow than did Ewen Cameron, who had by then left the AMI and was working full time in Albany. Appealed to on the subject, Cameron replied to McNaughton: "My recollections of her are that she was a person with whom we had a great deal of trouble, but when I wrote to the present Secretary of the Diploma Course in the AMI, she dug up nothing of this. Am I correct? And did we not consider her to be suffering from schizophrenia, and was she not the person who threatened to sue all kinds of people in the MNI and the Allan?"

After the American rebuff, Mary suffered another bout of what had stricken her in 1959 in Montreal—deep depression; and she again attempted suicide. It's a sign of the darkness of her life at that time that upon hearing of Ewen Cameron's death she got down on her knees to thank God for it and was over-excited for the following two hours. She pursued her lawsuit after he died, and in fact is still pursuing the suit in the upper reaches of the Quebec courts, the Jarndyce *v.* Jarndyce of

Canadian psychiatry. And in 1980, after years of solitary legal war, she joined her name to the list of plaintiffs in the suit against the CIA. She is determined that Cameron, whose quick judgement turned professional disaster into something close to tragedy, will one day be punished, if only in memory.

CHAPTER TEN

In the Sleep Room

Allan Memorial Institute Procedures Book
Treatment Routine—Sleep Treatment
June 1964
Committee on Therapy
A. Triple waking technique

1. Patient awakened 3 times a day: 8am, 2pm, 8pm.

2. During the waking period T.P.R. [pulse rate] and BP [blood pressure] taken before moving the patient out of bed to be cleaned and toileted and given medication.

3. Food at will. The minimum amount of caloric intake 1500; the minimum amount of fluid intake 2000 cc daily.

4. Medication:
Basic Formula—
Seconal 100 mgms
Nembutal100 mgms
Sodium Amytal 150 mgms (or Veronal)
Chlorpromazine 50 mgms (or Promazine 100 mgms)
To this Phenergen 50 mgms may be added.

The amount of medication should be adjusted according to the patient's level of wakefulness. Very deep sleep should be avoided.

b) Vitamin B and C (Beminal 1 capsule daily or 2 cc i.m. [intramuscularly] every other day, Vitamin C 100 mgms, P.O. daily)

c) Milk of Magnesia 30 cc with night sedation

d) Enema if no bowel movement in 3 days.

e) Catheterize if no urination in 12 hours and if other routine measures have failed.

f) If patient restless during the night 50 mgms Chlorpromazine or 100 mgms Promazine i.m., or H. and A. (Hyoscine 1/60 gr. Apomorphine 1/150 gr.) before 5am.

g) Patient's position changes every 2-3 hours and Oxygen with 5% carbon dioxide if respiration is shallow.

h) Foot of bed slightly elevated (anti-phlebitis precautionary measure). If deep sleep, passive movement and massage may be added.

i) In cases of thrombophlebitis, consultation with Haemotology Dept. should be requested.

Peggy Edwards is still a psychiatric nurse, the senior out-patient nurse in the psychiatry department of Sunnybrook Hospital in Toronto. From 1956 to 1960, she was head nurse on South 2, the ward with the sleep room, the ward where patients undergoing the heavy physical treatments were cared for. Sleep treatment, sub-coma or somnolent insulin therapy, depatterning, and Cameron's particular combination of sleep treatment, depatterning, and psychic driving—Peggy Edwards, then Peggy Mielke, was part of the team that delivered them all. The constant murmuring of voices, from wall speakers and pillow speakers, the sight of patients wandering the halls in their johnny gowns with football helmets on their heads, or prone under the onslaught of sound, were the backdrop of her working day for four years.

In her office at Sunnybrook, with its jungle of plants and a little sign that reads, "A cluttered desk is a sign of genius," not even a name-tag on her breast identifies Peggy Edwards as a nurse. She discarded the traditional white uniform and stiff little cap ages ago, along with the attitude that patients were there for her to tend. Now patients are partners in their therapy; she would never presume to force them into treatment, or dictate to them, or even write the kind of observations on their charts that were commonplace in her days at the Allan, where charts were not open to patient scrutiny and damaging things were often recorded. "A lot of what patients said was used against them," she remembered. "We'd try to impose what we thought was right for them."

She said that looking back on her early days in nursing, and especially her days with Ewen Cameron, gave her qualms: her voice flattened and got a little louder in her effort to be an honest judge of those times. Peggy Edwards is one health professional who has welcomed the advent of informed consent, patients' rights, advocacy groups, and ethics committees—not only because she believes involving patients in all aspects of their treatment is morally right but because she had first-hand experience of how easy it had been to surrender her own judgement to the man in charge. She hedged a little; she still held the man, Dr. Cameron, in high regard: "With everything written and reported since his death, I never think of Ewen Cameron as an unscrupulous man." But she had thought long and hard about how he had persuaded her and other responsible and sensitive people to do the things they had done.

She was young, only twenty-four, when he put her in charge of the ward where the most intensive research and treatment was conducted. She found Cameron overpowering, intimidating, authoritarian, and charismatic, a cocktail of qualities exceedingly heady to his nurses. In the early fifties, Peggy had chosen to enter psychiatric nursing out of a strong desire to gain some understanding of her father, a "highly productive man" (her words) who became an alcoholic. His addiction eventually broke up the family, leaving her mother to bring up four children on a social worker's income.

Peggy came from the Maritimes to train at the Verdun and at first her career's aspect was bleak. Large wards, minimal staff, and "people who had been living inside their own heads for years and hadn't been able to look after their own personal hygiene and were often nude and giggling, totally preoccupied with the inside of their own minds, lying on benches, or on the floor." She was advised to set her sights low, to look for small rewards, to find satisfaction in treating with dignity and respect patients who had been essentially warehoused and forgotten. "There were a lot of very regressed patients at that particular time...and if one was able to get them to brush their teeth, those rewards were the things that kept me going."

But she was so placed that she was to witness a big transformation. Heinz Lehmann was clinical director at the Verdun when Peggy was a student there, and she watched the results of his introduction of chlorpromazine. Lehmann was a self-taught scientific researcher of little means: the only resources his position at the Verdun hospital could offer were freedom and a chronic patient population grateful for anything he might try. As he was to say later, he found himself ahead of the English-speaking researchers at the Allan (and in the rest of North America) because, unlike Cameron, he had learned French and spoke it at home with his Québécoise wife. When a French drug company salesman came around with some literature, also in French, about a new drug called Largactil (chlorpromazine) developed in France, he could pick up the brochure and read it and see that here was something new: a drug that could control states of excitement without the toxic effects of long-term barbiturate use, but also a drug that might have the potential, given in a small steady dose, of warding off psychotic episodes altogether.

"There were no ethics committees," Peggy Edwards said, "and Dr. Lehmann was able to bring chlorpromazine to Montreal and start using it and within three months have dramatic results. Today such a process would take five years." The nudes lying lost on the benches, the non-stop gigglers, and the frenetic pacers started dressing themselves and brushing their teeth and talking coherently. Some who had been labelled patients for life got well enough to leave the hospital and, more amazing, didn't come back. There was a downside to the psychiatric drug revolution. The drugs could cause permanent Parkinsonian-style brain damage; they could be used as a kind of chemical strait-jacket, a prescribed version of the old padded room; and they permitted the de-institutionalization of thousands of chronic patients whose symptoms could be drug-controlled but whose coping skills for life outside the mental hospitals were nil. But these effects did not really hit full force for at least a decade. To Peggy, who had witnessed the change, even more dramatic change seemed possible and imminent.

Dr. Cameron charismatically expressed that spirit of optimism and advance. It may have been true that he himself didn't use the new drugs all that appropriately; he often mixed the old barbiturates, the new antipsychotics, and the even newer antidepressant drugs in counter-productive fashion, or at least in such a way that it was impossible to tell which drug was causing which effect. Still, he saw the potential of the new drugs clearly enough to call together the first conference on psychopharmacology in North America. On staff at the Allan, Hassan Azima was studying reserpine, a derivative of the plant rauwolfia, which seemed another potent antipsychotic. (It was later dropped from the psychiatric repertoire because it produced deep depression, and is now used as a drug to control high blood pressure.) Azima was also doing the second set of controlled studies on the effects of chlorpromazine, after Lehmann. Later, Cameron picked up a mention in the Australian literature of Lithium, a new drug in the treatment of manic-depression, and got one of his chief residents, Eddie Kingstone, to do the first published North American clinical trial. Neither Kingstone nor Cameron, who as the senior researcher should have, picked up on the drug's potential and, after one article (for which Cameron would take no credit), they let the matter drop. But Cameron was for the most part remarkably prescient (for example, he began calling for a revolution in attitudes towards and care of the elderly in the forties and fifties when others were eagerly watching the baby boom). For those on his staff who were forward-looking and progress-minded, Cameron was an excellent leader.

Peggy admired him most, however, for other qualities. Coming from the huge Verdun hospital, where patients were lucky to be individually reckoned with, she liked Cameron's attitude to patients: "I remember him as a man who was actively involved with his patients. He knew all of them by name and saw most of them twice a day, which was outstanding at the time because he treated large numbers of them."

Then there was his apparent hope. "I have this recollection of him coming to the ward every day with his entourage of people behind him—he walked very briskly and was very outgoing in a group. He called all the nurses 'Lassie' on the ward. He called me 'Girlie'—I never dared to ask him why I was Girlie when they were all Lassie. He'd say things like 'Girlie, we're going to cure schizophrenia.'"

Girlie, like many of the rest, believed in him utterly, and was flattered to be included as a soldier in the campaign. "We were sort of imbued with the spirit. We were not unlike a group of...." She stops short of saying religious converts or cult members, and ends, "We had this sense of privilege...that he was on the verge of a discovery and that we were going to be there with him. So when he started things like his LSD experiments, his psychic driving—we all just accepted it. When one looks back at it now it's kind of horrifying."

He also persuaded his head nurse that the patients he chose for his triple-barrelled treatment were people others had given up on. "We'd think, 'Isn't that great—here we are—everybody else has given up and we're going to help these people.' And in the psychic driving—these people were put to sleep, of course, and they had this combination of chlorpromazine and barbiturates, this cocktail, this whole big cocktail. And with that they were given ECTs, and the Page-Russell ECTs, and the button was often pressed several times, and they were given Page-Russells at least a couple of times a day until the point that they were confused in all three spheres [time, place, and self]. Which is totally horrifying to think back on."

Her voice turned wry as she remembered how she coped with the heavy nursing demands such treatments made. "We prided ourselves on caring for those patients and treating them like we did unconscious patients when we were doing medical nursing. In the sleep room, we turned those patients every two hours, we got them up and fed them their meals. We had this table in the centre of the room if they were awake enough and we would get them up, lift them, sit them down and we would feed them and care for them. Nobody ever got any kind of bedsore or break in the skin. We were priding ourselves, if you can imagine, on how well we were caring for these people."

Also, to the nurses—after tending their patients so carefully, washing and dressing them, and helping them through the horrid stage of confusion and incontinence—the improvement at the end of the entire cycle looked very much like a change for the better, worth every bit of their intense effort. If they didn't get better they were, after all, hopeless cases, and at least they had tried. A nursing colleague of Peggy's remembered feeling badly at the time over one patient who was brought from Verdun to the Allan as a research subject. A then-popular theory of schizophrenia held that bad mothering was a cause of the disease, and a whole style of therapy evolved around that idea. This particular regressed patient was made the special charge of a male doctor (not Cameron) and a female nurse and was, in effect, re-parented—indulged and loved as one would an infant—for an entire year. At the end of it the patient was sent back to the Verdun chronic wards as if the whole episode had never happened. To the nurse that didn't seem right.

But whenever they doubted, Dr. Cameron was willing to help them regain their perspective. He was at his best, said Peggy Edwards, when helping the nurses with some specific problem in patient care. And when he wasn't being hearteningly practical he was inspirational: "Dr. Cameron used to say that you have to risk if you want to get anywhere—you've got to risk. And he was willing to risk, because nobody had found a cure for schizophrenia and he was convinced—and he convinced us—that he was going to find the cure.

"I never for a moment doubted his motives. I think his motives were good. I do not think he was a malevolent man. In any way. Maybe misguided. Those of us who worked for him, if he was misguided, were also misguided.

"To go through that kind of learning experience as a nurse—one is conscious ever since of the dangers inherent within."

Whether by design or by instinct, over the years at the Allan, Ewen Cameron insulated himself from people who might have criticized his research from an equal footing. Peers tended to see what students and staff at the Allan might not notice, that the "overpowering, intimidating" Dr. Cameron was often anxious about how others perceived him. Dr. Frank Braceland, an American who worked with Cameron on the founding of the World Psychiatric Association in the early 1960s, described Cameron as like a cat on a hot tin roof during some of the European negotiations, nervous where Braceland had assumed such a dominating and rather abrasive man would be assured.

In *Life Is for Living* Cameron described the search for prestige as one of the major human motivators; he even described how prestige stuck like old chewing-gum to people who no longer deserved it. He won great quantities of it in his own life but apparently never quite enough to make him sure that he deserved it. With students he could be generous in handing out contacts and making connections, especially if the students were bright, self-motivated, and took his gifts and used them well. With peers—people he thought might do him some harm—he could behave in a fashion several of them described as petty.

Harvard psychiatry professor Jack Ewalt, for instance, found himself on Cameron's wrong side after he had failed to include him on a presidentially ordered commission of inquiry into mental health; Ewalt hadn't thought to do so because Cameron was working in Canada at the time, not in the United States. Cameron's attitude towards GAP, the Group for the Advancement of Psychiatry, which brought together forward-thinking American psychiatrists in a lobbying and reform effort after the Second World War, also revealed some touchiness about his status. Cameron's speeches about the professional future could have been written by a GAP member, so closely did their visions jibe, but Cameron kept well away from the group, treating them as a bunch of dangerous interlopers. Ewalt, who belonged to GAP, believed Cameron opposed them because they had not gone out of their way to solicit Cameron's support: "It wasn't his show."

Given his own institution and university department to run, Cameron had quickly gotten used to holding all the cards in most games. Peer review threatened the progress of the game, threatened his status, and had already brought him grief. Dr. Jack Griffin, who had been in charge of Canadian military psychiatric services during the

Second World War, remembers bringing a small group of prominent Allied psychiatrists to visit Cameron in Montreal soon after the war was over. Cameron considered one of them, British Brigadier-General J.R. Rees, a friend, and was acquainted with another, the American psychiatrist Bill Menninger. He launched into a long description of his adrenalin desensitization work before the group, describing how he was injecting increased doses of adrenalin into anxiety-ridden patients in the hope that he could immunize them against their "autonomous reactions". As Griffin remembered, almost in one voice Cameron's audience replied that the research was "ridiculous, childish, naive and a waste of time". Cameron argued vehemently and left them still angry; he did not stop the adrenalin experiments.

Cameron did not shy from hiring giants for the Allan, but that was the difference—he had hired them. On his staff, any light they generated also shone on him; in the fifties students flocked to the Allan partly because Cameron had recruited at least one representative of every new field in psychiatry, and usually a brilliant one. Peggy Edwards said the Allan gave off a charge of excitement just because of the minds at work there, "all of the greats in Canada". In psychoanalysis, there was Dr. Clifford Scott, who had been in analysis with Melanie Klein and was a past president of the British Psychoanalytic Society; and the doctors Johannes and Friedl Aufreiter of Vienna. In geriatrics, psychiatrist and neuropathologist Dr. V.A. Kral was doing ground-breaking work with his associates Dr. Bernard Grad and psychologist Dr. Blossom Wigdor. Dr. Eric Wittkower was heading up a drive into a new field suggested to him by Dr. Cameron, transcultural psychiatry. The senior men in biochemical work in Dr. Cleghorn's area were Murray Saffran and Ted Sourkes; Dr. Charles Shagass was exploring neurophysiology. The Allan's chief of psychology, Dr. Robert Malmo, was working on finding accurate quantitative measurements of mental illness; Hassan Azima was investigating both psychopharmacology and Freudian principles. Dr. Robin Hunter served for many of the residents as the mentor Dr. Cameron couldn't seem to be and went on to head first the department of psychiatry at Queen's University and then

Toronto's Clarke Institute. Dr. Bruno Cormier led the way into a study of forensic psychiatry.

Fern Cramer Azima, who came to the Allan at the precocious age of twenty, already an MA in psychology from Cornell, said, "Cameron was a pioneer in letting himself think originally and letting others conceptualize. He was very open to ideas on how we could change the understanding and treatment of mental patients. He allowed us the freedom to fight to understand these things. If we had an idea, he said run with it."

In consequence, they were usually far too busy at their own research to spend much time considering his. "We weren't involved with what the man was doing himself," said Cramer Azima, who worked in a research partnership with Hassan Azima (she later married him). "He was shy with his own peer group, and dreadfully shy socially, but he had a tendency to want to bring young minds to the Allan. I think he used us to inspire himself." They'd be flattered by the Chief's interest in them. When he called on them to be a sounding board for his own views, his ideas were usually in the speculative area. Cramer Azima said her phone would ring at any hour, she'd pick it up, and the distinctive Scots voice would say, "Fernie, I'm thinking about something, can you come over?" She would find him in a small room somewhere in front of a blackboard working out some thoughts on the genetic code; he was fascinated by the notion that either DNA or RNA might be the physical substratum of memory; in an experiment he had read about, flatworms were trained to move away from a source of light, then ground up and fed to other flatworms who seemed, in the eating, to gain some knowledge that light was a thing to be avoided. Cameron's interest led to a long series of experiments with injecting first DNA and then RNA into elderly patients in an effort to improve their memories, but Cramer Azima remembers more strongly the experience of sitting exchanging ideas on the very forefront of medical knowledge with her Chief.

Few of the teacher/researchers had an overview of the patient population at the Allan. Until 1954, Bob Cleghorn said, Cameron "kept a large proportion of patients under his sole control, treated by residents with little or no supervision". It was only after Cleghorn made a parting protest before leaving for a year to work in Boston that Cameron decided to give senior staff members at the Allan a little more hands-on responsibility for patient care; but even then he allowed them only six-month stints of rotation on one of three wards. Occupational therapists and art therapists, also caught up in the great spirit of innovation and impressed by Cameron's insistence that they were integral to patient treatment and not just the busy-hands departments, saw patients Cameron thought were ready for them; social workers provided after-care and support for a patient's re-entry into the world outside the Allan. But other than Cameron himself, only his residents and nurses witnessed the whole course of a patient's treatment.

As far as the administrative structure of the Allan and the McGill department of psychiatry went, that was pretty much solely Cameron, too. "He was very much the Chief in the Continental style," said Cleghorn—in other words, he did not think it his role to fraternize with his staff nor theirs to make decisions for the institute. He appointed assistants to the director, but never an assistant director. He would delegate decision-making to a committee, but only when he was certain the committee would come out right. Cramer Azima said, "He knew who was on his side and who wasn't. He was the leader, and he wasn't about to let someone upset his applecart." Cameron's word was the only accepted authority at the Allan Memorial Institute.

People in the larger Montreal medical community did know, in varying amounts of detail, the nature of Cameron's research. He valued publicity; press clippings on his tenure still fill a big binder in the AMI's library. Daily newspapers from the 1940s onwards carried elaborate if uncritical descriptions of all his research work. As a matter of course, Cameron also sent full treatment details to each patient's referring physician on a regular basis, describing the sensory deprivation, the psychic driving, and the depatterning: there's no evidence that any of those doctors, whether general practitioners or psychiatrists, registered a protest. When Dr. Charles Roberts left his government-research-funding job in 1957 to come to Montreal to help reorganize the Verdun Protestant Hospital (largely at Cameron's urging), he said he encountered no professional sniping about Cameron's care of his patients—only some comment about his ruthlessness with other professionals who got in his way.

Roberts was later to taste some of that. He worked hard as part of Cameron's volunteer team to organize the World Congress of Psychiatry that took place in Montreal in 1961. It, in turn, was the springboard for Cameron's last organizational coup, the founding of the World Psychiatric Association. About that time, Cameron told Roberts he had put his (Roberts') name forward for a teaching position at McGill, which certainly would have been a plum. But Roberts had also become involved in the 1961 Bédard inquiry into mental-health care in Quebec. An exposé, called *Les fous crient au secours* (*The Mad Cry for Help*), written by an ex-inmate of the St-Jean de Dieu Hospital, a huge asylum run by Catholic nuns on the eastern outskirts of Montreal, had become a best seller in Quebec. The author, Jean Charles Pagé, had also once been hospitalized at the AMI. The government determined to answer the plea in Pagé's title. Appointing two Francophone commissioners, they were looking for a third who spoke English. Because of Roberts' federal government background and his current experience as an administrator at the huge Verdun hospital, the government thought he was a good choice for the third person.

Roberts didn't think to mention the appointment to Cameron; Cameron was enraged when the commission fulfilled its mandate to look into all mental institutions in the province by also investigating the Allan. Cameron's upset wasn't entirely blind ego. He was in the process of hard lobbying for his institutional dream, a research building for the Allan, and as a resolute Anglophone who had cornered a huge share of federal government money he wasn't having an easy time of it with the provincial government. As far as patient care went, the Bédard report pointed out that the institution that used the most electro-shock in the province was the Allan; it also pointed out the disproportion in research funding. The McGill posting was never forthcoming for Roberts, and Cameron made it clear that Roberts' role in the inquiry was the reason why.

Still, Roberts said, when he thought seriously of the depatterning and psychic-driving techniques back then it was much in the way that Cameron himself seemed to think of them—as heroic intervention into the course of a hopeless life. "Anyone who had seen patients lying in their own excrement in a chronic hospital wasn't going to object to even heavy ECT," he said.

Some people say Cameron's depatterning was seen as the electro-shock equivalent of lobotomy, an operation that became an enormous treatment fad in the late forties and fifties, largely owing (in North America) to the efforts of one man, American neurologist Walter Freeman. Other psychiatrists and neurosurgeons seized on lobotomy for reasons similar to those that drove Cameron to try first insulin shock and then depatterning; lobotomy was an even simpler vent for therapeutic frustration—it seemed, for a time, to be a one-stop surgical cure.

Freeman soon discarded the operation as devised by the Nobel prize winner Egaz Moniz in favour of his own version—transorbital lobotomy. With instruments he fashioned for the purpose (and usually carried around with him in his breast pocket), Freeman achieved access to a patient's frontal lobes by driving steel probes up into the brain alongside the optic nerve. According to Elliot Valenstein's account of the fast rise and thorough fall of lobotomy in America, *Great and Desperate Cures*, Freeman felt that his operation was such a beneficial and minimal intervention that he even performed one in a motel room, asking the patient's relatives to hold him down.

In the scheme of things, depatterning was viewed as less drastic than lobotomy: Cameron himself advised against lobotomy, saying that if at all possible nothing irreversible should ever be done to a patient. But even though Cameron's method fell well within the purview of a psychiatrist's skill (unlike surgery), no one outside the institute itself picked up on Cameron's depatterning. There may not have been much public criticism of it, but no one proved eager to try it; the nursing care it needed was too time-consuming and costly, the number of ECTs and the memory loss it prescribed too troubling.

As for Cameron's literal-minded attempt at patient programming, in light moments in the medical community, psychic driving was simply joked about. There was the one in which Cameron settled a patient gently on the couch in his office, turned his tape machine on, and then slipped away to the Allan coffee shop, only to encounter a man who looked awfully familiar to him also having a cup of coffee. "Doc," the man said, "I figured you just turn your machine on so I brought along my own tape. We can both take the hour off."

Then there was the apparently true story that made people laugh even harder. Cameron liked to ask his driving patients to repeat their message to him so that he could check up on whether they were hearing it straight. On rounds one day, trailed by the usual number of residents, psychologists, and nurses, he stopped to question one patient whose problem was learning to like sex with her husband. One line of her message was, "You are at ease with your husband." What she had been hearing, repeated *ad infinitum*, was, "You are a tease with your husband." The implications of that piece of programming were something the entourage was able to dine out on.

Cameron's science was not what the local community respected him for; he himself was charismatic but his research ideas were neither infectiously straightforward nor intellectually interesting. Charles Roberts defended Cameron's right to do the research and the spirit in which it was undertaken with great conviction. But when he thought back on the time, he stated with some surprise: "You know, I referred patients to the Allan, but I never referred one to Cameron."

Fred Lowy, who more than twenty years later would write an evaluation of the ethics of Cameron's controversial experiments for the Canadian government, came to the Allan in the early 1960s not expecting to think much of Cameron at all. Before switching to psychiatry Lowy had been in the McGill department of psychology working with Donald Hebb, and the McGill psychologists were the first group of local professionals to scoff openly at Cameron's scientific abilities. "Blow the whistle on him," is how some of those former postgraduate students phrase it.

Hebb said that if any of his students had come to him with a set of concepts like those being put into practice by Cameron he would have laughed him right out of McGill; that Cameron's political position alone allowed him to get away with such simplistic scientific thinking. After the CIA controversy broke, Hebb (who died in 1985) was even harsher: "Cameron's experiments were done without the patient's consent. Cameron was irresponsible—criminally stupid—in that there was no reason to expect that he would get any results from the experiments. Anyone with any appreciation of the complexity of the human mind would not expect that you could erase an adult mind and then add things back with this stupid psychic driving."

Lowy, who was Cameron's resident for three months, said that barring Hebb, "most people at the time believed human behaviour was a result of a simple determinism, a follows b. People paid lip-service to there being multiple factors interacting, but believed there ·was one major problem at the heart of it." Cameron talked a storm of complexity about behaviour, Lowy said, but he believed with the deterministic majority. Belief and action in Cameron were never far apart. Said Lowy, "The Freudians had developed all these subtle methods of peeling the onion to get at the heart of the problem. Cameron wanted to drill right through and to hell with the layers. But, as we later discovered, the layers are all there is."

Compared to Hebb as a scientist, Lowy found that Cameron came up wanting, both in talent and in his apparent motivation: "Cameron didn't have a self-critical capacity and was easily self-deluded. By that I don't mean that he was married to his methods: if someone could show him a better way to go he might do it. If he could get his results, help people and win the Nobel prize he would be happy." Where Hebb surrounded himself with research teams of brilliant students, in Lowy's view, Cameron's personal research team was "not first-rate". Leonard Rubenstein, co-credited on many of the papers, wasn't even a doctor. Leonard Levy was more a clinician than a scientific thinker. The surviving remnants of research critiques exchanged between Cameron and Len Levy reveal a relationship in which the young doctor talked in quasi-critical and complicated terms in order to reassure his chief that the research was excellent and worthy.

Many former students and staff members at the Allan insisted that Cameron hated nothing worse than a sycophant; suffered dependent relationships badly; and didn't exactly mentor so much as allow people to run with the ball. Cameron seized on other collaborators and at least one of them, Dr. Thomas Ban, whose name appears on some of the papers sponsored by the CIA, went on to have a credible career specializing in psychopharmacology. He had been working with Heinz Lehmann, and that's where he wanted to stay, but Cameron was the head of the Allan, the most powerful man in Canadian psychiatry, and Ban, a foreigner new to Montreal, didn't think he had the right to refuse the work. In his own research efforts, Cameron didn't seem to miss the presence of a critical mind to check and balance his ideas.

On the face of it, students and staff members at the Allan had too much to be grateful to Cameron for to protest seriously the methodology of his experiments. He could articulate the hopes and dreams of his profession in a way few others could; the activism of the Allan stood in inspirational contrast to other eminent institutions, such as London's Maudsley Hospital, where many of the Allan residents had also trained. The Maudsley's (now knighted) Sir Aubrey Lewis might criticize Cameron's work as barbaric, but Eddie Kingstone, for one, had been to the Maudsley and found Lewis's institution "cautious and careful. Patients were studied and only treated if absolutely necessary. There was a long discussion before you ordered even one ECT." Bill Stauble, who had also done training in Britain, found the responsibility he was allowed to take on at the Allan awesome at first, and then exhilarating. Group therapy, the out-patient department, and undergrad teaching, plus six-month shifts in charge of a ward—all were his to do, whereas in England the hierarchy was such that Stauble's hair would have been as white as the Chief's before he was put in charge of anything.

"For those who didn't want to be caretakers," said Eddie Kingstone, "Cameron was very inspiring. We thought psychiatry was going to cure people, communities, the world, alter thought patterns and behaviour."

He and the other residents saw that Cameron was impatient, that his rounds with his public patients, as just one example, were too swift: "We saw that in his practice and we corrected it in a variety of ways." Kingstone was involved in the care of patients who were depatterned (he was the doctor who asked Mary Morrow to sign a refusal-of-treatment form): "What we saw was his impatience with methods. What drove him was a belief that people could change, and his role or the psychiatrist's role was to help them change.... He thought in a hospital something should happen."

Bill Stauble says that psychic driving seemed simplistic to a lot of the residents at the time. "In discussing those things with him, I'd guess we'd say, 'Well these [driving cues] are more rational, surface bits of information. You're dealing with deep inner conflicts. Do you really expect the information to get back into the childhood where it all started?' "

Cameron's residents, just like his nurses, loved the feelings of importance, the meaningfulness, the Chief could provide for their work. They may have criticized him, and some of them may have dreaded being assigned to the ECT work, and many of them had trouble taking psychic driving literally. Some of them found Cameron too domineering, ego-driven, power-hungry. But he was able to persuade most of them that what he did was justified. Said Eddie Kingstone, who went on from the Allan to head two major Canadian departments of psychiatry, "Cameron never hid either his successes or his failures—you could learn from both. I think that's why so many of us came away positive about him. We wouldn't have done some of the things that he did, but he never asked us to toe any line."

Kingstone thought a little further. "We now believe that change is limited. The profession has retreated from its belief that it could change the world. But psychiatrists still have to deny their limitations in order to maintain their optimism."

Cameron did a little more than deny his limitations. The seeds of his trespass against good science were sown in his absolute frustration with not attaining the objective experimental psychology he wrote so passionately about in the mid-1930s. He described his crisis of confidence in a lecture written in the early 1950s: "Deep concern, which I have felt since entering psychiatry, over the great difficulties occasioned in applying the scientific method to the study of human behavior...led me first to seek more 'steady' (that is, invariable) material which would be, for this reason, suitable for processing through the orthodox scientific method. The measurement of knee jerks was sought as an indicator of tension and blood sugar levels as measurements of emotional response. But after some years of this pursuit it became quite clear that one was sacrificing the really dynamic facts to what was more and more clearly visible as an unproductive conformity to a scientific methodology very suitable for dealing with the expansion of metals but useless in recording the expansion and constriction of the self image."

There followed "a determined attempt to tackle the philosophy of science itself, and to work out a series of methodological postulates suitable for tackling the highly adaptive but continually varying phenomena of behavior."

On the philosophy Cameron became eloquent; how he came to view the scientific method is best expressed in a 1948 paper published in *Science*, and titled "The Current Transition in the Conception of Science". The old method, he wrote, was "reminiscent of a dog with a bone. He [the scientist] dragged [the problem] off from wherever he found it to some secluded place of his choosing"—where he worried it to death in isolation and abstraction. Once solved, he took the revised bone back to where he had found it and saw if it worked. If the situation could be reduced to mechanistic enough terms of cause and effect, it usually did. But lots of bones, particularly in the social and biological sciences, resisted such abstraction and isolation—and then Einstein's comprehension of the physical universe made Newton under the apple tree a total cartoon. It began to sneak into the periphery of scientific consciousness that science was a form of human behaviour, too, not "a machine which may be set in motion without any regard for the man who operates it". That several astronomers tracking the course of a star might all perceive slightly different transits was a total upset of the possibility of objective science, and the pursuit of such objectivity began to seem a cultural rather than a scientific imperative.

That smashing of the dogma of objectivity, Cameron thought, was immensely liberating for the sciences of human behaviour, which had always been sniffed at as something less worthy (less rational) than the basic sciences of physics, chemistry, astronomy, and mathematics. Soft and not hard. "Now science itself must face its own bitter catalysis. For in very fact the world of thought is one world; and science, which has wrought such deep changes, must change with them." He permitted himself a small victory: "In this, our discipline…is a prime mover."

Reworking the scientific method to include the human factor was a bit of a problem: "how are we to rewrite the criteria of proof?" But his own science, whose justifications were entirely empiric, no longer had to feel so insecure and anxious since "it can no longer be asserted that abstraction and isolation of the problem is an essential part of the scientific method".

The trouble was that while Cameron's thinking on science was impeccable in the abstract, it was dangerous as he put it into prac-tice. While occasional attempts at validation of results showed up in Cameron's research papers produced at the Allan, by and large the only measure of success he came to use in his research was his own clinical judgement. After conducting his radical exploration of the phi-losophy of science, he came to believe that his own human judgement was as reliable an indicator of results as any other test of behavioural change yet devised. Maybe more reliable. And by the time he was pub-lishing papers on work funded by the Society for the Investigation of Human Ecology, his own criteria of proof were as lax as those he had railed against in his own youth, though in his eyes more intellectually justified.

Laughlin Taylor, a McGill-trained psychologist Cameron hired (with SIHE money) to do before-and-after tests on psychic-driving patients, believed that as a scientist Cameron had grown entirely self-serving. At first Taylor had been happy with the assignment because Cameron, as he always did, allowed Taylor his head: as far as Cameron was concerned the psychologist could choose whichever instruments of assessment he thought would prove the most accurate. And when Taylor mentioned to him that to get coherent results the patients at the before stage had to be in better shape—off all drugs and ECT for at least a week—Cameron concurred.

Taylor has said that he saw only patients doing psychic driving; he hadn't known at the time that Cameron was still doing the depatterning and driving combination. The first thing that bothered Taylor that he couldn't do anything about was the choice of experimental candidates: "There was no systematic selection of patients. I couldn't see any. Somebody happened along and somebody said, 'Well, what about trying psychic driving on them? What a good idea.' And on the project they went." According to Cameron, psychic driving was supposed to work best on psychoneurotics, but Taylor from 1958 to 1960 was also testing alcoholics, depressives, and schizophrenics.

After a woman burst into tears during a series of before tests, Taylor also came to believe that Cameron was not above coercing a likely candidate into the research project by threatening to withhold all treatment. The patient didn't want to do psychic driving, she told Taylor, but Cameron was going to send her away from the Allan if she didn't. Worse (under the dictum that if a treatment worked it was justifiable to force it on a patient), Taylor's test results showed him no real change for the better that could be attributed to psychic driving: "I couldn't see a difference."

Taylor, who needed the job, for the most part swallowed his reservations until a meeting with Cameron in 1960 where Cameron baldly outlined his opinion of what scientific results were all about. In the process of choosing ten case histories to support another paper on psychic driving he was going to deliver at an international conference, Cameron made it clear that the ten best cases were all the cases he was planning to report. Taylor argued that every test result had to be included or the research would be skewed, that Cameron couldn't just ignore the ones that showed either no change or that the patient had become worse.

Cameron replied that yes, he could. As far as he was concerned, controlled research in the style that Taylor was proposing did not produce the results he wanted. He had already tried it. The way he now worked was much more scattershot—he threw everything but the kitchen sink at the patients and reported only the best results. Roughly a third of all mental patients improved no matter what the treatment, so he could always report good results.

Taylor's memory of the next crucial interchange is as follows:

TAYLOR: That is not scientific research.

CAMERON: That is the way we do research here, Mr. Taylor, and if you don't want to be associated with it, you don't have to.

Taylor resigned a few weeks later, and no psychologist was hired to take his place. In papers published at that time the Cameron team seldom failed to mention that it found psychological testing less reliable than clinical assessment.

Bob Cleghorn, a basic scientist who became a psychiatrist after he joined the staff of the Allan and who has spent most of his career campaigning hard for a rigorous scientific discipline in psychiatric research, in his memoirs looked back in horror on the scientific judgement of his former Chief: "[Cameron] lacked what might be called scientific discrimination, a faculty which computerizes evidence and emerges with an answer weighted in the direction of reality. In a minimal way he shared with Freud the character of a conquistador." Even after closely examining Cameron's published papers, Cleghorn couldn't condemn him. He ended up comparing Cameron's assault on schizophrenia to the Dieppe raid, as "valiant but ill-conceived".

At the time, they all admired Cameron's valiant spirit, his unceasing therapeutic optimism; they put up with his bad science because they didn't see that it did any real harm. Few approached close enough to see what Laughlin Taylor did. Cameron allowed no one to point out a bad conception to him unless the critic had something better to suggest; few did. Laughlin Taylor's criticisms could slide off his back because in Cameron's view psychological testing was just as empirical as clinical observation. What he saw was as valid as any test, until he was proved wrong.

Three years after Laughlin Taylor left the project Cameron reported in a research paper that he had found the researcher's own mind a better instrument than any test: *"The experimenter is capable on the basis of his natural facilities of a far more subtle range of responses than any battery of tests."* The italics were his own.

CHAPTER ELEVEN

The Wrong Road Travelled

The research scientist that Ewen Cameron's former colleagues most often compare him to is Heinz Lehmann, his one-time "poor relation" from the Verdun Protestant Hospital. Early on in his tenure at Montreal, Cameron had turned Lehmann down when Lehmann applied to the Allan for a job. Later, there was no need for Lehmann to apply. His introduction of chlorpromazine into North American psychiatry in 1954 secured him status and research funding independent of Cameron's influence, and made him, in one fell swoop, far more important to the long-term development of the profession than Cameron. Lehmann, as Bob Cleghorn pointed out, had the natural scientific discernment and judgement many considered so lacking in his own Chief. Charles Roberts, too, noted that if Lehmann claimed a new drug worked best with manic-depressives or schizophrenics, one could trust that both his initial diagnoses and his findings would be accurate and repeatable.

Lehmann was not opposed to taking risks. The first people on whom he tried chlorpromazine were his staff; one fell asleep within ten minutes, others fainted dead away as a result of the drug's fairly drastic lowering of blood pressure. "For all I knew," he said, "they might have died from it. We didn't know how toxic it was." Luck, he says, as much as science laid the biggest breakthrough at his doorstep and not Cameron's: his drug worked while Cameron's various methods didn't. Yet if one compares Lehmann's first paper on the effects of chlorpromazine to Ewen Cameron's introductory papers on psychic driving and depatterning, the differences between them are clear. Cameron's papers, however academic in tone, are full of conjecture and unvarnished hope; Lehmann's (co-authored with G.E. Hanrahan) is level-headed, methodical, almost completely devoid of grand statement, and—given that he was doing clinical experiments with a new drug whose mode of action was unknown, a dangerous thing in itself—relatively careful.

In that first paper, based on tests on seventy-one patients running for an average of four months, Lehmann outlined not only the drug's therapeutic potential but touched on many of the effects that have since plagued the widespread use of such neuroleptic (nerve-seizing) drugs. Allergic reactions, jaundice and liver damage, nausea and "epigastric distress", a wooden "Parkinsonian" appearance, low blood pressure and irregular heart rhythms, dry mouths and noses, and a general interference with mucous production that rendered patients susceptible to colds—through careful observation Lehmann perceived them all. His failure to notice the most lasting effects of chlorpromazine (and the other drugs since developed in the phenothiazine and similar drug families) was only due to the fact that four months of fairly small dosages was not long enough to produce them.

Psychiatrists now have a name for these effects—EPS, or extrapyramidal symptoms. Translated in the bodies of the patients EPS means abnormal muscle reactions. There are dystonias, or uncontrollable and painful cramps—from spasms in the eye muscles that lock them in a fixed upward stare, to wry neck, in which neck muscles contract to pull the chin toward one shoulder or the other, to muscle seizures in the lower back, to life-threatening spasms in the mouth and throat that interfere drastically with breathing. There are dyskinesias (uncontrollable writhing, squirming, twisting, grimacing); akathisias (restlessness, pacing, foot-tapping, finger-rolling); Parkinsonisms (rigidity and trembling, stooped posture and shuffling walk);

and akinesias (the zombie effect). There is also tardive (late-appearing) dyskinesia, a form of brain damage that afflicts from 20 to 55 per cent of people taking neuroleptics for two years or longer, and that can include any of the effects listed above. TD, as they call it, lasts long after the drugs are stopped and may even be a permanent condition—the new, pharmacologically induced stigma of mental disorder.

In his 1954 paper Lehmann carefully noted that there had been only one drug-related death reported in the French literature, caused by treating a man with cirrhosis of the liver for delirium tremens; liver damage proved to be a contraindication for the drug. In the present drug-company literature on neuroleptics, sudden death is listed as a "side effect", the most commonly reported cause being the drug's interference with the gag reflex: the patient dies from aspirating vomit directly into the lungs and suffocating on it. The drugs can also cause not only constipation but a life-threatening paralysis of the bowels.

Any clinical researcher in medical science weighs the risks and benefits of the introduction of a new treatment; *primum non nocere*, as a principle to practise by, gets knocked into Cloud-cuckoo-land in medical school. If Lehmann did not turn up all of chlorpromazine's powerful, dangerous, and unwanted effects, he turned up enough to have an idea of what the stakes were. The major difference between his approach and Cameron's was what he compared his new treatment option with. Cameron consistently justified drastic measures by citing the apparent hopelessness of the conditions he was up against; he compared his experimental treatments against the effects of the supposed disease and was left rudderless. Lehmann was more scientifically palatable because he compared the effects of chlorpromazine to those of the treatments then available by asking several clear-minded specific questions. Was the new drug better or as good at controlling symptoms? How did it compare on side effects? Was it more or less easy to administer than other options? Was it less risky? Did it control symptoms alone or did it affect the underlying pathology? And then the question that Lehmann felt set psychiatric research aims apart from the aims of general medicine: did it "permit sustained psychotherapeutic rapport?"

Manic-depression was a particular concern of Lehmann's. Prior to chlorpromazine the options he had for treatment were ECT and barbiturate sedation, including prolonged sleep therapy. ECT could control symptoms, he wrote, especially when administered intensively; the catch there was that it also could "by its disorganizing effect on the higher brain functions, produce a new set of symptoms, characterized by confusion, restlessness and aggression". ECT was simpler to administer than chlorpromazine but "it is associated with the unpleasant side-effect of amnesia". Also manic patients tended to relapse.

Barbiturates and the other available sedatives often failed to control symptoms because they often suppressed a patient's inhibitions instead. While temporary use of sedatives wasn't particularly dangerous, the risks of sleep therapy, Lehmann wrote, were "serious and manifold" in nature and only warded off by costly and intensive nursing care. All three options—barbiturates, ECT, and sleep therapy—clouded the patient's consciousness. As Lehmann wrote, "Many of us have in recent years lost sight of our essential task of understanding our patients, as we subject them to a sequence of comas, shocks, convulsions, confusion, and amnesia, all of which render them incapable of relating to the psychiatrist in a consistent and meaningful way."

Using such criteria, chlorpromazine looked like the best therapeutic weapon Lehmann had ever seen: "Perhaps the greatest advantage of this drug lies in its power to quiet severely excited patients without rendering them confused or otherwise inaccessible." Quiet, he stressed, did not mean happy. Patients told him that while on the drug they felt hugely fatigued, washed-out, as if they were suffering the aftermath of an exhausting illness. The French researchers prior to Lehmann had reported that patients tended "to remain silent and immobile and to reply to questions in a slow monotone"—responsive only when asked to respond. The upshot, Lehmann wrote, was that "patients receiving the drug are often aware of their improvement without showing any euphoric reaction". Well, but not feeling well.

Such a condition was considered therapeutically useful. "Although a patient under the influence of chlorpromazine at first glance presents the aspect of a heavily drugged person....the higher psychic functions are preserved to a remarkable degree, and the patients are capable of sustained attention, reflection, and concentration." He added (cultural or professional bias obviously affecting him here): "One has the impression that this drug promotes an attitude of sober resignation and of critical reflection, even in acutely disturbed patients."

Heinz Lehmann hoped that chlorpromazine would be used as a kind of cast to hold the broken psyche in place while the patient and therapist worked together to effect the healing. The revolution its introduction caused did not have quite that effect. "Mental aspirin" was the tag phrase soon applied to the drug, and to the minor tranquillizers and antidepressant drugs that followed in quick succession. Pope Pius XII was given chlorpromazine to soothe his anxious nausea and burping; French military psychiatrists prescribed chlorpromazine to help soldiers overcome stress and fear while fighting in Algeria. (Chlorpromazine turned out not to be the answer to that question but, thirty-three years later, American army researchers apparently are close to producing a mind drug that will eliminate fear, the aim being to turn ordinary, human soldiers into killing machines built to withstand the horrifying conditions of a potential conventional war.)

Living better through chemistry. The temptation for psychiatrists faced with nasty or time-consuming cases became to substitute the medical act of writing on a prescription pad for the act of empathy and communication. The temptation was largely succumbed to. Biochemical psychiatry is still in the ascendant position; much of the institutional treatment of patients can now be described in terms of the proper adjustment of brain chemistry, with drugs to control the initial symptoms, and drugs to control the unwanted effects of the drugs, which produce other effects that researchers seek to find drugs to control in an endless chemical hall of mirrors.

Freudian psychology and other forms of talking cure, which in the 1950s had the intellectual upper hand, are out of fashion in psychiatry. Biologically oriented doctors, though the long-sought-for lesions of psychiatric disorders are still elusive, are certain that biochemical, hormonal, or lithium-salt-style adjustments make talk relatively unnecessary. Lehmann, in his eighties still an active teacher and speaker in his field, now rails against the single-minded pursuit of psychopharmacology. First because of its major side effect, the large-scale deinstitutionalization of mental patients that governments in Canada, the United States, and elsewhere found so economically appealing. Even paying for their massive drug plans and subsidizing their boarding-house rooms is cheaper than maintaining chronic patients in mental hospitals. Second, because Lehmann believes that doctors use the drugs to block exactly what he hoped chlorpromazine would effect—communication and understanding between patient and therapist. In a speech he gave in 1986, Lehmann said, "I am anxiously awaiting the next revolution in psychiatry which, I hope, will be a return to the humanities in psychiatry." He's waiting and hoping for the revolution in care which will bring the drugs and the effort at human comprehension back together again.

As far as Ewen Cameron was concerned, he had already achieved to the level of a Heinz Lehmann. He had taken a revolutionary new treatment from abroad, insulin-coma therapy, and been one of the pioneers of the method in North America and had worried over methodology and results and applications. Lehmann might be intrigued by questions that coherently tested the efficacy of treatment; Cameron was bored insensate by the straightforward logic demanded by objective experimentation. He wanted to fly without a net, up in the ether with the creative scientific geniuses; in a running file he kept on creativity he noted, "Creative thinking is not like ordinary thinking.... It is much more of a viewpoint, or a glimpse of something occurring in association with a particular feeling, a kind of 'letting go.' "

Mixed into Cameron's disenchanted Scots Presbyterianism was a touch of the Celtic mystic. He loved to hike in the mountains not just for the satisfaction of getting to the top of them but because being with the very trees led him into thoughts about "what causes living to be, as it were, everlasting".The man who revered twentieth-century science was also a water-diviner, who equated the letting-go feeling of creativity in science with the state he was in when his forked stick found water.

He also wrote notes to himself measuring his relationships to patients on the basis of how creative he was able to be ("Jan. 12, 1955. Note the failure to think creatively with Kelly today, but the ability to go on thinking creatively when Valette was in therapy.... also on this particular day there was no creative thinking with Dumas. With Kelly I was irritated by matters at the University, and with Dumas I was merely day-dreaming"). He was eager to make the Allan an institution that fostered scientific creativity, and even put together a committee of those he considered most creative as of 1957 (Cleghorn, Azima, Lehmann, Malmo, and his technician, Rubenstein, among others) to help him formulate guidelines to ensure that. The group's description of a creative person recorded in the minutes of the first meeting could have been a portrait of Cameron: they decided that "the individual had to be a worker...; that he had to have talent, naivety as in a child, openmindedness, curiosity, and an urge to complete the 'unclosed circuit.' He must also have strong motivation, and must enjoy inquiry. He must not be afraid to be in a minority."

Great men of science (and Cameron thoroughly endorsed the "great man" myth of scientific progress) had to have the strength to bear up under the weight of their divining; and walk alone if they had to. Ordinary men did all the tedious sorting out and refining of the great inspirations. When Cameron asked himself, "How does the scientist go about asking questions?" he was not thinking of criteria of proof. In his first speech on his psychic-driving research he wondered, "What are the factors which tend to make one man ask highly productive questions and others to put questions which lead to little, dull and dusty blind alleys?" He included himself in the category of highly productive.

But nine years after the start of his great foray into brainwashing, it was beginning to dawn on Ewen Cameron that, although his alley was never little, dull, or dusty, it was proving to be blind. In mid-1960, the Society for the Investigation for Human Ecology had stopped funding him because the results he claimed were just not satisfactory to them; executive secretary Colonel James Monroe had tried to secure replacement financing from the U.S. Air Force but there's no record that it ever came through.* Then psychologist Bob Malmo made one tiny semantic distinction apparent to Cameron: he pointed out that all of Cameron's efforts had been directed at forcing patients to pay attention to the driving tapes. But attention was not necessarily an active condition; one could pay attention to the words and let the meaning wash over. Wasn't involvement and not attention the thing that Cameron was seeking?

By February 1963, Ewen Cameron was standing up in public before the American Psychopathological Association in New York City—the same Cameron who had published twelve papers on psychic driving expressing never a shadow of doubt—to tell the world he had made "a wrong turning". When he had asked, "How could we block the mechanisms which the human being sets up to protect himself against adaptation...?" it had been the wrong question altogether.

He had then "continued to walk without a glint of success for a long long time.... Let me say simply that we vastly increased the number of repetitions to which the individual was exposed, that we continued driving while the individual was asleep, while he was in a chemical sleep, while he was awake but under hallucinogens, while he was under the influence of disinhibiting agents. We tried driving under hypnosis, immediately after electroshock, we tried innumerable combinations of voices, of timing and many other conditions, but we were never able to stop the mechanisms."

Confused, amnesiac patients were not good subjects for personality change; the upset and damaged brain did not take to new learning, and was far too complex an organ for an outsider to reprogram. In a patient, Cameron decided, it was "his thinking and feeling—in a

---

* The Canadian government, in fact, became the new funding source, providing $57,750 from 1961 to 1964 for a project on the files as No. 604-5-432, "A Study of Factors which Promote or Retard Personality Changes in Individuals Exposed to Prolonged Repetitions of Verbal Signals".

word, his involvement—[that] fundamentally…brings about reorganization". After years of believing that more repetition brought better results, that more amnesia and more confusion not only broke down old patterns but cultivated the neural ground for his own planting, Cameron quite simply decided he had been wrong.

After reading the years of research papers claiming that success was his, one is not prepared for Cameron to abandon his ground. But just as he had the freedom and the strength of ego to pursue a bad idea beyond the bounds of common sense and care for his patients, he had the intellectual freedom and the strength of ego to drop it when he was at last convinced it did not work.

One of the patients who came fresh to Ewen Cameron in his last years at the Allan Memorial cannot believe that the Dr. Cameron she knew could ever have been a party to brutal treatment. With her, Karralynn Schreck, he had done everything right.

Karralynn Schreck's last name, in the German, means terror, but it's been a long time since she was ruled by that emotion. Twenty-four years ago she was a patient of Ewen Cameron's at the Allan Memorial Institute, one of those hopeless cases sent to him as the doctor of last resort. Calling her by the pseudonym "Sonia", he described her in a paper as "an exceedingly complicated 23-year-old girl…who from a very early age showed serious neurotic tendencies with strong feelings of hostility toward her mother, expressing themselves ultimately in frank statements of hatred. She also had profoundly disturbing incestuous preoccupations with and fear of her father and hatred of her own body."

The old description causes the present-day Karralynn Schreck hardly a moment's pause; she left those conflicts behind her years ago. What distresses her is what she sees as an incomprehensible attack on her saviour. How could Ewen Cameron, her Dr. Cameron, be this person the news reports bill as a kind of Dr. Frankenstein? Without him, she believes she would still be that extremely ill person; she would have either spent her life in a mental institution or been a suicide. With Cameron's help, Karralynn Schreck has been able to live what anyone would call a normal life since she was twenty-four. For the past eighteen years she has been married to a doctor. He and she now live in a house on Easy Street in a small town in Pennsylvania. Karralynn says that Easy Street is both literal and figurative.

Other than to mention that she was born and raised in Moncton, N.B., Karralynn won't talk about her childhood; her relatives are still living, and even in defence of Dr. Cameron she will not drag the contributing factors of her illness into the light. She will describe just how sick she was: even as a child she had a propensity towards depression when under stress, as other people have towards a bleeding ulcer. At fourteen she came down with a severe attack of dermatitis that her doctor could only attribute to psychosomatic causes. Told by him that she was going to have to see a psychiatrist, the young Karralynn Mollins brightened and asked, "What kind? A lay analyst or a medical psychiatrist? A Freudian?" Probably no other child (or even parent) in Moncton in the 1950s knew that such distinctions existed; Karralynn, who read voraciously and knew she had what they called mental problems, harboured an ambition to become a psychiatrist and was actually happy to be sent to one.

Her disorder forced her to quit school after Grade 9. By the time she was twenty, after a series of shock treatments and a stay in the local hospital's psychiatric ward, she had exhausted the possibilities for help that existed in Moncton. Her doctor told her she had two choices: she could go to the Allan Memorial Institute in Montreal or she could go to the Institute of Living in Hartford, Connecticut—which he favoured because it was said to have better programs for young people. Lana Turner's daughter, who had murdered her mother's lover, was there; and Jonathan Winters, the famous comedian, also spent time in the Institute of Living. So that's where Karralynn went.

The label that went with her, in November of 1961, was "anxiety neurosis". The young resident assigned to her thought he knew better; as far as he was concerned Karralynn Mollins was a schizophrenic. He was her major care-giver; she was supposed to see him four and five times a week. She found him cold and unfeeling and felt like some object in a specimen case. She started to have full-blown fits, ten or more a day. She fell on the floor, flailing, her smouldering cigarette flying any which way out of her hands.

"Epilepsy," her resident said bluntly. "You're a hopeless epileptic"—and he turned and walked out of the room. He put her on the standard epileptic medication of the day, Dilantin with Phenobarbital, and seemed just to write her off. Karralynn began to use her cigarettes with a purpose, to burn holes in her thighs, hands, and feet. "The day my resident found out I was burning my feet," she says, "he sent me to the lowest unit of the hospital where fifteen to twenty women were locked up in a glass cage. I slept with ten other women. There were nurses on the other side of the glass wall looking in; we were always under surveillance. Women were masturbating, urinating on the floor, people would hit you. He put me down there for five days."

He might have kept her there longer, but his senior resident disapproved and moved Karralynn into a ward where, though she "had to pee in public—even the washrooms were under surveillance", the other patients weren't likely to hit her. Epilepsy drugs and all, her seizures grew so bad she was finally admitted to the institute's hospital wing, and there she lay, very depressed, asleep as much of the time as she could.

The *deus ex machina* was the New Brunswick health-insurance scheme, which about that time informed her parents that it would not continue paying Karralynn's hospital bills because she could receive the same treatment in Canada. Her mother, remembering the Allan, got on a train to Montreal. She had a lot of trouble getting in to see Dr. Cameron, and when he finally could spare a moment he told Mrs. Mollins that the Allan just had no room for Karralynn. Then Cameron's colleague, Dr. Frank Braceland, who happened to be director of the Institute of Living, interceded for Karralynn; on his own weekly rounds he'd taken a shine to her. He more than likely felt badly that she had entered his institute depressed and neurotic but walking on her own two feet and within seven months was exiting diagnosed as both schizophrenic and epileptic. In July of 1962, Karralynn went home to Moncton for three weeks and thereafter checked into the Allan.

Her initial treatment by Cameron was as peremptory as anything described by Val Orlikow or Mary Morrow—with a difference, of course. On Karralynn Mollins it worked. Doctors at the Institute of Living had burned into her mind that she was never to be without her epilepsy medication, that she had to take it for the rest of her life. But for the whole first week at the Allan the nurses kept refusing to give her the medication, on orders, they said, from Dr. Cameron. Panic-stricken, Karralynn insisted on seeing the doctor: "He just looked at me with this look in his eyes and said, 'Do you want to be the kind of person who has to be helped across the street for the rest of your life?'

"I said, 'No.'

"Then he said, 'Throw away the damn pills!' and he made a gesture like he was throwing them away."

Only after Cameron had made the guess that she was not an epileptic and got her to stop demanding her pills did he send her to Dr. Lloyd Smith at the MNI for a thorough neurological exam. Smith found certain small seizure patterns in Karralynn's brain and recommended that she should have her medication, but Cameron said no to him, too. Karralynn has never had a seizure in the twenty-five years since Cameron took her in hand. He performed a faith healing, told her to throw away her crutches and walk. "The damnedest thing," says Karralynn, "is that you do."

After that, when the nurses came to tell her that the next morning she would be starting psychic driving, Karralynn had no qualms and fewer questions. They gave her earphones and her negative tape (all about how she had no confidence in herself, was weak and inadequate) and told her to lie down on her bed to listen. She fell asleep. She consistently fell asleep. Dr. Cameron got very angry (his standard question—"Don't you want to get well?") and ordered driving injections for her. To Karralynn, the sodium amytal and desoxyn injections felt wonderful; three times a week she'd get the drugs and her tape and would write and listen and listen and write for two hours or so, pretty well as long as she wanted to listen. She worried that she liked the drugs too much, and that they might be addictive. Cameron said, "I know you—you're not the kind to get addicted to anything. Don't worry." So she didn't worry.

Karralynn's progress was not steady. In November 1962 she was released into the day-hospital program; she went home for Christmas and when she came back suffered a relapse that caused Dr. Cameron to admit her to hospital again. A psychologist's report at about that time described Karralynn as having a "schizophrenic character operating at a highly obsessional level" and stated that "prognosis was poor". Cameron was convinced that she was an anxiety hysteric, not a schizophrenic, and that she was treatable; from January to May 1963 he kept her exclusively under his care. The female voice on her positive driving tape upset Karralynn; her nurses rushed to inform her, awe in their voices, that her tape had been changed and Dr. Cameron himself was reading it. When he released her once again into the day-hospital program, Karralynn told him that she had to go home—her insurance would only cover stays as an in-patient. Cameron began treating her free of charge.

She was somewhat of a patient prodigy—young and articulate, despite the truncation of her schooling. There was no doubt that she was dependent on her doctor. "He infused you with part of himself, something special you could use until you could use your own resources," Karralynn says. For years after her stay at the Allan, when she started feeling low, she would remember his confidence in her. "I still had a poor self-image, and I'd begin thinking, 'You're worthless and ugly and so on,' and only stop myself when I thought, 'That's not right. Dr. Cameron thinks you're a very worthwhile person.' " But she was also struggling to be independent, to come into partnership with him. As much as she was drawn to depend on him she fought to stay emotionally free. As healer and patient they suited each other: "Dr. Cameron gave you genuine caring if you needed it," says Karralynn, "but he didn't want you to cling."

Psychic driving worked for Karralynn, in the context of an excellent relationship with Cameron, because it actually made her feel in control of a part of her healing. An excerpt Cameron published of her driving diary is full of the first person singular: "Each time I reveal something particularly painful, it is like lancing a boil. I feel a sense of relief for days afterward. Each time I uncover or admit to something I had previously been consciously unaware of, I feel myself become stronger, more able to cope. Weller! God, it's a good feeling!"

Cameron was an eager participant in her drive to become stronger. A note from him that survives from the tail end of her therapy praises her determination "to try and break out of the business of being a pt. The very fact that you can stand back and see how much you have tended to slip into the rut of being what you call 'an interesting psychiatric patient' means that this phase is coming to an end. I want you to go on trying to think of yourself not as a patient, but as a woman; a woman with a history and a woman with a future."

In the note he also advises her to think twice about clinging: "With regard to your feelings about me, these still are as neurotic as all get out. When you say 'If I cannot crawl back to you with my tail thumping for a few kind words and a scratch behind the ears, then why bother making the effort at all,' I feel like giving that dog a resounding kick that distance below the tail which would do the most good. There should be a relationship and I am sure there will be a relationship between you and me, but it should be a relationship of two people who have tried to do something together and have acquired a great deal of satisfaction [from] the success of their mutual achievement."

When it came to the end of things it was Karralynn, not Cameron, who broke the relationship off. In the summer of 1964, he told her that he would be moving to Albany and offered to help her find a job there so that she could keep seeing him, but she refused. Instead, she left the safety net behind and moved to Liverpool with her parents. She and Cameron exchanged a few letters over her future plans and how she was liking England: "Please tell me more about that high school equivalent when you write next," Cameron asked. "I am very anxious that you should get it if possible." The letter ends, "I do hope that you won't go on feeling frightened—if you do it will be a sad reflection on my extrasensory powers—I think of you very often, and in the nicest possible way! Are you sure you aren't feeling a little something. With very best wishes, yours sincerely, D.E. Cameron."

Karralynn can't remember if she replied to that letter, just that she soon stopped writing and that when she stopped so did he.

The cure they achieved together, however, was lasting. Karralynn went to work, and married, and then at the age of thirty-nine entered college in Connecticut, without benefit of a high school equivalent, and graduated a BA *summa cum laude* in 1983. At present she is working on a master's in psychology; her aim is to become a therapist in order to repay a little of what she thinks is owing to Ewen Cameron: "I want to treat people who can't afford to pay." Just as Dr. Cameron treated her.

The trouble with a recovery like Karralynn's was that there was no science in it. It didn't prove that psychic driving worked, only that the patient-therapist relationship had worked. Its first act had been a faith healing; its last, a parental letting go of a newly mature child. It had been good doctoring, but the process of good doctoring, or healing, wasn't enough for Cameron. In some unpublished reflections on his leadership of the Allan he wrote, "If [a leader] keeps his eyes fixed on the running tide of events, he will see that the public demands advance and hence he will not let himself fall into the trap of seeking only the immediate gains of clinical work and by gains, I do not mean only financial, but the approbation, the praise and gratitude of no doubt properly admiring patients. If he does so, he may become a good doctor but he will not be a leader in his field."

Having tossed out at long last the overpowering element of force in psychic driving, Cameron's struggle in his last years was to find the value in it. Instead of using brainwashing as the metaphor, he began to imagine an automated but patient-driven form of therapy. In a note titled "Forward Looking" he proposed a sophisticated thought detector: "Can we make the automation of psychotherapy self-regulating?…could we hook up the recorder with an index of special importance to the patient, for instance, blood pressure, muscle tonus, or the EEG…. If we do this, then we could automatically keep the patient on a particular topic to which he was continuing to show an emotional response. We could think of various ways of modifying this, whereby he was moved off a hot area, and onto a neutral area, and then…brought back to the hot area again, all automatically."

After a long and fruitless digression Cameron had come back to his starting point—that the impact of repetition lay in the firestorm of insight it sometimes set up in the patient. So he started to tackle the problem the other way around. Could he invent a mechanism to replace the therapist's therapeutic listening—some sort of intuition machine? Was psychotherapy so delicate and complex it defied automation?

But the last paper he published on the subject was in 1964, and thereafter Cameron's efforts were largely rhetorical. In the speech where he confessed to the wrong turning, he also had to say: "We are still far away from being able to set up the truly compelling patterns of behavior which sometimes occur naturally as, for instance, in the sexual patterns of behavior, nor can we set up patterns with anything like the durability that one finds in some habits or in imprinting in animals, but we have made a beginning." He may have continued to speak optimistically, but by abandoning the field he showed that he did not think that a beginning was good enough.

Though Cameron continued to recommend patients for it, he was also beginning to experience diminished expectations for depatterning. Psychiatrists in the early 1960s thought that they'd at last got ECT slotted into its proper empirical place as a treatment for depression and depression alone. Injections of muscle relaxants had reduced the ugly aspect of total body convulsions to a twitching of eyelids; when the treatment was used in moderation, the troubling confusion and amnesia could be minimized. The new weapons against psychosis were the prescription pad and the neuroleptic drugs; to suppress psychotic symptoms with a shock machine seemed increasingly barbarous. Depatterning, wrote Dr. Bob Cleghorn in his memoirs of those days, was "therapy gone wild with scant criteria".

It was not something, however, on which anyone wanted directly to confront the Chief, or even felt there were grounds to do so. In 1962, Cleghorn was left in charge of South 2 while Cameron was on a tour of Japan; though Cameron had been depatterning patients since 1953, it was Cleghorn's first "intimate contact" with the treatment's effects. "I was early struck by the zombie-like, repetitious, brief greeting given me daily by a girl known to me as a former classmate of my elder daughter," he wrote. "I can't say I was emotionally distraught nor did I develop a fanatical opposition to the goings-on I had inherited on a short term basis." His wartime research on wound shock on the battlefields of Italy "doubtless left me armoured against an immediate affective reaction". To mount an effective challenge, Cleghorn felt, he had to examine the literature thoroughly and try to knock the pegs out from under the treatment on a scientific basis. Though the treatment did bother him, he did not feel driven to take the assignment on.

In the end it was Cameron who started the proceedings that ended in the demise of depatterning at the Allan, by appointing Cleghorn as chair of a committee to oversee and rule on the cases of all patients recommended for the treatment. Several doctors at the Allan had tried depatterning with patients they viewed as otherwise intractable: Dr. Lloyd Hisey, Dr. Carlo Bos, Dr. Jacques Beaubien, and Dr. Peter Roper. Hisey, Bos, and Beaubien used it rarely; Roper vied with the Chief himself for the numbers of patients committed to the treatment. Cameron, who had once hoped that depatterning would become the treatment of choice for paranoid schizophrenics, had hired Dr. Roper against the advice of the only other staff member who had interviewed him and had taken a decided shine to the personable young British psychiatrist. But he was worried enough about Roper's use of depatterning to ask a formal body to second-guess his clinical judgement, which meant that they also had to second-guess Cameron's own. Wrote Cleghorn: "When my committee met we dealt with each patient recommended for regressive ECT and found that we could not agree that many such cases fell under the rubric of schizophrenia, which was allegedly the diagnosis qualifying the subject for such treatment.... Hence we cut the cases for ECT drastically." Soon Cleghorn was put in a position where he could stop the practice altogether.

In April 1964, Ewen Cameron stunned his staff by resigning three years before he reached McGill's mandatory retirement age of sixty-five. To everyone else in the world, even men who had also invested up to twenty years in the Allan, Cameron *was* the institute; they could not think of the place without him. To this day, they speculate as to why he left so suddenly, with so little fanfare, as if he had to cut them and the institute he founded out of his life. The simplest answer is that he had a great reluctance to retire from anything; if something was over he wanted to be out the door and onto something new.

He also had an offer he couldn't refuse. The medical school at Albany together with the U.S. Veterans Administration had offered him both a position and a laboratory he didn't have to abandon at sixty-five. It was a chance to keep working in an area where he still had some hope of making a big breakthrough, the effect of RNA on memory deficits in the aged—a well-funded stab at licking at least one of the debilitations of the ageing process he considered so tragic. His son Duncan says that Albany also applied some pressure; if Ewen Cameron wanted the opportunity he had better leave the Allan and take it or the money would go elsewhere.

But, as far as the ever-striving Cameron was concerned, there was not much left to detain him in Montreal. He had pulled the last rabbit out of the hat in 1964 with the opening of the McGill Research Building. He had the space at last to house the world-class psychiatric researchers who had for two decades camped out in any spare cupboard or stray inch of hallway. But his influence on the psychiatric scene was waning. In 1961, the province of Quebec had established a psychiatric division in the Ministry of Health that annexed back to the province the grant-application process that Cameron had for so long overseen. The Quebec government had then made a strong pitch that the research building be shared by McGill and two French-language institutions, Laval University and the University of Montreal. Cameron successfully fought off what he considered an unwarranted encroachment.

But he couldn't deny that the Allan had always had a disproportion-ate share of government research funding and that French researchers were now in a good position to compete for and win those funds. He did not exactly win political favour in a changed situation when he excluded the French from the new facility; the French-speaking med-ical community boycotted the building's opening ceremony. As for

Cameron's attitude towards the French—the dedicated anti-nationalist became almost a Francophobe. More than one of his contemporaries remember his state of near panic over the rise of separatism in Quebec. Says Charles Roberts, the ex-federal bureaucrat, "He was so anxious about the Quebec thing. He had almost irrational fears. He'd say make the river the boundary...we'll hold the south side. But Cameron was not naive. He knew English research was receiving disproportionate amounts both in federal and provincial funds. But the heyday of health expansionism was over. Since then we hold our own and that's about it."

Holding his own was not Cameron's style. Neither was the possibility of betraying in public any feelings he held for the AMI or its staff. Bill Stauble was assistant to the director in his last months there. He remembers Cameron telling him that he had just been to a retirement dinner where the retiree had actually cried. He swore to Stauble, "Doc, they're not going to do that to me!"

Cameron announced his resignation at a regular Thursday staff meeting. He allowed no holding of fêtes. The one gesture his staff made towards the Chief—commissioning a portrait from a respected local painter—did not come off. Cameron was suffering from not only his usual hyperactivity but also a case of the boils while he was supposed to be sitting, and the artist did not catch a likeness in any way pleasing to either Cameron or his family. On August 31, 1964, Cameron left the Allan for Albany, leaving in his wake not so much an institution in mourning as one in a vacuum.

McGill's principal, Dr. Rocke Robertson, drafted Dr. Bob Cleghorn to try to fill it. A respected basic scientist who had come late to psychiatry, Cleghorn found himself for the six years of his own tenure as the director of the AMI in a constant, wearying state of opposing, rectifying, rearranging, having to live with—or try to exorcise—the shade of Ewen Cameron. Little things hurt; when he took over the reins Cleghorn found that Cameron had neglected to enter staff into the McGill pension scheme, including himself. (Which meant that in his eighties Cleghorn still saw patients out of financial necessity as well as interest.) Large things were boggling; Cleghorn had to rationalize

Cameron's wing-and-a-prayer form of institutional financing in an era when dollars were much harder to come by. He also had to deal with a bitter aftermath of staff wrangles and lawsuits.

One of Cleghorn's first edicts was that no patient should be subject to more than six ECTs in any two-week period, part of a strategy to discourage depatterning. But a remnant of Cameron's interventionary zeal lived on at the Allan in the person of Peter Roper. Cleghorn assigned the head psychologist, Dr. Alec Schwartzman, and a new psychiatric resident, Dr. Paul Termansen, the task of scientifically evaluating depatterning as a treatment. They tracked down sixty-nine former patients and, on the basis of interviews and psychological tests, reported that depatterning seemed no more effective than any other treatment of the day. They also noted that it was far more difficult to administer and seemed to have caused (here they trod carefully) amnesias in the patients stretching from six months to ten years into their lives before treatment. Report in hand, on November 10, 1965, Cleghorn banned depatterning. (Encountering Cameron at a professional meeting a few months later, Cleghorn remembers Cameron telling him, "I thought you would discontinue that method.")

Peter Roper proved impossible to convince. He continued to schedule patients for what he called "intensive ECT" against Cleghorn's orders. Roper wrote three memos in quick succession arguing against the ban, and on December 17, 1965, appealed to the Royal Victoria Hospital's medical board to referee. The board, not surprisingly, supported Dr. Cleghorn.

Roper continued to depattern his patients. For another six months Cleghorn continued to intervene case by case. Cleghorn has said his breaking point was finally reached in June 1966 when, while talking to a man who had had numerous ECTs on Roper's orders, Cleghorn realized that the man believed that they were not in the Allan Memorial at all, but in Belfast, Ireland, and that Dr. Cleghorn was an officer he had met in the Second World War. On August 15, Cleghorn informed Roper by letter that his annual appointment would not be renewed the next January. Roper asked for a hearing in front of the hospital medical board, and before the hearing the two men got embroiled over yet another patient.

The board ruled against Roper. In November so did the full board of governors of the hospital. In January 1967, Roper sued for wrongful dismissal and stuck with the suit all the way to an appeal at the Quebec superior court level, where he finally lost. The Roper suit opened the first major crack in Cameron's reputation. On trial was not merely Dr. Cleghorn's right to dismiss a disobedient employee but, implicitly, Cameron's depatterning treatment.*

The Roper suit was also the impetus that finally won Mary Morrow the chance to take her suit to court. Lawyers and potential witnesses began to consider it possible that something terrible might have happened to her.

Cameron died in 1967; for the twenty years since his death, his methods and character have been subjected steadily to the scrutiny of the legal process in Quebec and now in Washington. It's a black-and-white adversarial world that has a hard time coming to grips with a character such as Cameron. Dr. Cleghorn himself, in the Roper case, testified to the barbarity of depatterning; in the Morrow case, he was on the other side of the suit and testified that depatterning was a legitimate psychiatric treatment of the time. In the new cases brought by former

---

* Peter Roper, who presently has a private practice in Montreal and works at the Douglas Hospital as a psychiatrist attached to the behavioural conditioning team, to this day does not understand why he was fired over depatterning. "Why did Cleghorn have such strong leverage with the hospital to get rid of me? I knew he said I disobeyed him and eventually we found out that the depatterning was the reason. But why was that so important to the hospital? He accused me of doing something that was a psychiatric treatment of the time— why did that give him leverage? Then a lot of us wondered why Cameron left, why all the treatments were stopped, really without cause." As far as Roper is concerned depatterning was a thoroughly respectable and useful treatment of schizophrenia wrenched out of his hands by outside forces. When news of the CIA's involvement in funding Cameron's research came out, Roper felt compelled to travel to Washington to look at the released MKULTRA files to see if his name came up or if anything in them might explain to Roper's satisfaction Cameron's quick exit from the Allan. He found nothing elucidating in Washington.

patients of Cameron's against the CIA, where Cameron's reputation and memory are ultimately on trial, Cleghorn is torn in many directions. An attack on Cameron is an attack on McGill and the Allan and the Royal Victoria, all of which Cleghorn served for thirty years of his life. The distortions the process causes in the picture of Cameron (uncaring monster in the pay of a secret agency) strike him as absurd. In the abstract he has not much sympathy for the plaintiffs, yet he proposes some sort of judgement-free medical misfortune insurance that would compensate them for their pain.

One word comes to Bob Cleghorn's mind as he contemplates Ewen Cameron, and he intends all the classical and tragical implications. Hubris. In one of his unpublished papers he defines it: "If I were forced to name a single significant twisted bit of thinking, other than outright cheating, I would have to say a blind desire to make a discovery is the chief element. This is hubris and is accompanied by a failure to assess evidence and finally by a delusional belief in the set of assumptions erected to support, justify or explain the developed hypothesis."

If one word had to be chosen as a comment on the career of Ewen Cameron, Cleghorn is right. Hubris is the one.

CHAPTER TWELVE

Fall from the Pedestal

Wayne Lang, at age forty-two the oldest of Flo Langleben's three children, believed that there was nothing left on earth that could transform his relationship with his mother. From the earliest days of his Montreal childhood he spent as much time as he could as far away from her as he could get. His father, Moe Langleben, worked as a designer for the garment firm Auckiesanft. It made high-quality if not high-fashion ladies' coats and suits; he liked to mention that he had fitted and suited two prime ministers' wives, Mrs. Lester B. Pearson and Mrs. John Diefenbaker.

Moe was gone from 7:15 in the morning until after 6:00 at night. His wife would save up all the bad things the kids had done and recount them as he walked in the door. Moe would then mete out the punishments. He never asked if what she said was true, and his kids came to think of him as their mother's hit man. A lot of mothers in the forties and fifties handled discipline that way, but most of them, as far as Wayne could see, were not like Flo Langleben: "Other mothers would always be hugging and kissing. Ours wasn't. Mother was never a warm person. She was always nervous and had a real short fuse. The three of us—we suffered."

Wayne didn't really understand it at the time, but his mother had no more desire to be stuck in the home she had created than he had. Flo, who shortened her maiden name, Levitsky, to Levitt, was a frustrated singer originally from Winnipeg. She had passed through Toronto in the 1930s and proved good enough to make broadcasts on CBC radio. How Moe met and married her is beyond Wayne—perhaps beyond Moe, too, for as a wife Flo left a lot to be desired. She ignored dirty dishes in the sink, didn't make the beds, and after she had a hysterectomy in 1952 began to suffer great monthly cycles of depression in which she would stay in bed for weeks, lying so still, Wayne remembers, it was as if she were dead.

Then came the mental hospitals. In 1955 she spent four weeks in the Mayfair Hospital, a private place on MacGregor Street in Montreal. She received ten or so electro-shocks and chlorpromazine, which gave her jaundice. In 1957 she was admitted to the Allan suffering from depression, anxiety attacks, and loss of weight. The resident doctors, under Cameron's direction, tried using LSD as an abreactant agent. According to a note on her chart she did not take to it: "Under [injections of 100 mgs of LSD and 20 mgs of desoxyn], the pt. rapidly began to develop marked somatic symptoms, among them numbness of the hands and feet with a pin and needle sensation later. She became panicky and complained after she went home and her family called about her condition. She was most manipulative about it, and accused the hospital of mistreating her. Her diagnosis was, on the discharge, of a severe character neurosis, very hostile individual."

Two years later, in August 1959, she was readmitted, suffering from anxiety attacks and radiating pains in her chest; she had lost twenty pounds in a few months simply because she wasn't able to eat. She said she was impatient with—could hardly tolerate—her children, unable to do her housework, that she "never felt really well". She was obsessed with illnesses among her own siblings and the recent death of her sister-in-law, Rose. On the second admission she seemed to Dr. Cameron the kind of chronic psychoneurotic patient best suited for psychic driving, though so resistant to treatment he depatterned her first. In a discharge letter addressed to her general physician, Dr. David Barza, Cameron described the treatment and its apparent effect:

> It was decided to put her on driving, and this was started on September 22nd, the patient being depatterned.... She has had 15 ECT. By November 6th she has had 43 days of sleep, the last being on November 5th, 32 days of negative driving, 32 days of galvanic stimulation [in which Cameron had a shock applied to her leg with each repetition in an effort to reinforce the driving cue] and 11 days of positive driving. She had accepted the positive driving very eagerly ultimately, although at first showing some hostility and criticism towards it too.
>
> By November 14th, 1959, she was transferred to the Day Hospital and started going home in the evenings. By November 20th she was very much improved, cheerful, friendly and quite a different person to what she had been.

That's not how Wayne Lang, who was seventeen at the time, would describe the difference. However badly she had done it, and however often she had taken to her bed, before the second stay at the Allan his mother had definitely run the Langlebens' unhappy household. The family had never known exactly what happened to her in hospital and tended not to believe anything Flo said about it, but realized that after she came out she was simply incapable of any kind of work. From then on she suffered almost perpetual insomnia, she was always anxious, she had chronic back pain, and with the least bit of upset she lost her voice—was unable to speak—for weeks and months at a stretch. Unable to speak and, of course, unable to sing. Her voice, which Wayne remembers as the one beautiful thing about his mother, was gone.

She became the bane of the family, to be trivialized and pacified. Moe, especially by his own sisters, came to be treated like a long-suffering saint for putting up with Flo over the years. She tried suicide several times and came pretty close once in Florida, where the family moved after Moe retired. He came home one afternoon around 3:30 to find her sleeping on her back on the floor and assumed she was doing it, as she often did, to ease the pain. He turned on the TV and fell asleep himself, waking up hungry some three hours later to find her still lying in the same position on the floor. Moe called Wayne's wife, Carol, who got the ambulance there in time—Carol assumed immediately that it was an overdose. "When she was finally able to talk did she ever give me a rough time," said Carol. "I told her next time she should call me first so I'll know not to rescue her."

Wayne, who was running an import-export business into Central America, had enough to keep him busy and away as much as possible from his mother. He admits he left the burden for the most part in the capable hands of his own wife. "I don't recall having a serious conversation with my mother for twenty-five years...just small talk and nonsense. I thought she was nuts, I thought she was faking. How can a person be speaking to you one day, and the next not be able to talk for four months at a stretch.... I used to think she would lose her voice so she could punish us, get us to kowtow to her—she was always that way.

"Then in 1982 I saw a big article in the paper that these people were suing the CIA. It was in the Montreal papers, too, and my aunts and uncles saw it. My uncle got in touch with David Orlikow, who said that the dates sounded right and that we should get my mother's records from the hospital." The family had soon contacted Orlikow's Washington lawyer, Joseph L. Rauh, Jr., who—after checking that Flo Langleben's hospitalization and treatment fit the time frame in which the CIA had been funding Cameron's work—agreed to add her to his roster of plaintiffs.

The CIA revelations caused a small revolution of guilt and anger within the family. "My father's sisters were guilty because they had always taken his side," says Wayne. "My father felt that he had been made a fool of by Cameron, and on top of everything had had to pay, too, for my mother's treatment." Wayne remembered all the times she had told him that she hated Cameron and had tried to hide from him, and how she had been afraid of the ECT. Flo Langleben felt a rare sense of vindication. She also found the right phrase to drive it deep into her family's conscience: "You thought it was always me to blame."

At first, David Orlikow had resisted the idea of pursuing anything so bold, so international in scope, as suing the Central Intelligence Agency for what had happened to his wife. He thought it made sense to approach the CIA to see if Val was actually one of the MKULTRA subjects; frankly, Val wouldn't rest until she found out. Within a month of the August 1977 *New York Times* story in which he'd first read about the covert funding, Orlikow had written to the CIA asking for information.

The director, Admiral Stansfield Turner, had just assured the U.S. Congress that the CIA intended to identify and contact MKULTRA's unwitting victims, and try to figure out "how to go about fulfilling the government's responsibilities in the matter". It was fair to assume that any responsibility extended to those affected in Canada, too. Orlikow was in favour of compensation; the financial scars left by his wife's illness were deep. The CIA's information and privacy co-ordinator wrote back to say that there were no names of unwitting subjects in the files so far discovered, but that, yes, the CIA was committed to tracking people down. By February 1978, David and Val Orlikow had become convinced that she qualified as one of the subjects and had engaged an Ottawa lawyer, James O'Grady, to try to coax a voluntary compensatory payment out of the agency. By June, David and Val had even decided on how much—"something in the area of $25,000", as O'Grady wrote to the agency's assistant general counsel, A.R. Cinquegrana.

The Orlikows thought the claim wouldn't seem like much to a bureaucracy the size of the CIA. Talking with Jay Peterzell, a Washington-based researcher then at work with John Marks on *The Search for the "Manchurian Candidate"*, David Orlikow wondered whether the CIA might give his wife the settlement in exchange for her silence. It was as if he had not yet been able entirely to adjust his attitude to Ewen Cameron. He found it hard, thinking back on his wife's illness, to find a clear-cut progression from bad to worse. To Peterzell he said, "I can't say that Cameron did make her worse. He certainly didn't help her, but...."

Any of David's hesitations were slowly worn away by the still considerable force of Val Orlikow's will—and the indications in letters coming from the CIA that it was ready to talk publicly about the necessity of tracking down victims, but it would also exercise the right to define those victims.

In fact, a bit of a battle was going on within the agency as to whether Cameron's work, sub-project 68 of MKULTRA, even fell into the category that had produced victims. A strong memo written by William J. Allard of the general counsel's office on October 31, 1978, laid the dispute to momentary rest:

> Although the overall project appears to have been initiated at McGill University prior to any involvement by this Agency, the substantial funds flowing from this Agency appear to preclude the determination that this Agency was minimally involved.... The use of the drugs identified and "particularly intensive electroshock" as part of the methodology suggest that long-term after-effects may have been involved. Also because the patients selected "were almost entirely those suffering from extremely long-term and intractable psychoneurotic conditions" [the quotes are from Cameron's grant application to the society] it is doubtful that any meaningful form of consent is involved in this case.
>
> It is recommended that this sub-project be set down as one in which further contact with the institution involved be initiated with the goal of identifying the subjects of the described research.

The subject who was clamouring on the doorstep was another matter. On February 5, 1979, Cinquegrana wrote (he hoped) a final letter to O'Grady on the Orlikow claim: "according to Agency records CIA was not involved in the support of this research program until after Mrs. Orlikow had ended her first stay at the Allan Memorial Institute and CIA terminated its support before she reentered the institute. Consequently, it appears at this time that Mrs. Orlikow was not involved as a subject by this Agency and CIA was not responsible for the treatment provided to her." The letter ended on a note of benevolent good wishes that sounded more like a dig: "I trust it will alleviate Mrs. Orlikow's concerns," Cinquegrana wrote, "to learn that she was not subjected to this treatment as a result of support furnished by this Agency."

The Orlikows found the reasoning specious, arguing that a penumbra effect on Cameron's research extended from the exact dates that money flowed from the SIHE to McGill. O'Grady wrote back that the Orlikows continued to assert their claim. On that front, passive assertion seemed their only choice.

But Val was determined that someone was going to say he was sorry for what had happened to her. She and David knew a Montreal lawyer named Phil Cutler. For $3,000 up front he said he would bring a suit not against the CIA but against the hospital that had paid Ewen Cameron's salary. In April 1979, Val Orlikow brought suit against the Royal Victoria Hospital, "declaring Defendant condemned for illegal, covert, inhuman experiments to which Plaintiff was submitted, all entirely devoid of any medical or other beneficial purpose and only for the purpose of reporting to the Society to Investigate Human Ecology [sic] and the United States Central Intelligence Agency". The literal defendant may have been the Royal Victoria Hospital, but it was clear that the person Val Orlikow wanted judged was Dr. D. Ewen Cameron, who had then been dead for a dozen years.

It still sat badly with the Orlikows that the CIA should get off the hook—they hadn't heard of a single "unwitting victim" the agency had actually traced and compensated. Telling the story to a friend one day, Orlikow wondered whether he shouldn't get a Washington-based lawyer, who would be on the spot and could push the CIA harder. He had a wild thought. Why didn't he try to get in touch with Joe Rauh? Here was a man who had been one of the key Washington lobbyists for civil rights, who had represented Lillian Hellman in front of the House Un-American Activities Committee, who had won an appeal for Arthur Miller, throwing out contempt-of-Congress charges resulting from Miller's refusing to name names for Joe McCarthy, who had taken major cases against big unions in which dead bodies figured and had emerged with victories that made union democracy stronger. His friend encouraged him—surely Joe Rauh wouldn't hesitate to take on the CIA.

David Orlikow called Joe Rauh on July 12, 1979, and to his complete surprise Rauh was willing. And as the lawyer eventually offered to take the case on a 100 per cent contingency basis (which meant that his expenses and fee would come out of the achieved settlement), David Orlikow could even afford to hire him.

Whether Joe Rauh ever came to rue the day is hard to tell; the word "rue" doesn't figure prominently in the vocabulary of a man who has made a five-decade-long career in Washington out of championing underdog and impossible causes. He had taken the suit for two reasons, stated in order of importance by his young law partner, Jim Turner: "One, to help the plaintiffs, and two, because we're a public-interest law firm and the law is the only check on a secret agency in a democratic society."

Rauh and Turner were to find, as the CIA regained and surpassed its former power in Washington under Ronald Reagan's approving eye, that the law was an unwieldy, slow-moving, and ineffectual check. They were to find that the CIA was as adept at revisionism as any Communist ideologue, entirely able to forget as the case wore on that it had ever vowed to make amends for the damage caused by MKULTRA.

William Casey, an old cold-war warrior with a long CIA background, was the only director of the CIA to act as a senior policy adviser to a U.S. president and to attend Cabinet meetings regularly. Joe Rauh, who had been through the cold war of the 1950s, watched almost disbelieving as, in the Washington of the 1980s, U.S. district attorneys defending the suit forgot that there was or should be a difference between the interests of the U.S. government and the interests of the CIA. Rauh's case, which dragged on and on, drawing in eight more plaintiffs and eventually the diplomats and bureaucrats of two governments, was like a litmus-paper test of the CIA's reborn influence.

Rauh took up correspondence with the CIA where the Orlikow's Canadian lawyer left off. He did not intend to push the matter to a trial. The age and variable financial and physical conditions of his plaintiffs (who, within months of his accepting the case, numbered five) made out-of-court settlement the sensible route. On October 11, 1979, CIA general counsel Daniel B. Silver wrote to Rauh: "While I would share your sense of dismay and regret if there was any certainty as to the facts, I do not find basis for any degree of certainty that the harm reportedly suffered by Mrs. Orlikow would not have occurred but for the funding or other actions taken by this Agency." He closed, "I trust that you will understand this letter is not in any way intended as a defense of Dr. Cameron's activities, which I personally find repugnant, nor do I wish to convey any lack of sympathy for Mrs. Orlikow. It is not possible, however, on the basis of the meager information available to conclude this Agency is responsible for Mrs. Orlikow's treatment at Dr. Cameron's hands."

The seeds of the CIA's defence were clear—nobody but Dr. Ewen Cameron was responsible for what had happened to people like Val Orlikow. But Rauh still found Silver's letter legally promising. Though he strongly argued for the penumbra effect on Val Orlikow's case, three of his four other plaintiffs had received the entire battery of Cameron's treatments while the CIA was funding the work:

> Jean Charles Pagé, who lived on a disability pension in a tiny house an hour's drive west of Montreal, was treated for alcoholism at the Allan from July to November 1959. He received four Page-Russell ECTs, thirty-six days of sleep, three days of semi-sleep, and thirty days of driving. Within a year Pagé ended up in St-Jean de Dieu asylum. He was the ex-inmate of St-Jean de Dieu who wrote the best-selling exposé of asylum conditions that sparked the Bédard commission.

> Robert Logie had been eighteen years old when first admitted to the Allan in 1957, on referral from a local hospital for aches in his joints and fits of trembling that his doctors presumed were psychosomatic. Psychiatric treatment, which included LSD, didn't help and Logie ended up back in the Allan in December 1958. He was given LSD again, and also depatterned and treated with psychic driving. A note by Cameron in Logie's chart read, "In retrospect we are inclined to think that Mr. Logie did have some kind of arthritic condition and that his joint pains

reached a fair degree of severity. Mr. Logie was given an injection of hydrocortisone to which the pains yielded." Logie had left the Allan after his second stay afraid of what might happen if he ever gave way to sleep again; twenty years later he still had insomnia, an inability to concentrate, and bad nerves. He was unemployed and living in Vancouver under the care of psychiatrist Paul Termansen, who had once carefully criticized depatterning in a joint report for Dr. Cleghorn. After treating Logie, he was not so careful, likening Cameron's human experiments to those of the Nazi doctors.

Lyvia Stadler, a Hungarian-born milliner who lost her first husband to a labour camp in the Second World War and emigrated to Canada with her second husband in 1952, began to go to Cameron for recurring depression in 1954. She was a patient on and off at the Allan from then until 1964. Confined to a nursing home in Montreal and suffering from a memory loss that covered that entire decade, she could not remember any details of her treatment. Her Allan Memorial records showed that she had been depatterned and had received large amounts of drugs and long periods of psychic driving.

Jeanine Huard, a Montreal housewife, had never been depatterned *per se*, but she had received many individual Page-Russell ECTs as both an out-patient and an in-patient of Cameron's from 1958 to 1962. She had also received intensive psychic driving and had been "immobilized in the area of repetition" with curare, among other things. Several experimental drugs had been prescribed for her (still identified only by numbers); and she had been treated with neuroleptics to the point that she had suffered extended periods of involuntary trembling. She had originally gone to see Dr. Cameron in 1951 for anxiety, weight loss, and a feeling of overpowering weakness, on referral from the public clinic at the Royal Victoria Hospital; she had just been treated for anaemia resulting from heavy menstrual bleeding due to endometriosis. Her subsequent child-bearing and gynaecological history reads like a female trip to hell: two of her four children suffered life-threatening illnesses and long hospitalizations shortly after birth; her monthly periods were so heavy she was eventually treated with blood transfusions and finally a hysterectomy. Cameron treated her for depression and psychosomatic tendencies ("Don't you want to get well, Jeanine?")

As each new plaintiff came to Rauh, some after reading about the Orlikows in their local papers, some after seeing John Marks on TV publicizing his book, Rauh presented their claim to Silver, asking for a settlement of $1 million apiece. When it finally came time for a face-to-face bargaining session between himself and the CIA, Rauh told Silver that the $1 million was a formality—he'd settle for $250,000 each. Silver, in the face of an escalating number of plaintiffs, had a one-word answer for Rauh, only he said it twice: no to the settlement; no to any negotiation whatsoever. He informed Rauh that as far as the CIA was concerned it bore no liability for any action of Ewen Cameron's. Since there was so far no evidence to the contrary, the CIA was assuming that the society had not actively recruited Cameron, but that he had gone to it soliciting funds.

That distinction was a slim one. The CIA had subsidized at least three and a half years of Cameron's experimental work, and Rauh's standard analogy was that a man who pays a hit man can't escape the charge of murder just because the crime was the gunman's idea. He filed a formal complaint against the United States of America in December 1980, asking for $1 million per plaintiff. His grounds were three: that the CIA had allowed the funding of experiments on humans to go ahead under the supervision of employees, such as Sidney Gottlieb and Robert Lashbrook, who had already caused the death of an unwitting subject in such experiments, namely Frank Olson (the army scientist who died of a fall from a hotel window shortly after being dosed with LSD). Secondly, those CIA employees did not exercise due care in overseeing projects involving dangerous human experimentation and did not insist the projects conform to already established ethical standards. Thirdly, the United States was responsible for knowingly funding an experimental program that violated those established standards. Clear negligence and clear liability: Rauh believed he could convince a judge that a tort had been committed. The CIA consistently tried to focus his attention on Cameron; he kept his eye firmly on the people who fostered the entire MKULTRA program.

The next phase in a lawsuit is the discovery and deposition process, in which major witnesses are examined under oath and lawyers attempt to collect all the documentary evidence in the case. The CIA effectively blocked that by immediately filing a motion to dismiss, on several grounds including that the United States could not be sued in its own courts by foreign citizens. U.S. District Court Judge John Garrett Penn had to rule on the motion. It took him until May 27, 1982, to make up his mind; he decided in the end that the suit could go forward. During the hiatus, Colonel James Monroe died; he had been the most crucial witness to the relationship between the SIHE and Ewen Cameron. As far as Joe Rauh was concerned the CIA had neatly prevented him from getting to Monroe as the opening salvo in a deliberate war of attrition against himself, his aged plaintiffs, and his case.

Rauh, who had just edged over seventy himself, soon assigned the newest member of the firm, twenty-six-year-old Jim Turner, to do the leg-work. Neat, fair-headed, and undemonstrative—but nearly as passionate as Rauh—Turner had fled the tedium of a job he had taken with the Interstate Commerce Commission out of law school. (He found dealing with disputes about which truck shipped what grapes where, even at the appellate level, "a dismal way to make a living".) He joined Rauh's firm in the winter of 1980. It turned out that after his undergraduate degree Turner had spent the summer working for the Church Committee, which had mounted an official attempt to get to the bottom of the CIA's mind-control experiments in 1975-76. Turner had seen most of the principal witnesses necessary for the Orlikow suit testify in front of Congress, and he'd watched men like Gottlieb elude probing questions because no one had yet discovered the surviving MKULTRA records. He did not mind at all having the chance to try to make Sid Gottlieb and the CIA accountable.

Though the case itself was still in limbo, potential plaintiffs continued to get in touch with Rauh in droves. In 1981, the Royal Victoria Hospital had settled with the Orlikows out of court for roughly $50,000 and costs. Since such a settlement did not establish blame, it did not set a legal precedent. The publicity was enough to see a reprise of the Orlikow story played out in the media, and another flood of letters from ex-AMI patients and their relatives to both the Orlikows and their Washington lawyers.

Among them were Mary Morrow and Flo Langleben, who were accepted as plaintiffs against the CIA. In the next two years Rauh added two more, to bring the total to the final nine. Rita Zimmerman, also from Montreal, had been under treatment by Dr. Cameron for anxiety attacks and alcoholism intermittently from 1946 to 1960. In 1959, she was put into sensory deprivation for thirty-five days, depatterned until she was incontinent of stool, and subjected to sleep and psychic driving.

The other new plaintiff was a frail and perpetually confused former Montreal businessman named Louis Weinstein. Weinstein's son, Harvey, a Stanford associate professor of psychiatry, had read John Marks' book when it came out and had got in touch with Rauh's firm in 1980 to see whether his father could join the suit. But it took until late 1982 before he and his two sisters could persuade their father that he deserved some recompense. Louis Weinstein tended to think that his treatment had been a punishment; he was guilty about it and had to be convinced to see himself as an innocent victim.

Harvey Weinstein had become a psychiatrist in order to figure out what had happened to his father. He had been on the cusp of puberty when Louis, who ran a successful Montreal dress-manufacturing firm, Theresa Frocks, began to suffer bouts of anxiety that affected his breathing and digestion. The breathing difficulty was the scariest; he couldn't catch his breath and was sure each time it happened that he was suffocating to death. His family doctor referred him to a local psychiatrist, who referred him to the Allan and Dr. Cameron. He was admitted and treated by Cameron in 1956, 1957, and 1962—with LSD, an experimental drug called MC4703, electro-shock, chemical sleep, and psychic driving. No longer able to run his business, by 1961 he was forced to sell both it and the Weinstein family home. He was never able to work again and even in his late seventies said not that he was retired but that he was unemployed.

His son, who is eloquent and obsessed about his father's fate, told the *Washington Post*, "When you're thirteen years old and you see your father—an independent, kind, smart person—become a different man before your eyes—it's impossible to accommodate that. I remember one of his first visits home from the hospital. He didn't talk much, and when he did talk it made no sense. When he wasn't sleeping he was drowsy. He asked us things about his parents, even though they'd been dead for years. His memory was gone. At night once, when I was in bed, I saw him come into my room and urinate on the floor. He didn't know where he was." Harvey Weinstein also said that there were days when he couldn't stop being ashamed of his profession and nights when he couldn't stop thinking of Ewen Cameron, who "ruined my father's life...left him with nothing...a poor, pathetic man with no memory."

The addition of Weinstein was especially useful to the case. It was beginning to be clear to Rauh and Turner that they had to find some extra edge to push the CIA not only into proper discovery but to a settlement. Public opprobrium wouldn't really do it because the agency's *mea culpa* days were over. The American media weren't particularly interested in the case because the plaintiffs were not Americans—like it or not, Americans are generally a self-regarding bunch. The Canadian government was the likeliest ally. These were Canadian citizens Rauh was representing, after all, and the government itself had surely been trespassed against by the CIA's secret funding of a Canadian researcher.

In Rauh's view, David Orlikow was the logical person to rally the Canadian government to a confrontation with the U.S. government over the plaintiffs; but as a long-time member of the NDP—the third and smallest party in the House of Commons—Orlikow hardly had a huge amount of lobbying power. He also believed it was indelicate and unseemly for him to try to use his position to get justice for, among others, his own wife. Among the plaintiffs and their close relatives, Harvey Weinstein, a psychiatrist who held a teaching job at a major

U.S. university, was the spokesman with the most credibility. And Weinstein did become partly responsible for the role the Canadian government played in the case.

It was Harvey Weinstein's long talks with Jeremy Kinsman, then a political-affairs officer at the Canadian Embassy in Washington, that convinced Kinsman in 1983 to start loudly pushing for justice for the plaintiffs—the first loud words from any Canadian government official for some time. Allan Gotlieb, the Canadian ambassador to the United States, remembered the Orlikow affair from 1977 and 1978. He had then been under-secretary of state for external affairs. It was his words on the matter that had alerted the American Embassy in Ottawa to telex a warning to the Eur/Can desk at the U.S. State Department: "Possible Claim against USA: Embassy infers from Gotlieb comments that GOC [government of Canada] is seriously concerned about potential political fallout from this case and would therefore like to see quiet resolution which in some measure accommodates Mrs. Orlikow. While such action would satisfy GOC, quite obviously it could be extremely difficult or impossible from point of view of USG."

The issue, of course, was not so much what had been done to Val Orlikow (though the fact that she was the wife of an MP counted for something), but that the United States had once again infringed Canadian sovereignty by funding work in Canada without letting the government or even the CIA's liaison in the RCMP intelligence service know what was going on. The same issue has vexed, in one form or another, every Canadian government since Confederation. In similar disputes (for instance, the many involving the American military presence in Canada), sovereignty has usually meant letting the United States go ahead and do what it wants but demanding that it keep Canada informed.

Shortly after news of the MKULTRA funding broke, Security and Intelligence Liaison director general John Hadwen summoned Stacey Hulse, the CIA station chief in Ottawa, to come and explain the matter: Hadwen says that Hulse expressed regret for both the infringement of sovereignty and the results of Cameron's experiments. Two days later, in Washington, another Canadian secret-service official, Percy Sherwood, went to see a representative of the American administration who told him that the Cameron affair had been "a regrettable occurrence". The Canadian government then received, in the diplomatic phrase, reassurances from the U.S. State Department that, under Jimmy Carter's new oversight procedures governing the CIA, such a thing would not happen again. In the copy of those regulations that the U.S. government sent to External Affairs, however, there appeared to be no new regulation preventing covert funding of projects in allied countries.

As far as Jeremy Kinsman could see, "no one was going to get seriously upset about [the compensation of] these wrecks." His rationale was that the situation could be viewed not as an intelligence matter, nor as a crisis of bilateral relations, but as a direct consular matter in which Kinsman could work on behalf of the interests of Canadian citizens trying to get justice in a foreign court. Joe Rauh grew to like Jeremy Kinsman alone among all the Canadian officials he was to encounter, possibly because Kinsman himself has said that on the issue he became a loose cannon.

Trying to help Rauh press his case seemed the logical tactic; in 1983 the CIA was still blocking him at every available turn. Says Kinsman, "We wanted to make sure, on a consular basis, that the plaintiffs were getting access to due process. We were saying, 'Look, you've got two alternatives. Let due process go forward or settle out of court.'" He and other Canadian officials sent these comments through the proper channels in the American State Department. Jim Medas, on the Canadian and European affairs desk, was frank. He told Kinsman that so-called consular pressure was only going to work "if Canada was going to make it an issue politically. How pissed off were we politically?" If the State Department was going to send a message to Justice and the CIA, it had to know if there was truly going to be a political, bilateral flap. Which was what Kinsman had originally been trying to get away from.

In May 1983, as its first actual attempt to help forward the case, the Canadian Embassy asked permission of the U.S. government to release to the plaintiffs' lawyers documents relating to the case that had originated in the United States. In July 1983, the Canadian minister of external affairs, Allan MacEachen, had to let Rauh and Turner know that the American government had refused the request.

By the end of 1983, Rauh and Turner had managed to locate and take depositions from John Gittinger, Richard Helms, Sidney Gottlieb, and Admiral Stansfield Turner, among others. Partway through examining Gittinger, Rauh had got the piece of testimony he needed to refute the CIA's contention that Cameron had been the one to ask for funds. Gittinger testified that he had directed Colonel Monroe to approach Cameron after reading Cameron's first published article on psychic driving.

Gittinger, who lived in a kind of commune for older couples in Norman, Ohio, and brought his wife with him to the deposition for moral support, followed what was to become the steady line in testimony from the men who had run MKULTRA. As far as he was concerned, he had hired responsible researchers and left it up to the researchers to handle such ethical matters as seeking informed consent. He had had no personal interest in Cameron's work and now felt no personal regrets about what had happened to individual patients.

Rauh could get no overall moral satisfaction from Gittinger (at one point he felt compelled to say, "Look, my friend, you and I are both pretty close to our Maker and let me tell you that I think you have done something terrible, but lying about it today you ought to think about.") But in a way Gittinger's sworn indifference proved something Rauh considered crucial to the case. The people in charge of MKULTRA never did stop to think about the consequences of their work on unwitting human subjects and themselves confirmed that they did not ask their researchers to do so either.

Sid Gottlieb testified that he personally had taken a vial of anthrax to Leopoldville to put on Patrice Lumumba's toothbrush (an assassination attempt that failed) and had mailed a poisoned handkerchief to an Iraqi colonel in the hope of incapacitating him for a time—not, in Rauh's books, a person with an overzealous regard for human life.

CIA and U.S. Justice Department lawyers were present as the depositions were taken, stopping testimony where they could on the grounds that it might be damaging to national security. They also visited the former CIA employees before their depositions to remind them of their oaths of loyalty and their criminal liability if they let slip anything the agency did not want to slip—which was more and more. The CIA was by now denying that it had ever expressed remorse about unwitting victims or apologized to the Canadian government. Nothing exists in a lawsuit except what is admitted into evidence. It didn't matter a damn if "everyone knew" that the CIA had expressed regret to the Canadian government. The CIA now said it hadn't done so and efficiently prevented Rauh and Turner from gaining solid evidence that it had. Rauh was sure that there had to exist some written form of apology between the two governments that would clinch the matter. But the Canadian government continued to say it couldn't release any American-originated documents without the approval of its correspondent.

So Rauh and Turner decided to up the domestic pressure on the Canadian government by opening their files and their hearts to a team of television reporters from the CBC's *The Fifth Estate*. The episode, which aired on January 17, 1984, brought Val Orlikow and the Cameron affair to millions of Canadian viewers and editorials to the pages of almost every major Canadian newspaper demanding that the government arm-wrestle the CIA to a settlement. Before the month was out, the Canadian government had felt enough heat to let the American State Department know that it was finally pissed off politically. On January 20, 1984, it delivered its first-ever formal diplomatic note of protest at MKULTRA's incursion into Canada.

Rauh watched and waited, and nothing happened. His case was now thoroughly hooked to an issue of bilateral politics between Canada and the United States. He took to asking any Canadian he met why their government was so obsequious. Why in hell didn't they stand up to the CIA? His increasingly outspoken and contemptuous views on the situation did not endear him to his "careful and reasonable" new allies in the Canadian government—who as far as they were concerned were doing all they could think of to help.

By December 1985, Joe Rauh, six years into what was supposed to be his last and glorious case, was beginning to feel a bit too much like living history, venerated and useless. Perhaps it was his own hubris, thinking that he could take the CIA on and win. It seemed that half the time when the phone rang these days in his office, whose windows overlooked Farragut Square in downtown Washington, it was a history professor asking for his recollections of past triumphs.

There he sat, uncomfortably, since arthritis had taken a massive hold in one hip, with his walls covered with the artifacts of those victories. Framed, a pen used to sign the Civil Rights Act into law, given to him by President Lyndon Johnson. For Rauh that fight really went back to the 1948 Democratic convention where he'd worked with Hubert Humphrey to push a first small civil-rights plank into the party platform. A group portrait hung on the wall from the 1964 Democratic convention in Atlantic City, where Rauh had represented the Mississippi Freedom Democratic Party. They had won a promise of desegregated delegations for the future. The inscription, in part, conveyed the party's gratitude for having "met a man like you who like us burns with the desire that all mankind be free...a white man that was also concerned with freedom for all".

Fifty years before Rauh had graduated *magna cum laude* from Harvard Law School and come to Washington to work for the New Deal. He was taken on as a law clerk by Supreme Court justices Felix Frankfurter and Benjamin Cardozo. There were photographs of both still on his walls; one autographed by Frankfurter, dated June 3, 1939, read: "For Joe Rauh who exercised for all too short a time his charming authority over the judicial process of his affectionate friend." Rauh had also served as counsel for several New Deal agencies. Thinking back on that time, he had commented to a *New York Times* writer, "There was a spirit in 1935 that has never come again. You had to be in it to believe it. The idealism was so great. We had night secretaries. We would work all night. We thought we were saving our country, and, you know, I think we really were."

During the Second World War he served on General MacArthur's staff in the Pacific. He came back to Washington, for a brief time working for government, and then going into private practice in 1947. That suited him. He was an advocate, though, not a litigator—he had to be on the right side of things. He was caught up in large ideas and Democratic politics. In the late 1940s he and Hubert Humphrey, Jim Loeb, Reinhold Neibuhr, Walter Reuther, Arthur Schlesinger, Jr., and others began to organize to mount a liberal, democratic answer to the intellectual allure of Communism. Their efforts resulted in Americans for Democratic Action (ADA), which in the 1950s fought Senator Joe McCarthy and the whole cold-war-inspired Communist witch-hunt. Rauh thought that one could fear Communist espionage or Communist military attack, but that it was crazy to fear and try to repress Communist ideas—those it was better to argue with openly. Most of the founders of the ADA were dead now, and few of the living were fit enough to speak. Jim Loeb had Alzheimer's disease. Rauh found that he was called upon to do the remembering for them all.

He had agreed to sort and donate his papers to the Library of Congress; he talked to the historians who phoned; but he wasn't a man for living in the past. To be stalled on a case was the worst frustration. To be treated like an impotent bundle of hot air by young U.S. district attorneys who didn't seem to know that they were employees of the government and not the CIA was humiliating. On the first day of the Gottlieb deposition they hadn't even let a man of his age take a supper break. Next day he had sent Jim Turner to ask the questions. Gottlieb, being polite, had poured a glass of water for Jim and pushed it across the table. Remembering Gottlieb's track record with unsuspecting subjects and tasteless substances, Jim had refused to take even a sip.

Surely, given his own much different track record, Rauh should be able to get a settlement. The best move might be to force it to a trial, but neither the firm nor the plaintiffs had the money to do that. Rauh knew that, and the CIA knew that, and the result was stalemate. The firm was already $10,000 out of pocket for expenses, and he and Jim had put in thousands of hours of billing time and couldn't expect payment until there was a settlement. Rauh thought that Orlikow could afford part of the expenses, but not the others. Jeanine Huard was living on her husband's unemployment insurance and hadn't even been able to afford the cost of having her AMI medical record photocopied. Lyvia Stadler was in a nursing home. Robert Logie was unemployed. Mary Morrow was already extensively in debt for her lawsuit in Quebec.

Rauh could just not figure Canadians out at all. Earlier in the year David Orlikow had hired a professional fund-raising firm to run a direct-mail campaign to raise money to cover the legal costs but, out of lists of thousands of likely supporters, hardly anyone had sent money. Orlikow had been so depressed by the lack of response he had himself barely been able to function for five months, and had been no help whatsoever to Joe.

A new government had come to power in Canada, a majority Conservative government, whose minister of external affairs (and former prime minister), Joe Clark, had talked very strongly of trying to aid the plaintiffs. He had apparently brought the case up in three sets of private meetings with George Shultz, but worse than nothing had come from it. Alerted at one point by Clark that the U.S. State Department had sent a clear signal that the Americans were ready to talk settlement, Rauh had gone to Scott Kragie, the lawyer then in charge of the CIA case, with an offer to lower the plaintiffs' demands to $150,000 each. Kragie responded with a suggested nuisance settlement of $25,000 each, which effectively ended the negotiation. Rauh then asked Clark to produce evidence of the "clear signal", and when Clark didn't, began to believe that he too was trying to lead Rauh down some garden path.

Then Shultz, as a result of his meetings with Clark, appointed his high-level new State Department counsel, Abraham Sofaer, to sort the issues out. After looking at the case, Sofaer decided that Rauh was out to get the CIA and the patients were only out for money—and furthermore that if the case went to court the CIA had a good chance to win. Needless to say, Sofaer's influence was detrimental to a spirit of negotiation.

Rauh himself was still waiting for the outcome of what he thought might have been a mistaken tactic on his part, inspired by his drive to nail down the missing apology. He and Jim had found Stacey Hulse, who had been CIA station chief in Ottawa in 1977, and John Knause, also of the CIA. Both men had been party to regrets or apologies from the U.S. government, and both had agreed to give depositions. The dates were set, when the CIA stepped in and stopped the men on grounds of a threat to national security.

Rauh and Jim Turner had gone to Judge Penn asking for a motion to compel the depositions, but they had filed that in January 1985 and by fall they still hadn't heard. Rauh had finally gone over Judge Penn's head to the administrator of the court to see if he could hurry up the ruling. One should never try to pressure a judge. As well, in the eleven months that Penn had been considering their motion, the Supreme Court had ruled in favour of the CIA in a Freedom of Information Act case, CIA *v.* Sims—in effect, saying that nothing judicial could touch the agency if the agency didn't want to be touched. (In the words of the judgment, "The national interest sometimes makes it advisable, or even imperative, to disclose information that may lead to the identity of intelligence sources. And it is the responsibility of the Director of Central Intelligence, not that of the judiciary, to weigh the variety of complex and subtle factors in determining whether disclosure of information may lead to an unacceptable risk of compromising the Agency's intelligence-gathering process.") The ruling didn't seem to consider the fact that by definition a secret agency has a tendency to come down in favour of secrecy.

The phone rang, interrupting Rauh's run-through of depressing circumstance. It was a friend asking his opinion of the one-woman show about Lillian Hellman running at the Kennedy Center. "I took Lillian for what she was," Rauh told him, "but people who resented her Stalinism—I think it would drive you crazy. I think you'd think there was some fakery about it. They took it from her writings—so it's not necessarily what happened. She spouted some pretty horrendous pro-Stalin stuff, but we got along fine and we did damage the House Un-American Activities Committee."

The actress Zoe Caldwell had reminded Joe so much of Lillian; on stage he said her face looked just as "beautifully tense". Rauh had written all of Hellman's letter to the McCarthy committee except the line that had made it famous, "I cannot and will not cut my conscience to fit this year's fashions." Rauh appreciated a good line. Hellman had also appreciated Rauh, writing of him in her memoir *Scoundrel Time*, "I like Rauh. Shrewdness seldom goes with an open nature, but in his case it does and the nice, unbeautiful, rugged, crinkly face gives me confidence about the mind above it." Rauh told his friend that he was taking the actress to lunch and hung up.

His hand had strayed to the pile of morning mail, and as he continued to rail against slow judges and toadying Canadians, he picked up and slit open an envelope. It was a copy of Judge Penn's ruling, which had been made two days before and mailed to him. Penn had been slow as a glacier and just as inexorable: he denied the plaintiffs the testimony of both Hulse and Knause. Rauh, who through his whole litany of complaint had not showed much real sign of defeat, suddenly looked caved in. "It's a real blow," he said, over and over. "I'll have to sit and think about it. I'll just have to take them to trial. It's a real slam." At 12:30 he attached a bow-tie to his open-necked blue-striped shirt and, cane in hand, limped off to have lunch with the actress.

He arrived back at his offices at quarter to three absolutely buoyant. Barely in the door he called out to Turner, "I've got my strategy worked out. I'm going to ask the Canadian government to send John Hadwen down—he's the other half of the conversation. Let's see them turn that down."

He asked Turner immediately to draft a letter to Clark for him to look at, a letter that would say, "You didn't help us get a settlement, now help us win this case. Give us Hadwen and the missing apologies documents."

Rauh decided not to release the ruling against him to the press until he had the letter ready for Clark. "We'll give both to Juliet O'Neill of Canadian Press to break, so it's positive sounding."

It was almost as if he had needed the blow from the judge to kick-start the motor of his case.

Releasing the letter to Clark along with the judge's ruling did not exactly ease Rauh's relations with Canadian officialdom. As one

Canadian Embassy staff member put it, "Rauh's game was to beat the horse in public to make it run faster." Beating Clark in public made him balk, and Clark refused to give John Hadwen to Joe Rauh. That made Rauh more incensed, and Jim Turner took to saying that he could carve a better man than Clark out of a banana. Two days after Clark's refusal, NDP leader Ed Broadbent, having been coached on the matter by Turner and Rauh, rose in the House of Commons to question Prime Minister Brian Mulroney as to why Hadwen was unavailable. Mulroney decided on the spot to contradict his secretary of state for external affairs. If Hadwen was crucial to the plaintiffs' case, they could have Hadwen.

Negotiations with the Canadian Justice and External Affairs departments began over the timing and parameters of the deposition. Canadian officials were trying to ensure that Hadwen wouldn't be overly badgered; Rauh viewed any reluctance or carefulness on their part as an act of betrayal of their own citizens, his plaintiffs. He did not have time to wait while the wheels ground slowly on. He had said all along that the CIA was trying to win the case by attrition. While he was waiting for Hadwen, Flo Langleben had died in a Florida hospital.

Rauh frankly thought that some kind of game was being played with him, especially by the Canadian Department of Justice. The previous fall, reports that the Canadian government had supported Cameron's research on psychic driving after the CIA funding had stopped had spurred John Crosbie, then justice minister, to appoint Halifax lawyer George Cooper to study whether the Canadian government could be considered legally or morally liable for what had happened to Cameron's patients. Cooper's mandate also included finding out whether informed consent had existed between Cameron and his patients, which could have given him the latitude to talk to the plaintiffs in the CIA case; but Cooper confined his inquiries to people who had been employed by the Canadian government. To assist him in assessing Cameron's medical ethics and integrity Cooper appointed a panel of three eminent Canadian psychiatrists, who also did not talk to the plaintiffs or the plaintiffs' lawyers. Then, at the beginning of March 1986, a Canadian Justice Department lawyer, Mark Jewett, was dispatched to Washington to be briefed by U.S. authorities on the CIA case, as one more result of Clark's meetings with Shultz. Scott Kragie had been threatening Rauh that if he took the case to trial Kragie would wrap the Canadian government's involvement with Cameron around Rauh's neck. Rauh was wondering if the Canadians were going to help him do it.

He and Turner flew to Ottawa to take Hadwen's deposition at the end of March 1986, hoping that at last they'd nail the matter of the apology down. But Hadwen, in a room filled with CIA lawyers, Canadian Justice Department lawyers, and External Affairs officials, faced so many people looking after various national interests that he uttered nothing remotely useful to Rauh's case. He was not allowed to say that the CIA official who had tendered to him what were now generally called "regrets" was Stacey Hulse, though everyone at the deposition knew it.

After the exercise, all Rauh had as proof was a memo dictated by Hadwen in 1984, seven years after the exchange occurred, confirming that an unnamed American representative had indicated that the U.S. government regretted both the infringement of Canadian sovereignty and Cameron's experiments themselves. As one sympathetic Canadian External Affairs official put it, "We couldn't even give Rauh the usual contemporaneous diary account of the conversation. Hadwen, who was leaving almost immediately afterwards to take up a new post in Europe, orally debriefed to the deputy who took over for him. No one wrote anything down."

Within a week of the Hadwen deposition, Joe Rauh had decided to leap-frog over the heads of both John Crosbie and Joe Clark (who had refused to meet with Rauh while he was in Ottawa) and take his plea for the missing written apologies to Brian Mulroney, writing him a letter—with copies to the press.

Dear Mr. Prime Minister;

Although I am 75 years old and have been a lawyer for almost 51 years, I have never before considered writing a head of state in connection with a lawsuit in which I was engaged.... In all honesty, I was reluctant to undertake so massive a struggle against so powerful an opponent as the CIA in the twilight of life and career....In deciding to take the case, I assumed, of course, that I would have the full support of the Canadian Government on behalf of its citizens and have been thunderstruck watching the opposite happen.

The letter went on to detail every instance of Canadian behaviour that Rauh had viewed as detrimental to his case, from the accusation that the Canadian government was still withholding the (in fact non-existent) written apologies; to the attitude of officials during the Hadwen deposition; to the fact that no one would give him a copy of either the Cooper report or Mark Jewett's account of his visit to CIA lawyers in Washington. The last complaint on Rauh's chest was that "the man who had ordered the destruction of all CIA documents about the brainwashing experiments is an invited guest to Canada's social activities....When Ambassador Gotlieb not only invited Richard Helms to the Canadian Embassy, but had the Embassy leak that fact to the *Washington Post*, everybody in the Capital assumed Canada didn't care a tinker's dam about what the CIA had done there. Washington is a city of signals, only too often sent through the society pages."

Rauh asked Prime Minister Mulroney to rectify these things, before all his plaintiffs had passed away. He ended, "For myself I had intended by now to retire from the practice of law and do some of the things that have not been possible for my wife and I up to now. But, health permitting, I am determined to remain at my post until some modicum of justice is done these plaintiffs and I continue to hope your Government will walk this long last mile with me."

Before Mulroney answered, John Crosbie decided to release the Cooper report to the public—only days after a Justice Department official, John Tait, had refused to give Rauh and Turner a copy. The CIA immediately annexed the Cooper report as evidence and filed a motion for summary judgment in the suit (asking Penn to rule on the issues without going to trial). Although Cooper was supposed to consider only the Canadian government's responsibility, he had included a twelve-page section on the CIA case. He first commented that, because he didn't have all the facts at his fingertips (and in fact none of the plaintiffs' side at all), "any inferences I may draw in this regard are necessarily tentative and speculative". He proceeded none the less to give his opinion. "[T]he CIA was simply interested in 'buying results' in ongoing research which it in no way controlled or directed." The focus, Cooper wrote, should be on "whether the work that Cameron did was proper or improper." Though the Canadian government did fund the same research, it bore no legal or moral responsibility because it had subjected Cameron's applications to peer review and no one had brought doubts to the attention of those responsible for the funding decisions. Furthermore (here Cooper quoted the great British jurist Lord Denning), "we must not condemn as negligence that which is only a misadventure".

Rauh's second letter to Mulroney, dated May 15, 1986, began:

I write this letter on an airplane from Los Angeles to Washington. Yesterday in Ventura, California, I took the testimony of a former CIA official [Robert Lashbrook], who, although he was responsible for the death of an American Army officer through administration of LSD in 1953, was left in his CIA position where he participated in delivering CIA support to Dr. Cameron's brutal experiments upon unwitting Canadian citizens. Anger wells up inside as I ask myself why I go on overtaxing my strength with cross-country trips and seven-day workweeks, and I risk bankrupting my small law firm to help Canadian citizens whose own government works against them....

For your government has now, even after my personal appeal to you, inflicted the worst blow of all to the Canadian citizens' case against the CIA. I refer, of course, to the so-called Cooper report which will take its place among the shabbiest, most mean-spirited and error-ridden official documents ever produced by a Government following Anglo-Saxon legal principles of fairness and due process of law.... The whole purpose of the Cooper exercise was to prepare a press release for the CIA....

Possibly the most deplorable thing in the whole panorama of Canadian Government onslaughts on my clients is the repeated duplicitous assertion that their government is assisting them....

I have made many straightforward requests in my two letters to you. This last one should certainly not be too difficult to fulfill: Please send me word through a secretary or aide whether you intend to respond to these two letters and, if so, when.

Rauh's outrage did get him an answer. Mulroney replied that his government was doing all in its power to protest the violation of sovereignty, to provide assistance to the plaintiffs, and to help achieve a fair settlement.

Rauh wrote back, on June 2, "Most respectfully, sir, your letter of May 27th can only be described as a total non-answer":

I keep asking Canadians I meet why your Government is acting this way. Some say it's the usual Canadian fright of the Big Brother to the South, aggravated by fright of the CIA. Others suggest it is Canada's, now admitted, involvement with Dr. Cameron that holds you back. Still others say Dr. Cameron had to be protected to preserve the good name of Canada's intellectual flagship, McGill University. Many others keep muttering about your father-in-law, Dr. Dmitri Pivnicki, an avid Cameron disciple who still practices at the Allan Memorial Institute, and wonder whether he has improperly influenced your government's policy. I still do not know the answer to the question, 'why?'

With that series of three letters, and others he wrote in the same state of rage to officials in the Department of Justice—all of which he would hand out to visiting reporters—Rauh effectively lost the remainder of his quiet supporters in the Canadian government, particularly in the Department of External Affairs. He argued that if they were quiet, losing their support didn't mean much. Throughout the suit he had hoped to use the sticky bilateral politics of the situation to entangle the CIA at least to the point of settlement. He had allowed the quiet Canadian diplomats to be his guide and found them apparently better at seeing the other guy's side of the story than their own citizens' side. He could not understand it; he found such an attitude a complete cultural mystery. Instead of setting Canadian bureaucrats and politicians alight with his righteous indignation, Rauh found he cooled them off, breached some imaginary line of good taste and tactics. Even Jeremy Kinsman, who liked to talk about causing waves and was passionate about the fate of the plaintiffs (though unable to do much about it from his new, high-level position in the federal Department of Communications), found Rauh's anger unacceptable: "Joe is a confrontation artist. He resents deeply slights to himself, being marginalized. He has an enormous capacity for indignation against discretionary authority. He believes cover-up is a way of government. He's usually been on the underdog side where lashing out in the press is a good tactic. It wasn't so good in this case."

Whether Rauh's lashing out hurt anything but the feelings of those who liked to think of themselves as silent allies is a moot point. There wasn't anything else the Canadian government was prepared to give in any case. Rauh wanted Canada to take the United States to the International Court at The Hague, but the Canadians failed to see how that would help. Said Ray Boomgaardt, the Canadian Embassy official who paid detailed attention to the case after Kinsman left: "There's no embarrassment factor now, unlike say when the CIA was planting mines in Nicaraguan harbors. The first thing the Americans would do is offer to settle the claim on the basis that they wouldn't do it again, and then argue that damage claims are not relevant to the International Court of The Hague and that local remedies had not been exhausted." The Canadian government was not that pissed off politically.

The CIA's determination to win the case rose in direct proportion to their renewed status in Washington, said Boomgaardt: "The CIA were *mea culpa* only while the case was being investigated. Then the feeling was, hold on, they could win the case. Then it was they *ought* to win—they should not yield for reasons of policy related to the protection of the CIA. You can't have people ripping off the CIA every time it sticks up its nose. Now, their argument is that even if the CIA did something wrong the damage to the plaintiffs was caused by Cameron, who was not controlled by the CIA. If the Canadian government is not liable then neither is the CIA." Boomgaardt himself did not for a moment equate what the Canadian government had done in funding Cameron with what the CIA had done—even though the peer review committee that okayed the grant application for the money that sustained Cameron's psychic driving research for a few years after the CIA backed out had a pretty complete picture of what the doctor was up to. "We thought we were hiring a soldier who turned out to be an assassin," said Boomgaardt. "They say they were just contributing to the salary of a soldier, whereas they *knew* he was an assassin."

The distinction seems a little fine to those who've been on the receiving end of the attentions of either—soldier or assassin. In fact, the plaintiffs' case has nothing to do with whether the Canadian government is liable, but only with whether the CIA failed to control Ewen Cameron and researchers like him.

What they all seemed to want to put on trial was Ewen Cameron's practices and ethics. Rauh thought that was certainly a solid part of his case, but why was everybody forgetting the bloody, never-changing ethics of the CIA?

In the fall of 1986 Rauh and Turner felt vindicated at least in what had been their secondary aim—demonstrating that the law had to serve as a check on a secret agency. The CIA and the National Security Council had been caught playing the games that only excessive secrecy and power allowed; it had broken American law in the twists and turns of Irangate.

Rauh's health was not good, though he hoped to hold on long enough to make the oral arguments against the CIA's motion for summary judgment. His posture had been thrown off so badly by the arthritis in one hip that his healthy hip had broken down under the excessive strain. Both were now diseased and he was facing two hip-replacement operations. On January 3, 1987, his seventy-sixth birthday, he entered Johns Hopkins Hospital in Baltimore to have the first hip done. That surgery went well, but his recovery was complicated by a mild heart attack and a bleeding ulcer, for which he had a second operation.

He was not able to get out of the hospital before mid-February. He was still convalescent, and when he recovered he was supposed to go back into hospital for the other operation. Joe Rauh finally decided to retire from active law practice.

Jim Turner made their oral arguments before Judge Penn on March 10, 1987. When he dropped in on Rauh at home to fill him in on how he thought it had gone, Rauh was on the phone lobbying to try to prevent a Marine colonel named Oliver North from receiving a guarantee of immunity from prosecution in exchange for his testimony before Congress on the arms-for-hostages deal. The CIA might have outwaited Rauh himself, but he still had some influence in Washington.

Rauh and Turner had to wait another ten months to find out how the judge thought it had gone, and at last it was a break that wasn't their necks. In January 1988, Penn ruled that there was no way the legal issues could be resolved without a trial: "There are genuine issues of material fact in dispute which preclude a decision on many of the legal arguments presented." He rejected the CIA's argument that a two-year statute of limitations knocked all the plaintiffs out of the suit except Val Orlikow. The only one he could see his way clear to dropping was Mary Morrow, who by her own admission had known about the CIA's funding of Cameron for more than two years before she joined the Washington suit. Penn's written decision showed sympathy for the state the plaintiffs were in. He even paused to point out an irony: "Curiously, often a classic manifestation of people who are afflicted with certain psychotic disorders is the irrational fear that the CIA and FBI is [*sic*] conspiring to harm them. In this case, the CIA involvement is real and the covert nature of that involvement is not contested." He ordered the suit to proceed to trial, and a date was set for June 7, 1988.

Finding the money actually to go to court was a serious problem for the plaintiffs, but Jim Turner began to make arrangements to take the final depositions from defence witnesses and experts, hoping that the Canadian government's new murmurings about a "generous ex gratia settlement" of $100,000 on each of the nine plaintiffs would come true. It was, after all, what the government's own adviser, George Cooper, had suggested in his 1986 report, even as he had found that the government had no legal liability. Joe Clark was indeed soon announcing that the government recognized the plaintiffs' need for financial help, and awarded them each a fifth of the "generous" amount—$180,000 altogether. "It's a shameful situation when you have nine people who have been starving," said Turner, "and, instead of a loaf of bread, you give them crumbs."

Setting the trial date, however, didn't mean that the CIA lawyers were finished their attempts to hold things up. They soon filed a motion for what is called an interlocutory appeal, a manoeuvre in which certain legal issues are sent to an appeal court for resolution before the original court has even reached a verdict. Such an appeal is rarely granted; of the thousands of cases that had moved through the Federal District court in the last two years only two had even got through the first step of the process, and none had got to appeals court. But for the CIA something more important was at stake than stalling an ugly little case. In his ruling against summary judgment Penn hinted that a trial just might find the agency liable for acts committed in foreign countries— if the decisions that set those acts in motion were made in the United States. Even though the CIA had once again sworn off covert action in the aftermath of Contragate, a legal precedent of that sort was nothing the agency could welcome. Once again everything stopped while Penn considered. By late April no one had yet heard whether the case would actually get to trial in June. By late May Penn had ruled that the case would go to trial, but had granted a defence motion for a postponement. A new trial date was set for October 1988.

A pigeon had also come home to roost on the shoulders of the Canadian government. Linda Macdonald, a Vancouver woman, claimed to have lost the memory of the first twenty-six years of her life, including the births of her five children, during a few months of Dr. Cameron's care. Between May 1 and September 12, 1963, according to Macdonald's Allan Memorial files, she received more than one hundred electro-shock treatments, eighty-six days of drugged sleep and intensive psychic driving, from which she emerged "completely disoriented and [needing] complete nursing assistance.... She is incontinent of both urine and feces." She had to be taught how to eat, to dress, to read, to write, to cook, and to love her parents, husband, and children, none of whom she recognized. She had been in touch with Turner in Washington about joining the CIA suit, but everything that had happened to her began three years after the CIA stopped funding Cameron's research. The organization paying Cameron's research bills when Linda Macdonald came along was the Canadian government. Life for her literally began at twenty-six, and for that she wanted someone to pay. Cameron was long dead, so one Canadian citizen at last decided to sue the Canadian government.

CHAPTER THIRTEEN

Death at the Summit

Dr. Brian Robertson sets a fat correspondence file and another stuffed with newspaper clippings on a coffee table in Ewen Cameron's old office, prepared to defend the chief he never met. One's eye is drawn to the analyst's couch, covered in a pale-blue open-weave blanket and with a white-cased pillow on which to lay an introspective head. Robertson, a psychoanalyst, practises a specialty Cameron didn't have much use for. Otherwise—in fixtures and furniture and even the apparent age of the paint job—the room looks as if Cameron could walk into it at any moment and miss only his old tape-recorder.

Hard hats hang over coat-hooks, and there's the occasional eruption of jackhammers in the distance. Robertson is the first director of the Allan Memorial Institute since Cameron's day to add a new wing to its physical structure. But he is in no way eradicating the past. Cameron haunts him not just because of the apparently unending CIA controversy, and not just because he operates in a human structure that has changed only minimally since Cameron dreamed it out of thin air, but because each time the talk turns to the Allan's founder Robertson's tongue is forced to hit every one of his profession's sore teeth.

He comes from a family of New Zealand surgeons. His father did major pioneering abdominal operations in the 1920s and 1930s at the end of which many patients were dead. No one condemned him for it. His brother is a surgeon who specializes in cancers of the face, head, and neck; he tries to outpace the disfigurement of the cancer bursting through all the tissue planes with the surgical disfigurement of his attempts to cure—his five-year survival rate is only 15 per cent. Yet when the two brothers get together, it's the surgeon who says, "Look Brian, I don't know how you work with all those people who don't get better." And Robertson can only respond that at least more than 15 per cent of his patients survive.

For the benefit of his current interrogator he adds, "Psychiatry is not the most glamorous of specialties. We have a very hard time explaining what we do....We often feel a little bit like we're under siege." Psychiatrists feel hard done by, misunderstood, like medical outsiders still tarred by the ostracizing brush of madness. A doctor thinks he can isolate and treat a leg or a heart; a mental disorder is still relentlessly bound up in a person's being. After fifty years of activism and intervention, psychiatrists can treat, but they still can't reliably cure.

When Robertson thinks of Cameron he remembers his own professor of psychiatry in medical school, an outcast who viewed himself as *agent provocateur* to the conservative faculty establishment. In class one day he asked his students, "What's the first duty of a doctor?"

They dutifully replied, "To treat patients."

"No," he cried, "It's to hate disease!"

"Cameron," says Robertson, "hated mental illness. That's what drove the man. He had a Presbyterian vision of the world, a Manichean vision, you know, good versus evil. And I think he saw mental illness as evil and he saw himself as the knight who rode against it. And I think that's not a bad moral base, except it has to be tempered.

"See, he could *not* not treat. I think that's the man's greatest fault, and I think that's what has come to rebound on his reputation. I think he went too far with ECT. You just don't hit the brain with a sledge-hammer. The only way that makes sense is if you believe you have to treat. But if you get *furor therapeuticus*, as the Viennese doctors used to describe it, then you're bound to do some harm. The fury to treat—I think he had it."

A part of Brian Robertson finds that fury to treat admirable, an expression of defiance in a contest whose tough odds haven't changed much since Cameron's death. In the 1980s, Robertson waits for the next huge wave of therapeutic energy, acknowledging with a pained shrug that a portion of what passes for treatment these days is chemical custodial care. Activism directed at the brain, at the moment, is probably the last course a wise doctor should take: "Nobody now doing good brain research in the field believes that they're dealing with anything but an extraordinarily complex organ structure which is probably some sort of massive endocrine organ, a hormone secreter. And is so finely balanced and complexly interdigitated one part with another that you can't take a scalpel and cut it and think that you're doing anything useful.... It doesn't take to simple adjustments.

"There's a whole issue behind this," says Robertson. "It's extraordinarily difficult to deal with psychotic people. There are many routes away from it. One of the routes is to say that drugs and biology are the answer. Another is to say that ECT is the answer. Another is to say that psychoanalytic theory is the one and only answer. They're all defences—you're up against an agonizingly painful illness for the individual, the family, and the society. God knows what it costs us.

"So hard is it to treat the very seriously mentally ill, that there's a projected process down the chain. Society hands it over to psychiatrists who tend to hand it over to psychiatric nurses who tend to hand it over to orderlies and there you get your custodial stuff."

A whiff of futility rises in the air, then a trace of nostalgia. Robertson can give chapter and verse on Cameron's weaknesses: excessive ambition, lack of critical judgement, a spirit of adventure that badly marred his practice of science, impatience. And yet for Robertson, who never experienced it, the Allan of the 1950s was a Camelot where for one brief shining moment a king marshalled his knights, his nurses, the local Rotarians and journalists, the educators, the do-gooders, the bureaucrats and the politicians for a spirited assault on mental illness.

Though Robertson doesn't idolize Cameron he resents the tarnish on the king's crown. In the best of all possible worlds, he'd name the new wing after Cameron, in spite of the Orlikows, the CIA lawsuit, and all.

An attack on the grandfather still threatens the grandsons. The heirs in the end are defensive, worried that their own reputations suffer in the glare cast on Cameron. The layperson sitting across from Robertson finally gets tired of trying to empathize with the profession's anxiety. She asks the question the doctors have all avoided, the one they say is impossible now to answer, and whose answer would have to be weighed against the greater good.

"How much harm did Cameron do?"

"I really don't know," says Dr. Robertson. "I'd have to see the people. I'd have to have some knowledge of them before and after. All I know is that all medical treatment is hurtful, it doesn't matter what it is."

"Funny, then, to have 'Do no harm' as your credo."

"Well we try. But as soon as you invade the body, you're going to do some harm. You invade a person's privacy and you trample all over them. You've got to do that in order to treat the disease. As soon as you use drugs you're going to do some harm. We treat schizophrenia with drugs which cause permanent damage to the nervous system. Should we stop treating because of that?

"We're very cautious. But we've got to treat someone who's suffering from an acute psychosis because they are suffering so much and their life is so disrupted. The fear—to be in an absolute state of terror—you have to treat. But we do harm by doing that. Whether Cameron did more harm than anybody in another specialty in his generation, I would think not."

"In his own specialty?"

Robertson doesn't answer that one.

Ewen Cameron and his youngest son, Jamie, left their Lake Placid house early on the morning of September 8, 1967, to do one of their favourite things, take a long hike in the Adirondack Mountains. Jamie, a twenty-four-year-old law student at George Washington University, would soon be back at school and too overworked to come home for many weekends. His father, approaching his sixty-sixth birthday, kept to the frenetic pace he always had, occupied with patients and his research work into memory and ageing. His ambition there, he said, was to crack the RNA radical.

This morning they were heading out to try to fulfil another ambition of his father's. They drove south of town on Route 73 and turned right on the winding side road that took them into the Adirondack Loj, a kind of hiker's central to the high-peak climbs of the range. From the steps of the Loj, across a lake edged with conifers and birches, they could see their destination, Street Mountain, no more than a slightly bigger bump of green among the others on the horizon.

It was the one Ewen Cameron wanted to climb, a trailless peak. There was no one route up it, but a number of trails, some of them false. To get to the top you had to be good with a map and a compass, and once up accept the fact that there wasn't much of a view. The summit was entirely forested, and you couldn't see very far unless you climbed a tree. But that wasn't the point. Street Mountain was one of the more difficult climbs in the area, a mountain that took an experienced guide four or five hours to get up—a good mountain on which to test your limits.

No one but Cameron knew exactly what his limits were, or someone might have tried to change his mind about climbing Street Mountain, especially on the kind of hot and humid September day that masquerades very well as one of midsummer. His daughter, Airlie, also at home on a visit, was a cardiologist and knew that her father had been having some heart trouble for which he was taking medication. But he had told no one in the family that he was now on a much stronger dosage. He wouldn't, since he didn't want them to fuss, and he resented the increasing impingements of age.

He and Jamie started to hike at around 8:00 AM, following a beaten path that led away from the Loj. They walked only a little way before they had to strike off across country on the remnants of a ski trail. Then the ski trail ended, and they were left to find their way on their own.

They climbed for roughly four hours, Jamie mostly in the lead. His father, who never went anywhere without index cards and a pen, would stop every now and then to rest and to scribble down notes for a lecture he was working on. Shortly after noon, Jamie turned to see his father slumped over behind him. He rushed back down the slope and for endless minutes, breathing as steadily as he was able and blowing the air as deeply as he could into his father's lungs, he tried to revive him. Then he gave up. It took him only an hour and a half, running, to get back to the Adirondack Loj.

Jamie called the local coroner's office and his sister. Then he again climbed the mountain, with four others, reaching his father by roughly 7:00 that evening. They had planned that a helicopter would fly in to carry his body back down, but the winds were too high and they had to leave him where he was. A forest ranger named Harry Eldridge spent the night beside him.

In the morning a party of fourteen rangers climbed up and successfully carried the body down. All in all, the town of Lake Placid considered Ewen Cameron's death a good one for a man who loved the mountains.

He was cremated, and according to his wishes his family held no memorial service for him. They asked that the money that might have been spent on floral tributes go instead to the psychiatric research fund of the Albany Medical College. By that time, Airlie and the others had discovered that the heart medicine Ewen Cameron had been carrying in his pocket was strong indeed, and that he must have known the risk he was running in attempting to conquer his trailless peak.

Telegrams of support and condolences began to pour in, and the men chosen to write his obituaries for the major professional journals began to struggle with their memories of the man. Dr. Frank Braceland, who had worked closely with Cameron to get the World Psychiatric Association off the ground, wrote to its secretary general, Dr. Denis Leigh, "I just finished writing an obituary for Ewen Cameron. It was the hardest thing I ever did. I guess I got hit a little harder than I thought I had been.

"Ewen was a rough guy. But I traveled abroad four times with him for meetings on weekends in Paris and I got to know him very well....

"The obituary published in the paper at Lake Placid spoke of him as 'that warm, kindly, gentle, good man'; their 'most distinguished citizen'; a man who was helping a Catholic nun with her old folks' home and who wrote to the President about her.

"He kept that part of himself carefully concealed for he used to scoff at things religious, and found fault with me for being gentle with our erring comrades from France. Underneath he was this kind of fellow all along."

The editor and publisher of the Lake Placid area newspaper was Jim Loeb, who had worked with Joe Rauh for years in Americans for Democratic Action. Under the title "The Understanding Man", he eulogized Ewen Cameron on the Monday after he died: "His worldwide success in his profession was, of course, due principally to his great knowledge and brilliance. But surely a great factor also was the softness—one is tempted to say loveliness—of his personality. Those who were privileged to know him, even briefly, will not soon forget the warmth and the kindliness of this understanding man."

"Jim Loeb wrote that?" asked Joe Rauh, hobbling slowly and painfully back from lunch, twenty years later, on one of the last days he was able to come into his office. "If Jim Loeb wrote that he sure didn't know Ewen Cameron very well."

Afterword to the Second Edition

As the lawsuit moved towards a trial date, set for the fall of 1988, the stakes on both sides got higher. Having tried everything to stall or to get the suit thrown out, lawyers for the CIA now tried to break down the plaintiffs through a long summer of hostile psychiatric depositions. The subtext was simple: in the wreckage of their lives, how could anyone tell what damage had been done by Cameron, or whether he had done any damage at all? But the plaintiffs held up surprisingly well through this round of psychological warfare, and, by September, Jim Turner was receiving serious overtures of settlement. He was ready for trial—part of him longed for the catharsis of public contest—but, all along, he and Rauh had hoped for settlement. He wanted his surviving clients to live to see a resolution to the suit, and to have the satisfaction of some money in their hands.

Val Orlikow was the last to agree; she really had to struggle to balance the interests of the other plaintiffs against her own desire to see the CIA found guilty by a court. The trial was set for October 4; the out-of-court settlement was announced that morning—U.S.$750,000, which worked out to about C$100,000 for each of them. As their contingency share, Turner and Rauh took what was left, barely enough to cover their costs. Turner, in his usual low-key way, pointed out that although the CIA still admitted no liability in the matter, the money was some kind of concession. It was also the first time the agency had been pushed into such a corner. Celebrating the resolution of the eight-year battle in a bare-walled, carton-filled office—the remnants of Rauh's law practice—Turner had to take his satisfactions where he found them.

Since serving the public interest was always uppermost in Turner's mind, he didn't last long in private practice. He went on to work for the House Committee on Legislation and National Security, where he had a direct hand in making the Kennedy assassination papers public. After Joe Rauh died, in September 1992, Turner and the Rauh family raised funds to establish the Joseph L. Rauh, Jr., Chair of Public Interest Law at the District of Columbia School of Law, because "What this country needs is another Joe Rauh". In 1993, Rauh was awarded the Presidential Medal of Freedom, posthumously, though President Clinton, in the part of the speech that honoured Rauh, did not mention the CIA suit.

In the wake of the CIA settlement, Linda Macdonald and her lawyer, the eminent former judge Tom Berger, upped the legal pressure on the Canadian government. When it became clear, in the fall of 1992, that Berger and his client were ready to take the matter to trial, the government passed an order-in-council, the AMI-Depatterned Persons Assistance Order, authorizing a $100,000 ex gratia payment to any living person who was a permanent resident of Canada and could prove that he or she had been subject to Cameron's experiments in brainwashing. In return for payment, each person would have to sign a waiver protecting both the Royal Victoria Hospital and the federal government, and withdraw any court action. This, the government stressed, was a compassionate response to a medical misfortune, and not any admission of liability. To date, seventy-seven people have been awarded the payment.

But not Val Orlikow. The original plaintiff in the CIA lawsuit died of cancer on May 23, 1990, at the age of seventy-three. As far as her husband is concerned, each one of the seventy-seven who have been compensated owes his or her payment to his own efforts and the sufferings of his wife and daughter—all of them are riding on Val's coat-tails. The last battle of this long-drawn-out contest belongs to David Orlikow. He has flooded justice ministers, deputy ministers, access-to-information officers, MPs, and former MPs with correspondence. He is implacable and obsessed. In a letter to Allan Rock, dated February 28, 1996, he wrote, "You may be tired of hearing from me, but you cannot be as tired of the case as I am. Dr. Cameron's experiments on my wife... [have] dogged my life and that of my daughter for over thirty years. We want nothing more than [to] be done with it, but we are not prepared to permit the case to be finished until justice is done".

Over Christmas and into January 1997, he sent off fifteen more letters to Rock, each one containing a different request for information. He also complained to the Law Society of Upper Canada about what he saw as foot-dragging and a cover-up on the part of George Thomson, deputy minister of justice. Thomson took a forbearing tone in his response: "The Department of Justice has responded to every one of Mr. Orlikow's numerous, and sometimes repetitive, requests for money, information, material and explanations of the government's position. While our replies have not always been to his satisfaction, they have always been reasonably prompt, courteous and as complete as possible".

Orlikow is taking a leaf out of Joe Rauh's book in the art of making Canadian government hackles rise. You can feel them thinking, "We're being reasonable. We've done all we can. The rules say he doesn't qualify. Why won't the old crank give up?" Orlikow has a much simpler view. The Canadian government passed that order-in-council. The Canadian government should be able to change that order-in-council. It's only what Val deserves.

Source Notes

Chapter 1: The Sad Demonstration

From firsthand reporting of the demonstration, which took place on Oct. 6, 1986; interviews with participants and one of the organizers, Don Weitz; and lawyer Jim Turner. The mad movement's own assessment of the event's success is in "Justice for the Allan Memorial Victims", by Kali Grower, *Phoenix Rising, The Voice of the Psychiatrized* (Dec. 1986).

Chapter 2: Rejection

Val Orlikow, after some months of negotiation, felt unable to grant me an interview. She believed that she had told her story often enough; that she suffered too much when she had to tell it; and that it was important to save her energies for testimony in her Washington lawsuit. Luckily, there are hundreds of pages of depositions and testimony already on the record in the two lawsuits in which the Orlikows have been involved, from which I pieced together this account. The first is the current suit, *Mrs. David Orlikow, et al.,* v. *United States of America*, Civil Action No. 80-3163, United States District Court for the District of Columbia;

particularly Val Orlikow's deposition given in Washington on June 12, 1986. The second is *Velma Orlikow* v. *Royal Victoria Hospital*, Quebec Superior Court, No. 500-05-006872-798. Testimony was heard in early May 1981, before the suit was settled out of court for $50,000 and costs.

Excerpts of Val Orlikow's medical records from her stays at the Allan Memorial Institute in 1956-57 and 1963-64 were attached to her 1986 deposition. The description of the Allan's new wing and D. Ewen Cameron's thoughts on mental-hospital design are from an article written by Cameron, "The Open Hospital", *Mental Hospitals* (Oct. 1954), 3-5. Details on Ravenscrag and the Allan family are from S. E. Appleton's book, *Ravenscrag: The Allan Royal Mail Line* (Toronto: McClelland & Stewart, 1974).

Dr. Charles Shagass's work establishing the sedation threshold is described in his article "The Sedation Threshold: A Method for Estimating Tension in Psychiatric Patients", *EEG Clinical Neurophysiology* 6 (1954), 221-33. Cameron's first paper on his controversial research is "Psychic Driving", *American Journal of Psychiatry* 112:7 (1956), 502-09. Cameron's casual attitude towards LSD is nicely summed up in a letter dated June 6, 1962, to the medical director of Sandoz Pharmaceuticals, written in response to a drug company questionnaire on the use of LSD by Canadian psychiatrists: "We have used this drug now for several years in the Institute and have had no difficulties.... My impression is that both the effects of the drug and the dangers thereof have been considerably overrated." Cameron added that to administer the drug, "No special training is required." A copy of the letter is in the Public Archives of Canada (PAC), Records of the Department of Health and Welfare, RG 29, vol. 10, file 1600, Return by the Honourable J. Waldo Monteith, Minister of National Health and Welfare, 1962. Monteith was responding to a parliamentary request to provide to the House all the department's correspondence files on LSD.

"Automation of Psychotherapy", by D. Ewen Cameron, Leonard Levy, Thomas Ban, and Leonard Rubenstein, appeared in *Comprehensive Psychiatry* 5:1 (Feb. 1964), 1-14. Other details of Orlikow's second stay at the Allan are from interviews with a nurse who cared for her and with art therapist Marie Revai.

The account of Orlikow and Cameron's Lake Placid relationship is based on her testimony in the Montreal suit and an interview with Cameron's eldest son, Duncan. One example of a favour David Orlikow performed for his wife's psychiatrist is a letter to Cameron from Orlikow, dated February 24, 1965, in which Orlikow supplies figures on medical research in Canada for a speech Cameron was to give (Box 3, File 23, of Cameron's papers at the American Psychiatric Association Archives [APAA] in Washington, D.C.)

Chapter 3: Disclosure

The description of Val Orlikow's life post-Cameron is from her own and other witnesses' testimony in 1981 in Quebec suit No. 500-05-006872-798. David Orlikow, while hesitating to grant a formal interview, agreed to confirm some details, including the account of how he discovered that the CIA had funded some of Cameron's research. The specific *New York Times* piece was a group investigative effort headlined "Private Institutions Used in CIA Effort to Control Behavior", which ran August 2, 1977. Dr. Gordon Lamberd, now dead, testified on his opinion of Cameron's methods and his worry that Val was overreacting to the CIA link during the Quebec lawsuit.

Details of John Marks' pursuit of the MKULTRA story are from: interviews with Marks and researcher Jay Peterzell; Marks' own correspondence with the CIA, filed as an affidavit to the Quebec lawsuit; and depositions from Frank Laubinger, Richard Helms, Sid Gottlieb, and Stansfield Turner in CIA suit No. 80-3163.

Marks and Peterzell gave me permission to use not only their open files of MKULTRA papers kept at the Center for National Security Studies in Washington, but also background files of interviews, including transcripts of all those Peterzell did with Cameron associates for Marks' book *The Search for the "Manchurian Candidate" : The Cia and Mind Control* (New York: New York Times Books, 1979). Many of the documents Marks originally obtained from the CIA were heavily censored; Joe Rauh and Jim Turner won many uncensored versions from the CIA in the course of a long discovery, and allowed me to see them. The Rockefeller Commission's findings were published in June 1975 as *Report to the President by the Commission on CIA Activities within the United States*; the portions quoted are on pages 226-27.

Stansfield Turner's actions and reactions as Carter's director of Central Intelligence are recounted in his own book, *Secrecy and Democracy: The CIA in Transition* (Boston: Houghton Mifflin, 1985) and in his deposition in the CIA suit. The deleted part of Stansfield Turner's manuscript was obtained by Jim Turner for use in the suit. The basic picture of the CIA in the seventies and eighties comes from interviews and background reading; especially useful were Phillip Knightley, *The Second Oldest Profession: The Spy as Bureaucrat, Patriot, Fantasist and Whore* (London: André Deutsch, 1986); John Prados, *Presidents' Secret Wars: CIA and Pentagon Covert Operations from World War II through Iranscam* (New York: William Morrow, 1986, and the updated paperback published in 1988); Bob Woodward, *Veil: The Secret Wars of the CIA 1981-1987* (New York: Simon and Schuster, 1987); James Littleton, *Target Nation: Canada and the Western Intelligence Network* (Toronto: Lester & Orpen Dennys, 1986); and John Marks, *The Search for the "Manchurian Candidate"*. The long quotation from Allen Dulles on "the battle for men's minds" was found in *Acid Dreams: The CIA, LSD and the Sixties Rebellion*, by Martin A. Lee and Bruce Shlain (New York: Grove Press, 1985).

The joke that Hitler lost the war because he was out of date is quoted in Gordon Wright's *The Ordeal of Total War, 1939-1945* (New York: Harper and Row, 1968). I'm indebted to many people for the picture of the impact of the Second World War on the profession of psychiatry: primarily Gerald Grob, historian of psychiatry and professor at Rutgers University; Cameron's own writings and speeches; Dr. Charles Roberts; Dr. Robert Cleghorn; Dr. Jack Griffin; Dr. Jack Ewalt. Many people who worked with Cameron mentioned his admiration for Dr. Will Sargant's book, *Battle for the Mind: A Physiology of Conversion and Brain-washing* (London: Heinemann, 1959).

Chapter 4: Good Science, Bad Science

The description of the purposes and resources of the Defence Research Board is in PAC, Records of the Department of National Defence, RG 24, vol. 4217, file 700-0-171, Exchange of Information with U.S.A. 1950-63, memo headed "Major Phases of the Canadian Research Program, 1947", by A.L. Wright. Information on the Canada-U.S. intelligence relationship is from Littleton, *Target Nation*; Omond Solandt's affidavit in the Washington suit; and interviews with people active in intelligence at the time.

Minutes of the tripartite meeting at the Ritz-Carlton Hotel on June 1, 1951, have been published as Appendix 21 to *Opinion of George Cooper, Q.C., Regarding Canadian Government Funding of the Allan Memorial Institute in the 1950s and 1960s* (Ottawa: Minister of Supply and Services Canada: May 1986). Of the two CIA representatives at the meeting, Commander Williams is dead and Dr. Caryl Haskins says he has no memory that the event took place.

The best contemporary source on Hebb's thought is his own ground-breaking book *The Organization of Behavior* (New York: John Wiley, 1949). On Hebb's relationship with the Defence Research Board: correspondence, memos, and reports in PAC, RG 24, a sampling of which have been published in the Cooper report, appendices 22-24. The secret papers on perceptual isolation, which were circulated at the time to the armed forces of Canada, Britain, and the United States, included "The Effect of Isolation upon Attitude, Motivation and Thought", by Hebb, W. Heron, and W.H. Bexton (1952); Bexton's thesis, "Some Effects of Perceptual Limitations in Human Subjects" (1953); and a 1955 report by Hebb and Heron called "Effects of Radical Isolation upon Intellectual Function and the Manipulation of Attitudes". The first paper published under the cover story Hebb and the DRB created was by Bexton, Heron, and T.H. Scott, "Effects of a Decreased Variation in the Sensory Environment", *Canadian Journal of Psychology* 8 (1954), 70-76. Other details on perceptual isolation, from the Rockefeller Archive Center (RAC), 427A–Canada, Box R949,

McGill University Psychology 1951-54, Trustees' Confidential Report on Donald Hebb's "Studies of the Thinking Process", May 1, 1954.

The report on Communist "brainwashing" circulated in 1950 is included as Appendix 20 of the Cooper report. Basic sources on brainwashing were Artichoke, Bluebird, and MKULTRA documents released by the CIA; Marks' book; a special edition of the *Journal of Social Issues* 13:3 (1957), 1-65; Robert Jay Lifton, *Thought Reform and the Psychology of Totalism: A Study of "Brainwashing" in China* (New York: Norton, 1961); Harold Wolff and Lawrence Hinkle, "Communist Interrogation and Indoctrination of 'Enemies of the State' ", *Archives of Neurology and Psychiatry* 76 (1956), 115-74.

Hebb's summing-up paper is "The Motivating Effects of Exteroceptive Stimulation", *American Psychologist* 13 (1958), 110-12. The Hebb-Lilly connection is outlined in an excerpt from Robert S. Morison's diary dated April 10, 1954, RAC, 427A–Canada, Box R949, McGill University Psychology 1951-54. Maitland Baldwin's role is pieced together from the CIA documents; Baldwin himself is dead.

The Rockefeller Foundation ran its own McCarthy-era security check on D. Ewen Cameron before he was to appear at a trustees' meeting in 1954, and found that his name showed up in the McCarran-Jenner Committee Hearings on Subversive Influence in the Educational Process, 1953, Part II, 1039, because of a statement Cameron had made before the American Psychiatric Association convention in May 1953. Cameron is quoted under the headline "Rising Fears Held a Peril to Science", in the *New York Times*, May 5, 1953: "American scientific progress is in serious danger today because of fear-inspired rumors, unjust accusations and ill-advised investigations growing out of the tensions of the cold war."

Chapter 5: The Elusive Cure

Documentation of Cameron's public life exists in largest quantity in the Cameron collection at the American Psychiatric Association Archives (APAA) in Washington, D.C.; also in the Allan Memorial Institute Library; the McGill University Archives; the Rockefeller Archive Center in New York State; and the Public Archives of Canada. Most of the papers that survive Dr. Cameron have been heavily edited either by Cameron himself in the move to Albany before he died or by his heirs, who destroyed his patient records, for instance, to protect the parties concerned from a possible breach of privacy.

Biographical detail came largely from interviews; where possible I've attributed information to its source in the text. An invaluable reference on Cameron's career at the Allan is Dr. Robert Cleghorn's as-yet-unpublished memoir, *A Search for Meaning in Hormones and Humans*, of which he gave me a complete draft. Briefly, other sources of biographical material include: the "D. Ewen Cameron Memorial Lecture, Biochemistry and the Schizophrenias", by Cameron's American colleague Harold Himwich, published in *Psychiatric Research in Our Changing World* (Amsterdam: Excerpta Medica Foundation, 1969); Val Ross, "The Great Psychiatric Betrayal", *Saturday Night* (June 1979); some unpublished notes by Cameron, "General Thoughts about My Years as Director of the Institute", in the McGill University Archives; a manuscript by Cameron's long-time secretary, Dorothy Trainor, "Looking Back at 21 Years...D. Ewen Cameron, MD—A Pioneer in Canadian Psychiatry", dated July 20, 1965, a copy of which is in the Allan Memorial Institute Library; "D.E. Cameron, MD, President, 1952-53: A Biographical Sketch", by Gregory Zilboorg, *American Journal of Psychiatry* 110 [July 1953], 10-12; the foreword by Danial Blain to Cameron's posthumous *Psychotherapy in Action* (New York: Grune and Stratton, 1968); and obituaries by friends Dr. Will Sargant (*British Medical Journal* [Sept. 23, 1967], 803-04) and Dr. Frank Braceland (*American Journal of Psychiatry* 124:6 [Dec. 1967], 168-69).

Cameron's own description of the country in which he grew up is from a Nov. 16, 1964, letter to a former patient, Karralynn Schreck, a copy of which she sent to me. The idea that Cameron's early ambition was to be a research scientist, not a clinical psychiatrist, is confirmed by his widow, Jean Cameron—and is overpoweringly clear in his own first book, *Objective and Experimental Psychiatry* (New York: Macmillan, 1935). The quotation from Cameron on asylum conditions in the 1930s is from a copy of a preface he wrote to Dr. Sargant's memoir *The Unquiet Mind*, APAA, Cameron papers, Box 4, Folder 30.

The picture of psychiatry's scientific ambitions in the 1930s is pulled together from interviews with Andrew Scull, Dr. Jack Ewalt, Dr. Jack Griffin, Dr. Charles Roberts, and Dr. Robert Cleghorn; also from F.C.R. Chalke, "Presidential Address: The Psychiatrist As Scientist", *Canadian Psychiatric Association Journal* 19:6 (Dec. 1974), 533-42; Cleghorn's "The Development of Psychiatric Research in Canada up to 1964", *Canadian Journal of Psychiatry* 29 (Apr. 1984), 189-97; and Eliot S. Valenstein, *Great and Desperate Cures: The Rise and Decline of Psychosurgery and Other Radical Treatments for Mental Illness* (New York: Basic Books, 1986). Major sources of earlier psychiatric history are Gerald Grob, *Mental Illness and American Society*, 1875-1940 (Princeton: Princeton University Press, 1983); Andrew Scull, ed., *Madhouses, Mad-Doctors and Madmen: The Social History of Psychiatry in the Victorian Era* (Philadelphia: University of Pennsylvania Press, 1981); Pierre Pichot, *A Century of Psychiatry* (Paris: Editions Roger Dacosta, 1983); also, Cleghorn's "A Comparison of the Historical Roots and Developments in Medicine and Psychiatry As They Affect Research", *Canadian Medical Association Journal* 85 (July 1, 1961), 18-27.

The story of Henry A. Cotton comes from a draft of Scull's paper "Desperate Remedies: A Gothic Tale of Madness and Modern Medicine", which was scheduled to be published in *Psychological Medicine* 17 (1987).

Chapter 6: The Imperative to Treat

The portrait of Cameron's life in Brandon, Manitoba, is from: an interview with his widow, Jean, and his eldest son, Duncan; interviews conducted by researcher Arlene Waite with hospital staff who had worked with Cameron (and who wanted anonymity), with male nurse William David Willey, and with Brandon Mental Hospital archivist Lloyd Henderson; documents at the Brandon hospital archives; back issues of the local newspaper, the *Brandon Sun*; an interview with psychiatrist and archivist Jack Griffin; and Cameron's own writings while at the hospital.

Cameron's papers include a draft, "Treatment on the Acute Ward", APAA, Box 1, Folder 3; "Urgent Mental Health Questions", another draft, APAA, Box 1, Folder 3; "Red Light Therapy in Schizophrenia", *British Journal of Physical Medicine* 10:11 (Mar. 1936); "Training in Psychiatry", *Canadian Medical Association Journal* (Jan. 1936), 78-81.

A friend from Cameron's Lake Placid days, Dr. Ginger Weeks, told the story of Cameron's efforts to rig up an automatic baby-feeding machine for his children. The account of how Cameron got to Worcester is his wife's; another source on his work there is Dr. Bill Holtz, who was a member of his research team. Information on Manfred Sakel's insulin-coma therapy from Valenstein, *Great and Desperate Cures*, and Sakel's own "Origin and Nature of Hypoglycaemic Therapy of the Psychoses", *Archives of Neurology and Psychiatry* 38 (1937), 188-203. Cameron's papers on insulin coma are: Hudson Hoagland, Morton A. Rubin, and D. Ewen Cameron, "The Electroencephalogram of Schizophrenics during Insulin Hypoglycaemia and Recovery", *American Journal of Physiology* 120:3 (Nov. 1937), 559-70; Cameron, "Further Experiences in the Insulin-Hypoglycaemia Treatment of Schizophrenia", *Journal of Nervous and Mental Diseases* 87:1 (Jan. 1938), 14-25; and Cameron, "Early Schizophrenia", *American Journal of Psychiatry* 95:3 (Nov. 1938), 567-78. The doctor who described the positive effects of insulin coma as "tender loving care" is Dr. Charles Roberts.

The paper by Oskar Diethelm on somatic therapies, "An Historical View of Somatic Treatment in Psychiatry", and discussion, weres published in the *American Journal of Psychiatry* (Mar. 1939), 1165-79.

Chapter 7: At Last, a Mover and a Shaker

Several of Cameron's colleagues mentioned the fact that he was scornful of anyone who might be construed as a father figure, including Adolf Meyer, but scorn is definitely not the tone in a draft of a tribute

Cameron wrote to the memory of Meyer in February 1961 (APAA, Box 4, Folder 28), which is quoted here.

Sources on the founding and early years of the Allan Memorial Institute are: numerous interviews; Cleghorn's memoir; and documents in RAC, 427A-Canada, Box R949, McGill University Psychiatry 1936-43. Some of the details on financing are also found in the Cameron papers at the McGill University Archives. The rocky relationship between Cameron and Penfield, and Penfield's ambition to annex the department of psychiatry to the Montreal Neurological Institute, are also documented in the RAC files mentioned above.

Cameron's address on the opening of the Allan exists in draft form in the APAA, Box 1, Folder 3. His ideas on unlocking the doors of mental hospitals are best expressed in "The Open Hospital", *Mental Hospitals* 5:8 (Oct. 1954), 3-5.

The Montreal Neurological Institute's war effort and subsequent crisis are outlined in correspondence and reports in the Rockefeller Archives, 427A–Canada, Box 948, McGill University Brain Chemistry 1949-54.

Cameron's thoughts on old age are from a book written for the general public, *Life Is for Living* (New York: Macmillan, 1948). His role in and his reactions to the trial of Hess appear in his own article "Nuremberg and Its Significance", APAA, Box 1, Folder 4, Jan. 19, 1946, and in the Hess file at the McGill University Archives. On medical ethics and the Nuremberg Code, human experimentation, and war crimes, my sources are: Jay Katz, *Experimentation with Human Beings: The Authority of the Investigator, Subject, Professions, and State in the Human Experimentation Process* (New York: Russell Sage Foundation, 1972); Robert Jay Lifton, *The Nazi Doctors: Medical Killing and the Psychology of Genocide* (New York: Basic Books, 1986); Eric Stover and Elena Nightingale, eds., *The Breaking of Bodies and Minds: Torture, Psychiatric Abuses, and the Health Professions* (New York: W.H. Freeman, 1985); a lengthy interview with Dr. Peter Breggin; and a twenty-six-page affidavit on the development of medical ethics by Columbia professor David J. Rothman filed by the plaintiffs in the CIA suit. Rothman concluded that "a requirement for voluntary consent was widely recognized in an uncodified form by the medical community before the Nuremberg trials and that this requirement was [only] formalized in the Nuremberg Code."

On Cameron's professional innovations and network building: interviews with Allan Memorial Institute director Brian Robertson; Dr. Robert Cleghorn; Bill Stauble; Eddie Kingstone; Fern Cramer Azima; Anne Johnston; Peggy Edwards; and many others. Print sources: Cleghorn, "The Emergence of Psychiatry at McGill", *Canadian Journal of Psychiatry* 29:7 (Nov. 1984), 551-56; Cameron and Baruch Silverman, "Tale of Two Institutes", *American Journal of Psychiatry* 122:2 (Aug. 1965), 189-94; E. Legrand and G.E. Reed, "Psychiatric Facilities in Montreal and Quebec", *American Journal of Psychiatry* 105 (1949), 782-85; Cameron, "The Psychiatric Training Network of McGill University", *American Journal of Psychiatry* 120 (1964), 1039-44; Cameron, "A University Centered Postgraduate Training Network", *American Journal of Psychiatry* 73 (1955), 112-16. Also, Cameron, "Psychiatry Comes of Age", *Modern Hospital* 64:3 (Mar. 1945). On the day hospital: draft of a paper Cameron gave at an APAA meeting in New York in May 1947, titled "The Day Hospital: An Experimental Form of Hospitalization", APAA, Box 5, Folder 44; and L.D. Goldman and K. Arvantanitakis, "D. Ewen Cameron's Day Hospital and the Day Hospital Movement", *Canadian Journal of Psychiatry* 26 (Aug. 1981), 365-68. Comments on Quebec's medieval culture are from the Allan's own brief institutional history, "History of the Growth and Development of the Allan Memorial Institute, 1943-1955", prepared at Cameron's direction and dated January 27, 1956, in the Allan Memorial Institute Library.

Cameron's grantsmanship and impact on research funding in Canada, from an interview with Dr. Charles Roberts, and from documents in PAC, Records of the Department of Health and Welfare, RG 29, vol. 304, file 435-3-4; vol. 316, file 435-6-3; vol. 379, file 615-5-15; vol. 8, files 620-1-1 and 620-2-1; and vol. 9, file 620-2-5. Omond Solandt's attitude to funding Cameron is eloquently put in his affidavit for the plaintiffs in the Washington suit; and is confirmed by both Roberts and contemporary documents. For example, on a May 8, 1950, memo about the idea that McGill could become a national psychiatric research centre (for which Cameron was lobbying hard), Solandt wrote a postscript: "Dr. Morton: As you know I feel that DRB experience does not justify singling out Dr. Cameron for special support. I would like to see others better supported first." (PAC, RG 24, vol 124, file 4-60-53.)

Chapter 8: The Automatic Cure

From interviews with Fern Cramer Azima, Peggy Edwards, Bernie Goulem, Anne Johnston, Bill Stauble, Eddie Kingstone, Peter Roper, Robert Cleghorn, Duncan Cameron, and others; and transcripts of interviews conducted by Jay Peterzell in the late seventies with Thomas Ban, Leonard Levy, and others. Material on Cameron and Hisey's investigations into the Cerebrophone is from Don Gillmor, *I Swear by Apollo: Dr. Ewen Cameron and the CIA-Brainwashing Experiments* (Montreal: Eden Press, 1987).

Sources for the story of the girl from Bermuda and the beginnings of psychic driving are a paper Cameron delivered to the New York Center for Clinical Psychiatry in Dec. 1953 called "Observations on the Playback of Verbal Communication" (APAA, Box 1, Folder 2), and a speech and slide show he gave to the American Psychopathological Association a decade later (Feb. 1963) called "Adventures with Repetition: The Search for Its Possibilities" (APAA, Box 2, Folder 19). Azima's variation on the sleep cure is outlined in his paper "Prolonged Sleep Treatment in Mental Disorders (Some New Psychopharmacological Considerations)", *Journal of Mental Science* 101 (1955), 593-603.

Cameron reported in his paper "Psychic Driving: Dynamic Implant" (see end of Source Notes) that he had tried the technique on "more than 100" patients in the first two years. The common figure reported in the current press on the case is 53, which is a number plucked from a later paper. The actual number of patients on whom Cameron reported trying varieties of these experimental techniques is 332; there must have been many more, because in the later years of the work Cameron took to reporting only the cases that had what he considered interesting or positive results. Cameron's published papers on controversial experiments are listed at the end of the Source Notes.

The source for the origin of the term psychedelic and the description of Humphrey Osmond's work with alcoholics is Lee and Shlain, *Acid Dreams*. Other information on LSD and Cameron's use of it is from "Return by the Honourable J. Waldo Monteith...." Hebb's horror that Cameron might publish first is supported by a letter he wrote to Whit Morton of the DRB on Jan. 1, 1953, in which he said, "Don't forget that Cameron is now undertaking some work with this method and *he*'ll [Hebb's italics] talk about it freely" (included in Appendix 23 of the Cooper report).

Cameron's finer feelings on the worth of memory are documented in his Maudsley lecture, "The Process of Remembering", *British Journal of Psychiatry* 109:3 (May 1963), 325-40. His ideas on the concept of "cure" are from an essay, "Philosophy of Psychiatry", *Archiv für Neurologie, Neurochirurgie und Psychiatrie* 91:1 (1962), 31-36.

Cameron's early grant applications and his reports on the federal government funding of his Behaviour Lab are in PAC, RG 29, Box 29, File 604-5-14. A memo from Dr. J.N. Fisher to Dr. Charles Roberts dated Sept. 17, 1954, says that the project ended on March 31, 1954, "and $17,874 were expended". Given Cameron's later record it's interesting to note that in his final report on that early project he commented that he tried to replicate Hebb's work in "restricted stimulation" but that "unfortunately, it proved impossible to find patients to undergo the experience."

Major mainstream publicity on Cameron's work at the time includes Jacqueline Moore, "Canadian Psychiatrists Develop Beneficial Brain-washing", *Weekend Magazine* 5:40 (1955); Brian Cahill, "New 'Personalities' Made to Order", *Gazette*, June 18, 1956; and "Psychic Driving: Repeated Statements May Influence Glands", *Globe and Mail*, Oct. 31, 1956. The research grant to Cameron made by the CIA cut-out organization, the Society for the Investigation of Human Ecology (SIHE), was reported by the *Montreal Star* on Apr. 20, 1957. A sampling of the media coverage of Cameron's more aggressive experiments includes: Cahill, "Two-Month Sleep, Shock New Schizophrenic Cure", *Gazette*, Sept. 2, 1957; Fred Poland, "Use Tranquilizers in Sleep Treatment for Schizophrenia", *Montreal Star*, Sept. 17, 1957;

"Long Sleep, Shock and Then Amnesia Help Mental Patients Lose Symptoms", *Gazette*, June 14, 1960.

Sources on Cameron's relationship to SIHE include: Gittinger's deposition in the Washington suit, in which he admits that the CIA solicited Cameron; John Marks, *The Search for the "Manchurian Candidate"*; copies of annual reports and CIA documents from Marks and Rauh files; Gillmor, *I Swear by Apollo*; depositions by Sid Gottlieb and David Rhodes. The fact that the staff at the SIHE helped Cameron and Rubenstein with statistical analysis of their voice stress research is mentioned in a letter from Cameron on file in the records of Mental Health Grant 604-5-74, included in the appendices of the Cooper report.

Chapter 9: Mary Morrow, MD

Reconstructed from depositions taken in the American lawsuit and from her own suit against Cameron in Quebec Superior Court, *Dr. Mary Morrow* v. *The Royal Victoria Hospital and the Estate of the late Doctor D.E. Cameron and/or Legal Heirs*. The testimony includes that of co-workers, bosses, teachers, staff who treated her at the Allan, expert witnesses debating her sanity and the amount of damage she suffered, and her sister and mother. Evidence includes copies of her letters and medical records. Case No. 500-05-738532.

Chapter 10: In the Sleep Room

A copy of the 1964 procedure for sleep treatment is among the exhibits in the Morrow suit, No. 500-05-738532. The first portion of the chapter comes from several interviews with Peggy Edwards. Analysis of Cameron's own ability to use the new range of psychiatric drugs is from an examination of the available hospital records of plaintiffs in the Washington suit; and the observations of Dr. Cleghorn and residents and nurses who worked for Cameron. Praise for Cameron's inspirational qualities is an almost universal chorus among the psychiatric professionals I interviewed. That he suffered peers badly, however, is another common observation, put most bluntly in interviews with Ewalt, Cleghorn, Griffin, and Roberts. The overview of the way the Allan actually ran is put together from numerous interviews, but owes most to Stauble and Cleghorn.

The Roberts material is from an interview with him; the other members of the Bédard commission were Dr. Dominique Bédard and Dr. Denis Lazure, and their report was called "Rapport de la commission d'étude des hopitaux psychiatriques". Some documents and correspondence on the founding of the World Psychiatric Association are in the Cameron collection, APAA. Cameron's feelings about lobotomy are from an interview with Anne Johnston.

Fred Lowy's critique of Cameron as a researcher is published in the Cooper report; other material is from an interview with Lowy. Hebb's comments are taken from a series of interviews conducted with him in the late 1970s by Jay Peterzell. The surviving research critiques sent to Cameron by Leonard Levy are in APAA, Box 2, Folder 14; information on Thomas Ban is from Peterzell interviews. Aubrey Lewis's comment on the barbarity of Cameron's depatterning work is from Cleghorn's memoir.

Cameron's crisis of confidence in the scientific method is described in "Observations on the Playback of Verbal Communication" (APAA, Box 1, Folder 2), which I quote. The Laughlin Taylor material is from Gillmor, *I Swear by Apollo*. Cameron's own notion that the experimenter's perceptual tools are finer than any test is a recurring theme in his published research.

Chapter 11: The Wrong Road Travelled

Lehmann's introduction of chlorpromazine is outlined in Lehmann and G.E. Hanrahan, "Chlorpromazine: New Inhibiting Agent for Psychomotor Excitement and Manic States", *AMA Archives of Neurology and Psychiatry* 71 (1954), 227-37. Other information about Lehmann is from Peggy Edwards, Montreal contemporaries, and Gillmor, *I Swear by Apollo*. Details on the effects of neuroleptic drugs are from interviews with psychiatrists and psychiatric nurses, Dr. Peter Breggin, and *Dr. Caligari's Psychiatric Drugs* (Berkeley: Network against Psychiatric Assault, 1984).

Lehmann's simile for the action of chlorpromazine is from the *Gazette*, Jan. 3, 1956, in an unbylined article, "Drugs for Mind like 'Cast on Broken Leg'". That article also reports the use of chlorpromazine to drug French soldiers fighting in Algeria. The American army research into an anti-fear drug is outlined by a former Pentagon military intelligence officer, Richard A. Gabriel, in his book *No More Heroes: Madness and Psychiatry in War* (New York: Hill and Wang, 1987).

Cameron's notes on creativity and the minutes of the committee he convened on the subject are in APAA, Box 5, File 43, "Minutes of Discussion on Scientific Creativity Held on Wednesday, July 17, 1957, at 8 PM in the Allan Memorial Institute Library". The rhetorical question on productivity is from "Observations on the Playback of Verbal Communication". Cameron recorded Malmo's point that attention and involvement were two different things in a memo headed "Dr. Cameron's Notes—November 30, 1962", which was circulated to Levy, Ban, and Rubenstein (APAA, Box 3, Folder 22). Draft of the speech "Adventures with Repetition" is in APAA.

The section on Karralynn Schreck is put together from interviews and correspondence with her; the paper in which she is described as Sonia is "Automation of Psychotherapy" (see list of Cameron's papers, below).

Cameron's ruminations on leadership and doctoring are from page 3 of an unfinished memo called "General Administrative Policies—D. Ewen Cameron, MD", dated June 25, 1964, from the Cameron box, McGill University Archives. The note "Forward Looking" is dated Oct. 30, 1964, and is in APAA, Box 3, Folder 22. The account of the demise of depatterning is largely from Cleghorn and Peter Roper, and also from some documents filed in the Morrow suit in Quebec Superior Court. The Schwartzman and Termansen paper was presented at the Canadian Psychiatric Association meeting in Edmonton in 1966 and then published as "Intensive Electroconvulsive Therapy: A Follow-up Study", *Canadian Psychiatric Association Journal* 12 (1967), 217-18.

Chapter 12: Fall from the Pedestal

Sources on Flo Langleben are: her interrogatory filed in the CIA suit; interviews with Wayne and Carol Lang; and medical records held by the Langleben family. All the other documentation of the chapter comes from: interviews with Joe Rauh and Jim Turner; court documents filed in Civil Action No. 80-3163; documents on the case put together by the Canadian Embassy; External Affairs files; interviews with Jeremy Kinsman, Ray Boomgaardt, and three spokesmen in Washington and in Ottawa who stressed that they were only speaking for background; and depositions. The quote on Joe Rauh is from David E. Rosenbaum, "Joe Rauh: 50 Years, and Counting, of Doing Good", *New York Times*, Jan. 8, 1985.

Chapter 13: Death at the Summit

The account of Cameron's final years in Albany and his death on the mountain is pieced together from interviews with members of his family, Dr. Bill Holtz, and several Lake Placid friends; the Lake Placid paper at the time; and officials at the Adirondack Loj. That his ambitions were to crack the RNA radical and climb Street Mountain is from Daniel Blain's preface to *Psychotherapy in Action*. Dr. Frank Braceland's comments on Cameron were found in a copy of a letter to Dr. Denis Leigh, dated Oct. 24, 1967, in the Braceland papers, APAA, Box 3, Folder 22. Jim Loeb's editorial appeared in the *Adirondack Daily Enterprise*, a copy of which was given to me by Duncan Cameron.

A Partial List of Dr. Ewen Cameron's Papers

Cameron, Dr. D. Ewen. "Psychic Driving", *American Journal of Psychiatry* 112:7 (Jan. 1956), 502-09.

——. "Psychic Driving: Dynamic Implant", *Psychiatric Quarterly* 31 (1957), 703-12.

—— and S.K. Pande. "Treatment of the Chronic Paranoid Schizophrenic Patient", *Canadian Medical Association Journal* 78 (Jan. 1958), 92-96.

——and R.B. Malmo. "Effect of Repeated Verbal Stimulation upon a Flexor-extensor Relationship", *Canadian Psychiatric Association Journal* 3:2 (Apr. 1958), 81-86.

——, L. Levy, R.B. Malmo, and L. Rubenstein. "Repetition of Verbal Signals: Behavioural and Physiological Changes", *American Journal of Psychiatry* 115 (May 1959), 985-91.*

——et al. "The Effects of the Repetition of Verbal Signals upon the Reorganization of the Schizophrenic Patient subsequent to Intensive Physical Treatments", *Proceedings of the Second International Congress for Psychiatry*, Vol 3 (Zurich: 1959).

——. "Production of Differential Amnesia as a Factor in the Treatment of Schizophrenia", *Comprehensive Psychiatry* 1:1 (Feb. 1960), 26-34.

——, L. Levy, and L. Rubenstein. "Effects of Repetition of Verbal Signals upon the Behaviour of Chronic Psychoneurotic Patients", *Journal of Mental Science* 106 (Apr. 1960), 742-54.*

——, Thomas Ban, and L. Rubenstein. "Sensory Deprivation: Effects upon the Functioning Human in Space Systems", in Bernard Flaherty, ed., *Psychophysiological Aspects of Space Flight*. New York: University of Columbia Press, 1961, 225-37.+

——, L. Levy, Thomas Ban, and L. Rubenstein. "Repetition of Verbal Signals in Therapy", in Jules Masserman, ed., *Current Psychiatric Therapies*. New York: Grune and Stratton, 1961, 100-11.+

---

* indicates that research was conducted with support of the SIHE

+ indicates research funded by Dominion-Provincial Mental Health Grant No. 604-5-432

——, L. Levy, Thomas Ban, and L. Rubenstein. "A Further Report on the Effects of Repetition of Verbal Signals upon Human Behaviour", *Canadian Psychiatric Association Journal* 6:4 (Aug. 1961), 210-21.+

——, J.G. Lohrenz, and K.A. Handcock. "The Depatterning Treatment of Schizophrenia", *Comprehensive Psychiatry* 3:2 (Apr. 1962), 65-76.

——. "Repetition and Response", *Proceedings of the Third Congress of Psychiatry*, vol. 1. Montreal: McGill University Press, University of Toronto Press, 1962, 200-04.

——, L. Levy, Thomas Ban, and L. Rubenstein. "Automation of Psychotherapy", *Comprehensive Psychiatry* 5:1 (Feb. 1964), 1-14.+

——, L. Levy, Thomas Ban, and L. Rubenstein. "The Effects of Long-term Repetition of Verbal Signals", *Canadian Psychiatric Association Journal* 10:4 (Aug. 1965), 265-71.+

Acknowledgements

Many people helped me to pull the pieces of this story together. Of the dozens of people who worked with or were taught by D. Ewen Cameron (many of whom weren't eager to see their names attached to either their anecdotes or their opinions) I'd like to thank in particular Dr. Robert Cleghorn, Peggy Edwards, Dr. Bill Stauble, and Dr. Eddie Kingstone for the hours of time and depth of insight they gave me. For help in understanding how Cameron's actions fit into the history of psychiatry, thanks to Andrew Scull and Gerald Grob. Thanks to Arlene Waite for her research on Cameron's early years in Brandon, Manitoba.

I owe a large part of the CIA end of the story to Washington lawyers Joe Rauh, Jr., and Jim Turner, who allowed me to read seemingly endless numbers of depositions, affidavits, interrogatories, and documents revealed by discovery; and who kept me informed of each twist and turn in the long history of Civil Action No. 80-3163. Thanks also to John Marks, Jay Peterzell, and the Center for National Security Studies in Washington for access to their research files on MKULTRA and Cameron. Thanks to Jim Littleton for his stimulating interest in the project and his knowledge of the Canadian intelligence community. And to Don Gillmor, a friendly competitor who did me the favour of publishing first.

I'm indebted to Margaret Cannon Mays for walking me through the first steps of the paper chase; to Rodney Young and Bennett McCardle of the Public Archives of Canada; to librarian Julia Main of the Allan Memorial Institute; to Bill Baxter of the American Psychiatric Association Archives in Washington, D.C.; to Claire Collier of the Rockefeller Archive Center; and to Dr. Jack Griffin, who watches over the small archives of Canadian psychiatry housed at Toronto's Queen Street Mental Health Centre.

Then there are the people and the organizations that made the writing possible. First among them is Eric Rosser, without whom I wouldn't even try to do this sort of thing. Joann Webb, who is always there with paying work and good advice; she and John Gault and Dawn MacDonald are my first readers and constant sounding boards. I'd also like to thank my editor, Margaret Allen, and my publishers, Louise Dennys and Malcolm Lester; my agents, Lucinda Vardey and Linda Turchin, who never fail to support me professionally and personally; and my parents, Bill and Olive Collins. It took three levels of arts councils—the Toronto Arts Council, the Ontario Arts Council, and the Canada Council—to help finance the research, and I'm grateful to all three.

Finally, I'd like to thank Ewen Cameron's oldest son, Duncan, and his widow, Jean, for agreeing to be interviewed by me. Both will view the results with extremely mixed emotions, yet both decided at last to take the risk. And also, Cameron's patients, the plaintiffs in the suit against the CIA, for sharing their stories in whatever way they could.

Index

Adrenalin desensitization therapy, 168

Against Interpretation (Sontag), 44

Albany Medical College, 92, 242

Alexander, Leo, 111

Allan, Sir Hugh, 9-10

Allan Memorial Institute, 2, 9-17, 18, 48, 62, 64, 103-08, 115-16, 122, 141, 146, 150, 163, 170, 190, 209, 237

Allard, William J., 209

Allen, Morse, 55, 56

Allende, Salvador, 31

Alzheimer, Alois, 77

American Board of Psychiatry and Neurology, 158

American Civil Liberties Union, 28

American Journal of Psychiatry, 13, 81, 130

American Medico-Psychological Association, 76-77

American Psychiatric Association, 41, 62, 69, 127

American Psychopathological Association, 189

American Veterans Administration, 21, 199

Americans for Democratic Action (ADA), 223, 243

Annihilation ECT. *See* Regressive ECT

Archives in General Psychiatry, 86

"Artichoke" (code name), 55

Auckiesanft, 204

Aufreiter, Friedl, 168

Aufreiter, Johannes, 168

Automatic psychotherapy. *See* Psychic driving

"Automation of Psychotherapy" (Cameron), 19

Azima, Hassan, 126, 164, 168, 169

Baldwin, Maitland, 58-59
Ban, Dr. Thomas, 175
Banting, Sir Frederick, 119
Barza, Dr. David, 206
Battle for the Mind (Sargant), 42
Beaubien, Dr. Jacques, 156, 198
Bédard Commission, 171, 212
Beecher, Dr. Henry, 112-13
Behaviourism, 133
Bicêtre (hospital), 72
Bleuler, Eugen, 76
"Bluebird" (code name), 55
Boomgaardt, Ray, 232-33
Bos, Dr. Carlo, 198
Boyd, Dr. David, 158
Braceland, Dr. Frank, 167, 192, 242
Brainwashing, and psychic driving, 135-36, 196-97
Brandon Hospital for Mental Diseases, 69, 83, 85
Brandon Sun, 85
Brave New World (Huxley), 123
British Journal of Physical Medicine, The, 87
British Medical Association, 81
British Psychoanalytic Society, 168
Broadbent, Ed, 227
Burghoelzli Clinic, 67
Bush, George, 31
Butler Health Centre, 137

Caldwell, Zoe, 225
Cameron, Airlie, 241, 242
Cameron, Duncan (Jr.), 66-67, 119, 122, 199
Cameron, Duncan (Sr.), 65
Cameron, Dr. D. Ewen, 2, 3, 10, 11, 13-17, 18-23, 24, 27, 28, 42, 62-63, 64-71, 83-90, 92-99, 100-20, 121-41, 142, 144,

145-46, 147, 153-56, 157-58, 162-65, 166-81, 187-90, 192-96, 196-201, 201-03, 205, 209, 212, 215, 216, 220, 230, 233, 235-36, 237-43
Cameron, Jamie, 240-42
Cameron, Jean Rankine, 64, 67, 83-84, 90, 101
Canadian Neurological Association, 149
Canadian Press, 226
Canadian Psychiatric Association, 70
Cardozo, Benjamin, 222
Carter, Jimmy, 30-31, 219
Casey, William, 32-33, 211
Cassidy, Dr. Gordon, 149, 151, 152
Center for National Security Studies, 28
Central Intelligence Agency (CIA), 2, 4, 25-27, 28, 29-30, 31, 33-34, 35-36, 47-48, 54, 57-59, 137-39, 175, 202n, 203, 208-22
Cerebrophone, 122
Cerletti, Ugo, 93, 127
Chlorpromazine, 126, 163, 165, 182-87
Christian Science, 76
Church, Frank, 33
Church Committee, 215
Churchill, Winston, 36, 38
CIA v. Sims, 225
Cinquegrana, A.R., 208, 209-10
Civil Rights Act (U.S.), 222
Clark, Joe, 224, 227, 228, 234-35
Clarke Institute, 169
Cleghorn, Dr. Robert, 65, 66, 116-17, 144, 153, 168, 169, 180, 182, 197-98, 200-03
Climax (CIA project), 34

Colby, William, 31

Collip, J.B., 116

Cooper, George, 227-28, 229-30, 234

Cormier, Dr. Bruno, 169

Cotton, Henry A., 77-82

Cotton Award for Kindness, 77

Cramer Azima, Fern, 169, 170

Crosbie, John, 227, 228, 229

"Current Transition in the Conception of Science, The" (Cameron), 177-78

Cutler, Phil, 210

Dancey, Dr. Travis, 48

Defence Research Board (DRB), 46-47, 56, 118, 134

"Dehydration Method in Epilepsy, The" (Cameron), 86

Depatterning, 132, 172, 197-98

Desoxyn (amphetamine), 14, 128

Diethelm, Oskar, 97-99, 100

Dominion-Provincial National Health Grant, 117

Donovan, General William "Wild Bill", 40

Dulles, Allen, 35-36, 54

Duplessis, Maurice, 113

Edwards, Peggy, 161-66, 168

"Effects of Repetition of Verbal Signals upon the Behavior of Chronic Psychoneurotic Patients" (Cameron, Levy, and Rubenstein), 134

Eldridge, Harry, 242

Electro-shock. *See* Electrotherapy (ECT)

Electrotherapy (ECT), 7, 20, 70, 131, 165, 185

Ewalt, Jack, 167

External Affairs, Department of, 219, 227, 228, 231

Extrapyramidal symptoms (EPS), 183-84

Ey, Henri, 126

Field Experimental Station, 47

Fifth Estate, The (CBC TV), 221

Fischer, Ferdearle, 81

Fisher, Mrs., 10

Fleming, Grant, 103

Focal-infection theory, 78-82

Ford, Gerald, 28, 29

"Forward Looking" (Cameron), 196-97

Frankfurter, Felix, 222

Freedom of Information Act, 29-30, 225

Freeman, Walter, 172

Gamma 50 LSD-25 ("acid"), 13-14, 18; *see also* LSD

George III, King, 72-73

Geschickter Foundation for Medical Research, 26

Gittinger, John, 137-38, 139, 220

Goebbels, Joseph, 37-38

Gotlieb, Allan, 218, 229

Gottlieb, Dr. Sidney, 30, 33-35, 36, 56, 57, 138, 214, 215, 220, 223

Gouzenko, Igor, 47

Grad, Dr. Bernard, 168

Great and Desperate Cures (Valenstein), 172

Greenacre, Dr. Phyllis, 80-81

Gregg, Alan, 103, 104, 118

Grégoire, Jean, 117

Griffin, Dr. Jack, 167-68

Group for the Advancement of
Psychiatry (GAP), 167

Hadwen, John, 218-19, 226, 227,
228
Hanrahan, G. E., 183
Harcourt, Countess, 72-73
Haskins, Dr. Caryl, 48
Hebb, Donald, 48-50, 52, 56-57,
58, 66, 119, 129, 173-74
Hellman, Lillian, 210, 225
Helms, Richard, 30, 31, 36, 220,
229
Henderson, Sir David, 66
Hersh, Seymour, 28
Hess, Rudolf, 108-09
Hill, C.G., 76
Hinkle, Lawrence, 54
Hisey, Dr. Lloyd, 105-06, 122, 198
Hoffer, Ab, 24
Holtz, Dr. Bill, 92-94
House Un-American Activities
Committee, 210, 225
Howlett, Dr. John, 151-52
Huard, Jeanine, 213-14, 223
Hulse, Stacey, 218-19, 224, 228
Human Ecology Fund. *See* Society
for the Investigation of Human
Ecology (SIHE)
Humphrey, Hubert, 222, 223
Hunter, Edward, 53
Hunter, Dr. Robin, 168
Huxley, Aldous, 123, 129

"Imagination of Disaster, The"
(Sontag), 44
Informed consent, 111-12
Institute of Living, 191-92
Insulin-coma therapy, 91-96, 98,
102, 131, 187

International Court, 232
Interstate Commerce Commission,
215
Isolation Group, CIA, 59

James, F. Cyril, 103-04, 118
Jasper, Herbert, 149, 151
Jewett, Mark, 228
Johnson, Lyndon, 222
Josiah Macy Jr. Foundation, 26
Justice Department (Canadian),
227-28, 231
Justice Department (U.S.), 221

Kingstone, Eddie, 153, 164, 175-76
Kinsman, Jeremy, 218, 219, 232
Klein, Melanie, 168
Knause, John, 224, 226
Kraepelin, Emil, 76, 77
Kragie, Scott, 224, 228
Kral, Dr. V.A., 168

Lamberd, Gordon, 24-25, 28
La Mettrie, Dr., 72
Lang, Wayne, 204-05, 206, 207
Langer, Walter, 40
Langleben, Flo, 204-07, 216, 227
Langleben, Moe, 204
Largactil (anti-psychotic), 7-8, 163
Lashbrook, Robert, 214
Laubinger, Frank, 30
Laval University, 199
Lehmann, Heinz, 109, 126, 133,
163, 175, 182-87
Leigh, Dr. Denis, 242-43
Les fous crient au secours (Pagé),
171
Levinson, Ed, 136
Levy, Leonard, 132, 136, 174-75
Lewis, Aubrey, 101, 104, 175

Lewis, Nolan, 102, 108
L'Homme-machine (La Mettrie), 72
Life Is for Living (Cameron), 114, 119, 167
Lifton, Robert Jay, 60-62, 110
Lilly, John, 57-58
Lithium, 164
Locke, John, 72
Loeb, Jim, 223, 243
Logie, Robert, 212-13, 224
Lovell, Stanley, 40-41
Lowy, Fred, 173-75
LSD, 129-30, 165
Lumumba, Patrice, 34, 220
Lyons, Dr. Reuben, 8

McCarthy, Joe, 210, 223
Macdonald, Linda, 235
MacEachen, Allan, 220
MacEchern, Dr., 148
McGill perceptual-isolation experiment, 50-52, 56
McGill Research Building, 199
McGill University, 9, 48, 102, 118
McNaughton, Francis, 143, 144, 148-50
Malmo, Dr. Robert, 66, 136-37, 168, 189
Manhattan Project, 41
Manic-depression, 76, 77, 164, 185
Mao Tse-Tung, 53
Marchetti, Vincent, 29
Marijuana, as truth drug, 41
Maritain, Jacques, 105
Marks, John, 28-30, 33, 34, 39, 54, 55, 139, 208, 214
Matas, Dr. John, 7-8, 9, 12
Mathers, Lavin, 69, 90
Maudsley Hospital, 101, 175
Maudsley Lecture, 130-31

Mayfair Hospital, 205
Mayo Clinic, 7, 12
MC 4703 (experimental drug), 216
Mead, Margaret, 137
Medas, Jim, 219
Mein Kampf (Hitler), 37
Menninger, Bill, 168
Mental Hygiene Institute, 102, 116
Methamphetamine (barbiturate), 18
Metrazol-convulsion therapy, 93
Meyer, Adolf, 67-68, 69, 77-78, 80, 81, 90, 93, 100, 115
Midnight (CIA project), 34
Miller, Arthur, 210
Miltown (tranquillizer), 21
Mindszenty, Joseph Cardinal, 25, 49, 133
Ministry of People's Enlightenment and Propaganda, 37-38
Mississippi Freedom Democratic party, 222
Missouri Institute of Psychiatry, 158
Mitchell, S. Weir, 75
MKULTRA (CIA operation), 31, 32-33, 34, 36, 55, 60, 131, 137-38, 139, 202*n*, 208, 209, 211, 215, 218, 220, 221
Moniz, Egaz, 82, 172
Monroe, Colonel James, 27, 135, 136, 189, 215, 220
Montreal Neurological Institute (MNI), 66, 103, 107, 142-43, 149
"Moral therapy", 74-75
Morison, Robert S., 118-19
Morrow, Clare, 142-43, 153, 156
Morrow, Dr. Mary Matilda, 142-59, 176, 202, 216, 234
Morton, Whit, 50
Mosher Memorial, 101

Mulroney, Brian, 227, 228-29, 230-31
Mushatt, Cecil, 105-06

National Institutes of Health (NIH), 57, 58
National Security Council, 31, 233
Nazi Doctors, The (Lifton), 110
Neibuhr, Reinhold, 223
Neurasthenia, 75
New England Journal of Medicine, 112
New York Times, 25-26, 27, 28, 132, 208, 222
Nineteen Eighty-four (Orwell), 38
Nixon, Richard, 31
Normandy invasion, psychiatrists at, 38-39
North, Oliver, 234
Nuremberg Code, 111-12, 113
Nuremberg trials, 108-13

Objective and Experimental Psychology (Cameron), 71
Office of Strategic Services (OSS), 31, 35, 39, 40
O'Grady, James, 208, 209, 210
Olson, Alice, 29
Olson, Frank, 29, 214
O'Neill, Juliet, 226
Operational Research Group, of the DRB, 50
Orlikow, Arch, 17
Orlikow, David, 2-3, 5, 10, 17, 18, 25, 27, 207, 208-15, 217-18, 223
Orlikow, Leslie, 5-6, 12, 17
Orlikow, Val, 2, 5-23, 24-25, 27-28, 62, 208-16, 218, 221, 234
Orwell, George, 38
Osmond, Humphrey, 129

Overholser, Winfred, 41

Pagé, Jean Charles, 171, 212
Page-Russell electrotherapy, 132, 144, 153, 165
Parsons, Dr. Frederick, 92
Penfield, Wilder, 58, 65-66, 104, 107, 108, 119, 148, 149, 150
Penn, Judge John Garrett, 215, 225, 226, 230, 234, 235
Permitil (neuroleptic), 21
Peterzell, Jay, 208
Phipps Clinic, 67, 100
Pinel, Dr., 72, 74
Pinock, Thomas, 90
Pius XII, Pope, 186
Prados, Miguel, 105
Prisant, Peggy, 9
"Process of Remembering, The" (Cameron), 130-31
Psychiatric Clinic (Vienna), 68-69
"Psychiatric Tragedy of Rudolf Hess, The" (Scott), 109
Psychic driving, 13, 18, 19-20, 122-28, 130, 165, 172-73, 180, 194-95, 196-97, 206
"Psychic Driving" (Cameron), 130, 139
Psychobiology, 67-68

Queen Mary Veteran's Hospital, 48
Queen's University, 169

Rasmussen, Theodore, 150, 158
Rauh, Jr., Joseph L., 4, 207, 210-36, 243
Ravenscrag. *See* Allan Memorial Institute
Reagan, Ronald, 32, 211
Rees, Brigadier-General J.R., 168

Regressive ECT, 131, 132, 198
Repetition, power of, 123-27
Report, Rockefeller (1975), 29
Reserpine, 164
Rest cure, 75
Retired Records Center, CIA, 30
Reuther, Walter, 223
Revai, Marie, 21
Rhodes, David, 138
Ritz-Carlton Hotel, 47
Robb, Preston, 151-52, 153
Roberts, Dr. Charles A., 117, 120,
    170-71, 172, 173, 182, 200
Robertson, Dr. Brian, 65, 66,
    237-40
Robertson, Dr. Rocke, 200
Rockefeller, Nelson, 28
Rockefeller Foundation, 57,
    103-04, 118
Roosevelt, President, 39
Roper, Dr. Peter, 198, 201-02, 202*n*
Royal Medico-Psychological
    Association, 81, 134
Royal Mental Hospital, 66
Royal Victoria Hospital, 9, 11, 103,
    145, 148, 201, 210, 215
Rubenstein, Leonard, 13, 19, 27,
    125, 128, 132, 174
Rush, Benjamin, 73

Saffran, Murray, 168
St. Elizabeth's Hospital, 41
St-Jean de Dieu asylum, 171, 212
St. Mary's Hospital, 142-43, 149,
    150-52
Sakel, Manfred, 91-92, 127
Sargant, Dr. William, 39, 42-43,
    133
Scheider, Victor. *See* Gottlieb, Dr.
    Sidney

Schizophrenia, 76, 86-87, 91-92,
    120, 166
Schlesinger, James, 31
Schlesinger, Jr., Arthur, 223
Schreck, Karralynn, 190-96
Schwartzman, Dr. Alec, 201
Science, 177
Scopolamine, as truth drug, 41
Scott, Dr. Clifford, 109, 168
Scoundrel Time (Hellman), 226
Scull, Andrew, 72, 74, 76, 77, 80
*Search for the "Manchurian
    Candidate", The* (Marks), 30,
    139, 208, 216
Seconal (barbiturate), 7
*Secrecy and Democracy: The CIA
    in Transition* (Turner), 32
Senate Foreign Relations
    Committee, 31
Senate Human Resources
    Committee, 31, 33
Senate Select Intelligence
    Committee, 31, 33
Senate Sub-committee on
    Intelligence, 33
Sensory deprivation, 2
Sherover, Max, 122
Sherwood, Percy, 219
Shultz, George, 224
Silver, Daniel B., 212, 214
Sisler, Dr. George, 8, 9, 12, 15
Skinner, B.F., 133
Sleep therapy, 88, 126, 160-61, 185
Smith, Dr. Lloyd, 193
Society for the Investigation of
    Human Ecology (SIHE), 26-27,
    135, 138-40, 178, 188, 210, 215
Sodium amytal (abreactant), 11-12,
    14, 18, 55, 118, 129
Sofaer, Abraham, 224

Solandt, Dr. Omond, 47, 48, 118
Sontag, Susan, 44-46
Sourkes, Ted, 168
Stadler, Lyvia, 213, 224
State Department (U.S.), 219, 224
Stauble, Dr. Bill, 123, 141, 175,
  176, 200
Stern, Karl, 105, 156
Strecker, Dr. Edward, 41
"Study of Factors Which Promote
  or Retard Personality Change in
  Individuals Exposed to
  Prolonged Repetition of Verbal
  Signals, A", 189*n*
Sunnybrook Hospital, 161

Tait, John, 229
Tan, Dr., 146, 153
Taylor, Laughlin, 178-81
Taylor, Telford, 111
T. Eaton Company, 6
Termansen, Dr. Paul, 201
Thought control, Chinese method
  of, 52-54
*Thought Reform and the
  Psychology of Totalism: A Study
  of "Brainwashing" in China*
  (Lifton), 60-61
Tizard, Sir Henry, 48
Transcultural psychiatry, 168
*Transcultural Research in Mental
  Health* (newsletter), 137
Transference, 16
Trenton State Hospital, 77, 78-81
Turner, Admiral Stansfield, 30-33,
  36, 208, 220

Turner, Jim, 4, 211, 215, 217, 220,
  221, 223, 227, 233-34, 235
Tyhurst, Dr. James, 48

University of Manitoba, 8
University of Montreal, 199

Valenstein, Elliot, 172
Venecek, Dr. Donna, 152
Verdun Protestant Hospital, 20,
  102, 109, 116, 162, 170, 182
von Meduna, Ladislas, 93

Wagner von Jauregg, Julius, 68-69,
  85, 120, 127
Washington Post, 217, 229
Weekend (magazine), 134-35
Weinstein, Harvey, 216-18
Weinstein, Louis, 216-17
Wigdor, Dr. Blossom, 168
Willey, William, 86
Williams, Commander R.J., 48
Wittkower, Dr. Eric, 127, 168
Wolff, Harold, 26, 54, 135-36, 140
Worcester State Hospital, 90
World Congress of Psychiatry, 171
World Psychiatric Association, 70,
  167, 171, 242

Yerkes Laboratories of Primate
  Biology, 48
York Retreat, 74

Zimmerman, Rita, 216